MEETING THE LOVEFRIEND

Marline,
Allow your Love
expressiveness to be you in
all things.

Royal Sallele

ALSO BY THE AUTHOR
****

Second Reflections
> 1991 Royal Ideas Publications.

Watch for "Talking With Love."
A briefer explanation of Love's presence with Its central focus on how to talk with Love and thereby achieve a marvelous expression of Oneself.
> 1992 Royal Ideas Publications.

Watch for "Love's Group Meetings."
This booklet will explain how these groups can be formed and successfully heal their participants of all disappointments. These groups focus entirely on Love's solutions for their concerns.
> 1992 Royal Ideas Publications.

Royal Satterlee's
MEETING THE LOVEFRIEND

DICK HANNON

**ROYAL IDEAS
PUBLICATIONS**

Royal Ideas Publications
St. Charles, Missouri
Copyright © 1991 Royal Satterlee

Printed in the United States of America

ISBN #1-879227-03-7

ACKNOWLEDGMENTS

First and foremost, I am acknowledging the incredible gift of understanding given me from my Lovefriend. I recognize that my Lovefriend is the Lovefriend of everyone. Therefore I thank every reader who supports this sense of reality, for my Lovefriend is your Lovefriend and altogether we are One. All other people are involved with us, so I acknowledge that the Love of everyone has made this book possible.

I also express my warmest gratitude here to several particular people who have shown themselves to ably understand and assist me in conveying this sense of Love with considerable authenticity. First of all, I am mentioning three of the most special people in my life.

One of them is Richard ("Dick") Hannon, who has masterfully illustrated this book by integrating his "Sandy Sandbox" cartoon characters with it. He also formed the illustration for the book cover. Both in my earliest and later experiences of him, I became aware that he deeply feels life. He is also an international concert pianist and the director of a large music school. Presently, he is enrolled in ministerial studies in a nationally acknowledged metaphysical school.

My wife, Noreen, is one of these three, and has no close rival for my adoration of another human being. She has placed in the computer, over and over, the writings inspired by the Lovefriend. I adjusted various passages because of her wisdom and alertness to the meanings they were intended to convey.

Audrey Stewart has tirelessly and enthusiastically read and edited this manuscript and helped me learn how to better communicate myself through language in order that I might convey the place that Love deserves in all of our thought. She has shown herself to be unswerving and highly committed to transmitting the real meanings of these teachings.

I deeply appreciate Dr. Tom Johnson's participation in reviewing the book and writing the supportive foreword.

Walter Manka through his expertise in printing books unreservedly assisted me with his capacity. Also, he contributed his talents in designing the book cover. Randall Getz is a computer expert and has given a great deal of time in sharing his skills as needed. Debby Gordon, Phylis Clay and Bobbie Dixon were very helpful in reading and advising me about various parts of the developing text. I also gained significant help from Kay Tyson, Marsha Siefert and Joan Dow. Had these people not been there when I needed them, this writing would have appeared only after a considerable delay.

Royal Satterlee

NOTES FROM THE AUTHOR

****

I define some significant words and phrases differently than most people have been doing. Therefore, it would be helpful for the reader to become familiar with the glossary (in the back of the book).

This book teaches its readers how to live Love's Way. Anyone can become more loving day by day through reading any few pages of it daily. Some people will want to devour the whole book as rapidly as they can, and they too will become expressive of Love as never before. However, some readers will feel that the reading cannot be done as quickly as they think they will want to proceed. Or they may wish to read the "lighter" pages first. For example, one could begin with chapters one, two, three and fourteen. Or go directly to chapter three to observe my fundamental and experiential basis for understanding Love's presence. Then go back, and read the chapters that were missed. For those who appreciate the topic LOVE, every chapter is rich with Its presence. Above all, make it your foremost interest to meet the Lovefriend. You will always be glad you did.

Using the glossary and index will aid one's understanding of Love's presence. The words that are used in the book will sometimes carry "deeper meanings" than dictionaries will provide. The glossary should provide adequate clarification.

Capital letters are utilized throughout this writing to distinguish a difference in certain words such as Love, Intelligence, Good, etc. Although some of these extra uses of capital letters are explained in the text itself, the glossary more quickly makes clear the reasonings for many of them. Some words which are not capitalized and which could have been for similar reasons are not, because they would have complicated the reading. An example of such a word is "life."

PREFACE

This book is the first of several I am writing about Love's presence and empowerment. Although each will stand on its own merits, this particular one has a fundamental message which is a key to all of them.

Until we conceive of Love as the greatest Friend we will ever know and let Its Friendship be felt by us in everything we do, life and Love will remain elusive to our understanding. Let this guide encourage you to meet Love as the best Friend you can ever have. Nothing can compare to the joy, serenity and Self-fulfillment you will feel from knowing Love's presence.

There are depths of Love's Good that will enchant you and beckon you on toward the greater experiences of your spirituality if you act on the ideas of this book. Levels of greater living will open up endlessly, if you but let Love express you in these ways.

There is a means and an end in every beginning. Here the means is the study of Love's nature. Our being aware of Love's presence is the end that emerges through this beginning.

CONTENTS

❖ ❖ ❖ ❖ ❖

CONTENTS

CONTENTS

CONTENTS

By Children -- Imagination -- Support Groups -- Love's
Group Meetings.

FOREWORD

We are told that love is the healing power, that through the attitude of love we draw to us our creative good, and that the power of love protects us from anything unlike love. These are all true. Much has been written about love and all of it is important because love is the great power of the Universe. Someone recently told me that she did not believe in God and therefore considered herself an atheist. Because of this she felt alien to the Spiritual Life that I teach. I asked her if she believed in love. She replied, "Why, of course I do." "Well then," I said, "you believe in God because love is God." Or, I should say, Love is God. She accepted this and now has a whole new approach to life based upon a power within herself rather than outside.

There are four main areas of our life that must be fulfilled if we are to live fully and completely. Those areas are health, wealth, creative Self-expression and love. However, I believe that when we really understand what love, or Love, is all about, all of these other areas are touched by it and are completely alive and in action. When we are living and expressing love, we are free of criticism, judgmentalism, trying to control others, and taking away the good of others. When we are living and generating love, we are free of anger, jealousy, resentment, fear or hatred, which are the emotions that kill ourselves. Love blesses the one who is loving. It blesses the one who is loved, but blesses ourselves first of all. It is a feeling and an action. It is not really love until it is actively expressed. When we reach out to others in an open and accepting way, something glorious happens to ourselves. We find ourselves in touch with a vast, limitless inner power. This power is an Intelligence that guides our way into our creative good. This power is a Presence that is not only comforting, but strong in Its direction of how we should live our lives.

Royal Satterlee, in his outstanding book, "Meeting the Lovefriend," has explored and given to us the larger concept of love. It is capitalized so that now it is Love. Now it gives to us a greater meaning than what we know in a superficial way as romance or something that we give and receive. Now it is revealed as a Power that can do anything. Now it is revealed as that Intelligence that guides our way into the fullness of life and through each and every challenge that comes our way. When we connect with it we feel secure, safe, creative and fully alive. He tells us that this Friend is within everyone, no exceptions. All we have to do is acknowledge It, actively and consciously be at one with It, and It takes over and lives through our every thought, word and deed. The more we turn to It, the more It turns to us. This is not to say that It is separate and apart from us. It is the very essence of our own Self. Royal Satterlee clearly shows that the meeting with the Lovefriend is a meeting with our own Real or True Self.

We are always our own experience in that we see through our attitudes, our perceptions, our own consciousness. If that consciousness is distorted with anger, fear, negative memories, needs etc., we are not seeing clearly. However, it is through the consciousness of Love that we see in true perspective. The Lovefriend that is so real to Royal Satterlee becomes very real to us as we surrender to his enthusiasm for these meetings with the Lovefriend within each of us. He shows us the way to let this Presence fill every fibre of our being, which then opens up for us a life beyond our previous imagination.

While I was reading the manuscript of "Meeting the Lovefriend," I found myself filled with ideas for my own books, for my own lectures, for my own way of life. These ideas that were brought alive within my own Self were not necessarily the ideas that I was reading. Royal's presentation simply served as a springboard to that uniqueness that is within my own Self. I realized then the importance of this book. If he can do this for me, he can do it for anyone who chooses to experience Self-discovery. This is not to say that the ideas presented in this book are only to be used as a catalyst to our own way of life. He presents practical, dynamic, and inspiring answers that we can and should use. But his loving and caring exploration of the Truth of ourselves gives us the gift of awakening to Who and What we are as individuals. This is what any great teacher does. He or she gives us the gift of our own Self, our own reason for being.

"Meeting the Lovefriend," is so filled with Truths and is so Absolute in its presentation that it needs to be read again and again. Each time I went through it I found something new, something more. It is a book that must be studied and absorbed and lived. The Lovefriend doesn't deal with problems but with answers. It takes us above and beyond what went wrong. There are many support groups that meet regularly to let everyone talk about what they are going through, whatever that might be. They cover in great detail everything that is wrong with their lives. Here is a different way. A way that is the wave of the future. It is the way of being at one with what is right with us instead of what is wrong. It is a way of being at one with the answers rather than the problem. The Lovefriend within each of us has our own answers because each of us is unique. Experiencing the Lovefriend is why we are here. It is the answer to drug abuse, any addiction, gang warfare or loneliness. Meet your Lovefriend. Royal Satterlee will show you how.

Dr. Tom Johnson
Author of "You Are Always Your Own Experience"
 "Action Does It"
  - Many other books

THE LOVEFRIEND

When we meet with the Lovefriend regularly, and feel Its presence, we think with a LARGE SENSE OF LOVE. Therefore, our experiences and everything in our lives are especially GOOD FOR US.

LOVE'S SELF-GIVINGNESS

The presence of Love within me
cares for all my needs,
gives me my sincere desires
and heals me each moment
that I meet with It.

Love does all of this,
because It is my greatest Friend.

Love does not provide these needs
by giving them to me.
Love gives me Itself
through acting as me.

INTRODUCTION

I

Love is the great underlying reality of life! There is no absence of Love! Nevertheless, many people have invented the idea that Love (capital letter L) is fictitious, and they have replaced their idea of It with love (lower case l). It is as though they feel a need for Love, but they think it would be impractical to experience It. However, love is such a small sense of Love that only a small expression of Good can come from it. On the other hand, when we believe in Love, our experiences are immediately made splendid. Then happiness, success and harmony abound.

All of us have been involved in thinking of Love in a small way. It is no wonder that we have not liked some (or many) of our experiences; but how could they have been better when we have denied Love's greater reality? We can help ourselves now by turning to the great idea that Love is everywhere present. That idea represents Love as It truly is. As we think that idea, we feel Good about ourselves, people Love us, and we are made happy, resourceful, peaceful, prosperous and healthy. We find that our real experience of life is marvelous as we believe in Love.

In turning to the greater idea about Love, we must turn away from our small sense of It. This necessitates our becoming aware of how we have experienced mistaken conceptions of Love's magnificence. We must begin from where we are!

We have erroneously believed that for Love to exist for us, we were required to have a special relationship with another person. We have consequently had various experiences that have ended in disappointments. For instance, some of us right now have a relationship of dependency with another person which seems ideal, and we may feel fortunate. However, we have falsely presumed that being either in control or in the service of another is all that we can have of Love. We shall discover that Love is immensely greater. Such a small conception of Love is the result of believing that life has problems that are largely compensated for, or even resolved by, our being a controller or a follower of another. Beneath this thinking, but not as deep as is our essence, there is an insecurity within us that will someday become evident when we are truly ready to express Love. In the process of enlightenment, the mistaken conceptions become known, but need not be judged and sometimes can be easily discarded.

An increasing number of us have come to the belief that no one has become as special or as loving to us as we had conceived someone could be. We had thought that we would become intimate with someone who would sympathize with our disappointments.... with all of our dashed hopes, *and who would then treat us well.* Or we had presumed that we could help another, *to keep that person from falling.* But now we know that love which only leans upon or supports another is not what we really desire. Some of us have ceased looking for such a dependency. We have built a new hope, that of finding someone who would complement us and make us whole. This too has not fulfilled us, because we are not really lacking anything; that we lack is a negative idea, and an unnecessary one.

Our disillusionments with love are furthermore the result of our thinking that the only viable relationships we might ever have are those in which two or more entities have agreeable experiences with each other. We need to discover that there is a more essential kind of relationship, and One that is far more real. For two or more entities do not exist in our greater reality! They seem to exist in our fictional world, the one that we have invented out of the belief that our five senses entirely explain our natures. But the real world has but One life in it, and it is the experience we have of Love!

There is One especially beneficial relationship that all of us have; it is the relationship of the person who we think we are with the person who we are becoming. Deep within, we already are the person who we are becoming, but until we know this, we tend to feel we are something much less. Yet a deeper, truer feeling of Self underlies the lesser feeling. We will in time become aware of this greater feeling; we will discover that it is the feeling we have of Love.

Love is tender with us, gentle and giving of Itself. We can become aware of Its tenderness, of Its gentleness and of Its empowerment. This inspiration comes from deep within us; we are made from Love and we are being made into Love. This is wholly a feeling of legitimate friendship, of happiness, and of Self-fulfillment, because Love is really who we are.

Of course there are other people in the One life that we live! And to the extent that we know there is but "One life," we experience Love on a magnificent basis with these other people. But, when we think their lives are separate from ours, their relationship with us ceases to be as loving as we desire. Then we feel we must avoid them, resist their influence or change them. Either they seem to have many faults, or it seems that we do.

Our relationship is a no fault one when we acknowledge Love as the great reality, the only reality, and the sole relationship that we have in truth. There is no judgment in this, and other people are a wonderful part of it.

II

It is common to search for Love. Everybody does. We look into the lives of our parents, our friends, our heroes and our heroines for Love. We see something of Love there some of the time, but we do not find as much Love there as we want to, because the measure of Love that we see outside of ourselves is no more than that which we place upon others as we look upon them.

The degree to which Love benefits our lives is in direct proportion to our awareness of Love's Presence. We mislead ourselves for a long time by thinking that our dependencies are that Love. Nearly all marriages before the middle of the twentieth century were dependencies, and the idea that Love could be found because of them was an impossible dream. Many sham marriages still exist. Men and women are increasingly protective of their legal rights within their marriages. As a result, the thought that love could be lasting in marriages is growingly in question.

Most recent marital agreements have been entered into with considerable caution or fear, sometimes conscious and sometimes not. Caution has been sensible because marriage cannot bring about happiness. When caution has not been used, fear in some other form has usually intruded upon the hope for marital bliss. However, some people still cling to the naive thought that marriage can give them love and happiness. They are right that love exists, but they do not understand that its greater reality is Love. Marriage cannot cause Love to be, but Love can bring about a happy marriage. Love causes marital bliss when a husband and wife celebrate marriage as an institution for sharing Love rather than one for seeking love.

Before we are married or experience Love in any kind of relationships, we tend to search for It. All the time, we feel Love inside ourselves, but we act out our lives largely unaware of this feeling. We do not readily find Love, because as we seek It we constantly think we do not have It. We easily conclude that it is unrealistic to think we can ever find Love, and that we must make ourselves secure without It. Yet because Love is truly with us, we can discover that It is within ourselves by observing that It is Love that has inspired us to search for Love. We find that Love is who we are as we talk to ourselves with the idea of combining all of our actions to support the achievement of our heartfelt self-interests, and as we *let* Love be *all* that we are.

Love flows with ease in our lives as we think of a center within us that keeps us alive and effectively guides our search, and as we let ourselves know that that center is the Love we seek. At first we ask of life, where is Love? Gradually we let Love teach us Its nature. We come to feel It as guidance that is deep within ourselves. As we let Love prompt us from within, we see that our particular environment is another place of Love for us. All our friends and presumed enemies there are teaching us something about Love unawares. Sometimes, they teach us in the manner of their ordinary conduct as they reach the understanding of who they really are. Other times we learn of the need for Love when we see them living as though Love is nowhere to be found; their lives are not functioning well. We notice that something like that is happening with us too; this occurs when we are afraid to be true to ourselves. Still, at the center of who we are, Love is inviolable; it is only our doubts about Love that need correction.

We need only stop ourselves right where we are, and recognize that Love is *within* every thought we have, *within* every relationship and *within* every event. *Love is not every thought, relationship and event, but It is WITHIN ALL of them*! While we search for Love, we too often think we find Its absence. But when we know why we have searched, that It is something of our sense of Love reaching through us for a greater recognition, the search gives way to the realization that we are Love, and that we are manifesting more of the inherent Love that we are.

When we come to know that we are Love, we are enabled to greatly express the Good of life that we have longed to demonstrate in the past. How is it that Love then expresses us as never before? It is simply the result of our having discovered that giving to others what they most desire creates an ease in us. That is, *our believing* that they can do, be and have all that they have deeply wanted, but had given up as though it were impossible for them, has placed us into joyful living! Because of this, we really feel Love!

Then, Love simply means for us that we believe both ourselves and others will yet succeed in manifesting our hearts' sincere desires.

III

Really feeling Love enables many friendships to be enriched. Marriage especially becomes a happy, successful and meaningful experience. Nevertheless, Love is never found because of marriage. Love is brought into marriages and other relationships, through the deepening of the greater and more requisite relationship of the inner sense of Self with the outer sense of Self.

Gradually, a great sense emerges of the only relationship that we ever have which never knows conflict. That is, there comes to us an awareness that we are having meetings with the presence I have named "the Lovefriend." No one else ever sees these meetings of Love with you or me, nor can we see them with another. Yet, no human contact can compare in closeness to this experience! And many of us become aware that something marvelous is causing us to feel Good about ourselves.

At first the idea that a Lovefriend presence could exist seems too good to be true. Yet, as we embrace the idea, the Lovefriend in some way reveals Itself. And we find in our meeting with It, the essence of who we are. The Lovefriend is the Self within the self. It is our spiritual identity. It is when we believe we no longer need to search for Love that It announces Itself. Some of us imagine that we see this Friend; others of us feel Its presence. There are various ways through which we reach a state of conviction that the Lovefriend is real and that the proceedings of a meeting are being carried out through us. It happens at the same time that we really feel Love!

IV

Always, when we really feel Love we act with Self-reliance. It is through our finding Love within ourselves, and our becoming sufficiently aware of feeling It, that we find we have become very confident and resourceful. This is not through thinking of ourselves as superior to anyone, but rather by being aware of something in us that helps us and which we instantly know is also in everyone else.

Love is able to provide for all our needs and desires, and It enjoys doing so. Love is the great actor of the universe. Whenever Its acting is evident, we are aware that Its care is being given or received. Its care is implanted, and is to some degree, actively maintained in every single person. Therefore, all people are agents of Love. It is not possible for anyone to not care for the self or other people. However, it is possible for everyone to falsify their expression of care so that Love is not very recognizable in the forms of their behavior. Herein lies the dual possibility out of which all troubles arise. That is, we can choose every moment whether the care given through us will be positive or negative. In the most positive sense, the people in our lives, including ourselves, can be given our expression of Love through the esteem and confidence we place in them. In its most negative sense, our actions towards them and their reactions to us can temporarily destroy them, emotionally or physically. In all human relationships, both the initiator and the recipient of action have awesome responsibilities. However, when those who are "in our care," even children, rise out of their reactions and allow Love to express them or to tell them what to do, we cannot even appear to hurt them. Since most people presently live in their reactions, the need to feel responsible or to allow Love's presence to guide, exists with all who are willing to experience life's better possibility.

Let us understand that Love cannot be misused. If we care for ourselves or others in an abusive way, it is not Love doing this through us. It is the result of thinking erroneously that any care we give is an act of Love. Although Love is always with us and is actually the potential of Good that is in everything and every experience, Love is never misused. Rather, It is often ignored or misunderstood. When we ignore Love, we are unaware that It is. When we misunderstand Love, we are aware that It is, but we think we are receiving Love's guidance when we are alternately following some misguided thought about It. All this means that Love is misplaced in our thinking about life to the extent that we force our false ideas of care upon ourselves or others. Therefore, we are wise not to give ourselves too much credit for caring. Rather it is essential that we be open to Love, and that we let the action of Love provide Its care through us.

Although it is impossible not to care, but only to give either good care or bad care, we can eventually approach a desirable state of being that is as though we do not care at all. It is necessary for us to eventually discover how to do this and to implement it. When it happens, our sense of valuing care by naming it as good or bad will be replaced by an intelligent care that is neither good nor bad in the ordinary sense. Yet, it will be exceedingly Good and without any lack of this greater experience of Good. Acquiring the experience of "not caring" is not something we should do until we have first learned to care. The purpose of "not caring" is to establish the ability to step out of Love's way when we desire to let It act MORE CARE-FULLY through us and as us. The meaning and the way to express this mastery of care will elude us for a long time. When we are ready to "not care," Love will announce this to us.

V

Our understanding will ultimately include the awareness that Love provides us perfect care, and that we always receive Its care to the degree that we think and feel we can. Even when our guardians or so-called friends give us bad care, we have that experience from them because we have not yet made ourselves aware that care can be better. If we had that awareness, we would not appear hurt, because no one can even appear to hurt those who know Love's presence. The abused and the abusers both share doubt that Love (with Its care) is present. Even if our guardians or friends provide the perfect care that Love can give us through them, we are not guaranteed that we will not experience disappointments. This is because our reception of care often includes our feeling insecure about it. And if we feel insecure, care is not adequately felt in its completeness; we think of it as concern. Care is often felt that way, especially when we are too infiltrated with anxiety to discover any help in it. What are we to do? Love cannot improve Its care since It is already perfect, but we can improve our receptivity and our own further expression of it, by trusting Love more. We can trust Love more by understanding It more. *WE WILL UNDERSTAND WHEN WE OURSELVES BECOME AWARE THAT ON A DEEPER LEVEL WE ARE FEELING LOVE. AND WHEN WE EXPERIENCE THAT FEELING REGULARLY, NO ONE WILL APPEAR TO HURT US AND WE WILL NOT APPEAR TO HURT ANYONE ELSE.*

When we truly understand life, we will know that Love is never perverted, never misused; however, Love's care is often displaced by a pseudo care. If care could not be mistakenly perceived, we could only experience our caring as Love knows to give it. This would mean that we would not be free to accept Love's care as it is or to reject it. But we are free, because although Love is always the great actor, we can refuse It a great role on the stage of our lives for a long time. We cannot refuse to care, but we can temporarily pervert ourselves by using a mimicry as a substitution for Love's care. Love only acts perfectly, but when Its care is given through an agent who substitutes anxiety or concern for It, it appears that Love is not so pure or helpful. And when Love's care is misrepresented through our distorted ideas of care, our sense of Love's being present is to some extent dissipated, and remains as unexpressed potential. Our false understanding of Love's care dulls our interest in feeling Love and trusting It. The less we are aware of a sense of Love, then the less Love is expressed in the care we give.

We are slow to express Love's care without employing a lesser form of care, because to do better requires of us a greater understanding of Love. When we get enough understanding of Love, it is because we have become very aware of our feeling of Love; then we simultaneously let It care through us. We learn our best lessons about care, not by discovering how to use it, but by letting it show us even more of the Love we have desired to know. We cannot discover a greater sense of Love by modifying the way we care, but we can experience wonderful care as we acknowledge the feelings we have of Love.

We will really feel Love, and we will know that we do, when we cease fearing It. It seems strange that we would fear Love; but this happens because we touch Love within our thoughts, and there Its gracious ideas seem fanciful to us since other people have taught us a different idea about reality. Love whispers from within us that we are totally Good, that we can do any sensible thing, and that every desire can be. But people tell us that we are ignorant to think that anything really Good and inventive could come from us. Despite this, at times we draw near to Love's whisperings. When this happens, we sometimes feel afraid that other people will not approve of us if they discover our interest to be One with Love. And so, *we often fear our greatest resourcefulness.*

Love wants us to be different from everyone else. It wants us to dare live our own lives by trusting It for everything we do. Love desires that we be harmonious with all people, but through Its guidance. The guidance of Love is more wonderful than has been popularly thought and more constructive than has been practiced; it is helpful to everyone. However, we find that people in general do not trust this, and so we have to be courageous to become aware of Love; we have to be willing to be different from others, to let It help us.

Many of us have often distrusted Love because it seems to us that some human person whom we have trusted has let us down. If we do not begin to believe in the deeper, inner feeling of Love that we have in and of ourselves, the memory of that apparent hurt will continue to deprive us of our potentially better lives, and we will not know the one feeling that is solid and sure! *However, if we let this writing become our opportunity to believe that somewhere inside ourselves there is something that can be trusted without reservation, we will find the Love that never lets us down!*

It may seem that dependability is all that we could hope for. But there is something even better than never being let down. It is being lifted above a mere "fixing" of the problems of life, to an experience of reality that is truly helpful and healing because it is Self-fulfilling for us. *AS WE DISCOVER HOW TO LET LOVE ACT INCREASINGLY AS US, A HIGHER REALITY THAT IS WITHIN THE SEEMING AND ORDINARY REALITY WE HAVE BEEN EXPERIENCING IS REVEALED TO US. WE FIND IT AS WE ESTABLISH A FRIENDSHIP WITH LOVE....NO OTHER RELATIONSHIP WILL EVER FEEL AS TOUCHING, WHOLE OR PROMISING OF GOOD.*

At last, our relationship with Love becomes the only essential relationship of life for us, and we discover that we are Love. When this occurs, we observe that our other, more temporary relationships are freed of every disappointment we have had with them. But can this happen in this lifetime, right here on earth? *YES, IT CAN! YES, IT CAN! YES, IT CAN!*

LOVE'S FRIENDS

All people think they want to be loved by some person or several persons. Deeper than the longing to be near someone else or others, is the desire to feel Love's Friendship. When we let ourselves feel Love, we adjust our other interests so as to express Love's Friendship *WITH* others. How can we do this? I cannot point the way to a place or to a particular moment, because we do not meet Love in Its deepest essence through our arranging for a space or time. *YET LOVE DESIRES US TO MEET WITH IT, AND WHEN WE ALSO STRONGLY DESIRE THIS, WE ARE FOREVER THEREAFTER LOVE'S FRIENDS.*

If some readers are wrestling with the idea that meetings with Love should require of them a place and time, I suggest that a new thought be followed. The idea that well addresses this concern is to simply become *receptive* to Love's showing Itself wherever and whenever it might happen. No amount of exerting oneself can help us with this. Merely conceiving Love's Friendship will allow it to come about. Imaging that there is a Lovefriend is *ALL* that is necessary. Do not struggle with the text that follows; simply keep conceiving and imaging that the Lovefriend is with us; Love will show Itself.

It only takes a single meeting with the Lovefriend for us to become Love's Friends. *Being Love's Friends is a high station which means that we Love ourselves so much that we cannot help but Love everyone.* This idea quickly translates itself into an agreeable vision for planet earth. Many of us have envisioned that there

29

could be peace, plenty and happiness everywhere on earth. Some of us have tried to instigate that vision. Greater success comes for us as we sense Love's presence.

We begin with ourselves right where we are, for otherwise we cannot greatly discover Love. As we open ourselves to let Love express the truth of who we are, we let go the egotistical attempts to resolve our crises which are preventing us from acknowledging mistaken attitudes we have about our family and other personal relationships, employment, national and world views. This does not mean that there is a termination of our individualistic liberties or our involvement in resolving the difficulties we often experience in families, friendships, work or nations. Not at all. However, a new sense of Self, family, work, friendships, philosophy, nation and world takes place. It happens through our feeling Love more truly, wherein an awareness of how to express It without partiality or prejudice emerges. We unfold from a deeper sense of ourselves the interest and ability to be in Love with everything and everyone at once. We discover how to live in complete harmony with all, while feeling incredibly Good about ourselves. It includes that we die to the old attempts to merely sympathize with people's troubles, to sacrifice ourselves and to "act" nice, because we let go of the small ways we have thought Love must be.

When we let go that our past practices of love can really help or heal us enough, the Lovefriend within us shows Itself. The emergence of the depth of Love's care that heals us and everyone else, lies immediately beneath those old attempts to build relationships and experiences that are loving. The reason that the Lovefriend can build with us that which we have never achieved before, is that Love's heart is unlimited in Its vision of One People and Its knowledge that each person is able to feel Good within the situations that are experienced.

We understand this well as we conceive of the greater possibilities in our discovering "consciousness." We can all become conscious of the Friendship Love is providing us from within ourselves. As we act from this sense of Self, everything unlike it crumbles, and Love greatly grows in our midst.

First, the Lovefriend rebuilds our lives as we become determined to talk with It. On the heels of these very personal conversations, we gather in groups to support one another in being Love's Friends. Love's support is most authentic when we

We gather in groups to support one another in being Love's Friends

open ourselves to Its guidance, and even more, to Its activity of expressing us in everything. Regardless of the burdensome nature of the habitual experiences that have entrapped us, perfect solutions are available through Love. Love's answer is not to cope with problems. Love has a natural means of transforming our troubled actions into a well governed and uplifted expressiveness of wonderful living.

Love's support groups are forming themselves whenever we walk and talk enough with Love. We need not "try" to form such a group, but simply desire it to occur and expect that it will form itself through us and as us. The Lovefriend's will is that Its Friends will live abundantly through this means. Love's "support groups" occur as we build the individual practices of courting the Lovefriend. This solitary connection with Love is the reason that Love's groups can meet with great success.

Practical implications include that the movement of the twentieth century's support groups can be converted into the twenty-first century's supportiveness that Love's Friends build. Support groups are not sacrificed in this, but are expanded in effectiveness.

Let us then familiarize ourselves with Love's presence as the great beginning. As we go on, let us expect to be inspired by the Love within us that is greater than sacrifice and the past practices of sympathy and nicety. As Love's Friends, let us let Love rejuvenate our support groups so that Love greatly helps and heals, from within us and them. Our problems will then be both diminished and turned about until they are only seen as opportunities for effective living. We can do it! We can do it! We can do it!

CARTOON CHARACTER FACES

Sandy

Newton

Hypatia

Calvin

Veda

When we meet the Lovefriend, and feel Its presence, we think with a LARGE SENSE OF LOVE. Thereafter, our experiences and everything in our lives are especially GOOD FOR US.

CHAPTER ONE

LOVE IS A PRESENCE

Can you sense love as an ever present Friend who (which) is caring for you from within yourself, who (which) is also caring for others from within themselves, and who (which) is an infinite provider that flows through all thoughts and feelings? YES, YOU CAN! YES, YOU CAN! YES, YOU CAN!

Surgery had been completed for the removal of her brain tumor. Infection set in. Her condition deteriorated so that she lost her ability to speak intelligibly. Her physicians said that recovery was impossible. This was reported to me, and I came to her from a considerable distance. As I entered the immense hospital center where she was confined, I knew she could not remain so terribly diseased.

When I entered her room the Lovefriend[1] told me that this lady was well, but that I needed to say so. Throughout my conversation I assured her that her health was perfect. She uttered sounds in reply, but her inability to speak clearly made her words indistinguishable to me. I declared that right then

---

[1] We can hear the Lovefriend in a way that is similar to our sense of conscience speaking from within us. Unlike the conscience, Love does not speak *at* us and not even to us, but rather through us and as us. Until we identify Love as the moving Spirit and supreme motivator of our ability to express ourselves well, our lives tend to contain frequent disappointments and difficulties. As we imagine what the Lovefriend is like, and as we become willing, Love shows forth our lives very resourcefully.

Love's presence was being revealed from within her in a distinct and markedly observable manner. My prayerful declaration included statements that it could not be possible for anyone to suffer as it seemed she had.

Two or three weeks afterwards, I visited in her home and found that she was regaining her ability to speak. She asked me if I saw the garden that appeared in her room when I visited her. I indicated that I had not.

She said, "Did you see Him?" I was aware that she believed she had been in a garden and that someone of especial presence was in it. Again I said, "No," but I could tell that she had experienced an illuminated consciousness. I added that I greatly felt the presence that she saw. And both of us knew we were speaking of the same awareness. She was improving rapidly: the infection and most aspects of the condition that she had experienced were already gone.

The Lovefriend is a DEFINITE PRESENCE and is within everyone. Could we but see or feel Its immediacy in everything, life would be expressed perfectly every moment. Just as marvelously, we can feel It WITHIN OURSELVES as much as we desire to. However, the awareness of the Lovefriend is not manifested in our experience until after we contemplate the idea that It can be.

KNOWING LOVE'S PRESENCE

I was walking late at night, alone on a country road. For an hour, as was my daily custom, I spoke with the Lovefriend who was my sense of an unlimited presence, who loved giving Its unlimited resourcefulness through me. On this particular evening, as I gazed upward at numerous brightly lit stars, an impulse suddenly gripped me to pray for a young man who had been a friend for some time.

I tried to open my mouth to pray, as though I must cry out for his recovery from tuberculosis. Having visited him several times in a sanatorium, I recalled that one lung had been removed, but that the tubercular condition had then infected the other lung.

No solution for him was known by his doctors. Yet the Love-friend knew he was well. Right then I knew I need not cry out for him, so that he would become well. I need only announce that HE WAS HEALTHY.

The words that came forth were, "Nothing need be asked: HE IS ALREADY HEALED AS I SPEAK. I KNOW THAT IT IS TRUE." And he was made whole. Three days later I visited him, and he told me that all evidences of his ailing condition disappeared, that he was physically examined on the morning afterwards and was found totally healed. He still had but one lung; nevertheless, it was a healthy one. And the condition never returned.

LOVE'S CARE

It was early evening when his wife called me. She said that her husband had just been rushed to the hospital. He had suffered a severe rupture of the heart. The doctors said he could easily pass on at anytime. I thought of how we had first met after his having been told over and over that he could not live more than two weeks because of a heart problem. He had proven wrong all such longevity estimates. Yet a few months later, he seemed to be slipping away.

As I entered the hospital lobby his wife rushed up to me and said, "They will not let me enter his room now, but you will be allowed." I consoled her and prepared her for his healing or his passing. The Lovefriend spoke from within me that it would be one way or the other, and that the nature of the experience would be glorious in either case.

When I entered his room I am quite certain that his spirit watched me from above. A nurse sat at the foot of the bed. His very large body was not greatly covered, and he lay on his back. There was no movement from him. I moved to his side, coming quite close. I spoke to him of his wife, three other friends and myself. I had taken the time to call the three friends before driving to the hospital. I told him that I had done this, and that altogether we knew that he would stand up and walk away healed, or pass on peacefully and confidently into the arms of the Lovefriend.

The nurse indicated that I was wasting my time, that he was in a deep coma and could not hear anything from me. I thanked her and then told him that I would name all five of us, one at a time, and that I would expect him to know and acknowledge our certainty that he was healed, and that he would then either get up and walk or pass on quickly and peacefully, to express his regained health in his next life experience. I then named his wife. He raised his large body upward until his face touched mine. He pressed his cheek to my cheek so that I felt a warmth of feeling from the pressure of it. After about fifteen seconds he dropped his body back onto the bed. I named the others one by one, last of all speaking out my own name. Each time he raised his body to mine, and touched me similarly. The nurse scampered out of the room, thoroughly confused. But I simply knew the Lovefriend had brought us into a oneness.

After I spoke my name he fell back onto the bed and as my right hand grasped his, I said, "Do what you need to do now and experience it easily. I trust that all is right and good with you." Immediately he let go of his last breath, peacefully. The nurse, other nurses and several doctors came in then, but he was already wholly joined with the Lovefriend. I left quietly, but more confident than ever that all was well.

LOVE'S FLOW

My business was fifteen years old. Many sacrifices, including long hours of hard physical labor, usually seven days a week, had made it seem a chore. Yet I loved doing the service that I rendered. My company maintained numerous marine fish and invertebrates, as well as freshwater tropicals, in aquariums for people who could afford the best of such services. This venture was carried out with some employee assistance, and was pursued in a wide metropolitan area of Southern California.

I had made the decision to let the Lovefriend expand the business, bring customers to me and make me prosperous. Yet having done so, it seemed I was not assisted from anything within me or around me. Actually, it seemed to become harder to keep the business going. Day after day, I treated and affirmed that the business would grow. Because it was a service business, much of the income was profit. Therefore, I had decided that to increase my income progressively by $200 each month I would be satisfied. It would mean that there would be $400 in the second month, $600 in the third month, and so on. However, after six months had passed and no new income developed I became depressed and discouraged. It was then, in the midst of a long cry about it, that the Lovefriend seemed to be standing there by me and spoke through me in no uncertain terms that my desire was being fulfilled.

The next morning the telephone rang at 8:00 a.m. and I was provided an account immediately for $200 a month. In my enthusiasm I sensed that more was about to happen. On the next day a similar amount of repeatable business came my way. As rapidly as I could set up accounts, more and more business came to me. In two weeks I had $1400 of new monthly income. All of the new customers contacted me without any advertising or pursuit of them on my part. That rarely ever happened before with even a single customer. Never again did I have to seek out new business.

Because the new $1400 per month was seven times greater than my choice of $200 new business every month would have been, I declared to my sense of the Lovefriend's presence that such generosity on Its part was much more than I thought I had mentally conceived that it could be. Then I sensed Its rationale. Because exactly six months had gone by since I had first opened my beliefs to the idea that I could become prospered $200 more every month, the sum of $1200 was now necessary to meet my original desire. The additional $200 had to be included since it was Love's idea that each new $200 come to me a month in advance.

Thereafter, until I chose to set my direction towards changing my occupation, a new $200 increase in monthly income occurred on a dependable basis every month. These new customers proved to be the easiest ones for whom I had ever worked. I learned that the Lovefriend knows how to bring people together in the way that is best for all.

LOVE'S ALTERATIONS

A young woman in her twenties studied with me about her unlimited potential to experience happiness and wholeness. Many years before, her mother had taken much of the DES (Diethylstilbestrol) drug that doctors then prescribed. Before using the drug, her mother had seven miscarriages in a row, and then this woman was born.

There were internal complications from the beginning. By five years of age, the little girl was crippled with rheumatoid arthritis. Doctors said she would never walk again. She chose to disbelieve them. She then showed many recovery signs, and became able to walk without impediment.

Many daughters of mothers who had taken DES did not live past twenty. This was because of the deadly cancer that they experienced in their developing female reproductive system. Doctors often suggested that affected girls have hysterectomies performed as a measure of assistance. Like many others, when this young girl reached her teens, the evidences of precancerous cells were discovered within her body. Her doctors urged that a hysterectomy be undertaken due to the rapid changes of certain cells. She refused the operation. The condition grew more serious. Doctors examined her every three months. Biopsies were frequently performed. The evidences pointed toward the likelihood of cervical cancer, and she frequently felt considerable discomfit from the condition.

After studying metaphysics for a few weeks in my classes, she convinced herself that a technique called Spiritual Mind Treatment would heal her. She loved herself enough for the procedure to work well. Her very next checkup showed that she was stabilized. Now, years later, thorough medical examinations continue to prove her free of disease.

In the other instances cited, people's attitudes and environmental conditions were altered. Amazingly, in this case a chemical factor was shown to be just as amenable to change.

For the young woman described here, both her walking again as a little girl and the resolution of all later complications became possible because she loved herself enough to succeed. Love is the primary factor, the real cause in all healings and all experiences of life improvement. Love is our greatest Friend.

LOVE, BELIEF, DESIRE AND POISE

There are two elements in healing that we all need to know about. One of them is that Love's presence is both the cause and means of our being able to live, and of our further ability to experience life's opportunities richly. The other element which enables us to tap into the richness of Love's healing presence, is *our desire to believe* that Love can heal us.

When we activate our desire to believe that Love's gift is unlimited Good, we have greatly joined our thoughts and beliefs with Love's presence: *we have struck a poise.* Similarly, there are two elements in our experiencing places of poise in the physical

Our desire to believe that Love can heal us, enables us to tap into the richness of Love's healing presence

atmosphere of our planet. One of them is gravity, which is the basis for our being able to maintain an equilibrium and composure in our walking, sitting, lying down, running and jumping. The other is that we *already believe* that gravity will support us in these activities. That is, we do not have to consider whether we can walk, sit and jump, etc.. When we were babies, we saw people doing all of these things before we moved about very much, and as we matured, we simply began doing them too, not questioning in any way our ability to do so. However, most of us could not have conceived of floating an iron ship or building a machine in which we could fly. We had only learned how to do those things which we observed in others.

The pioneers of flying and floating heavy objects had to come to the belief that they could do something more than their understandings of specific gravity at first enabled them to do. They had to take notice that principles and laws existed which enabled them to use their earlier awareness of gravity to do things that had seemed impossible before. For instance, they had to employ the principle of "lift" to fly. Their ability to do this was primitive at first. "Lift" was not fully explained until after many planes were flown...not until 1939. Yet, the Wright brothers managed to convince a large part of the general population in 1903 that flight was possible. From whom or what did these pioneers gather their larger awarenesses? It was from a deep place in their imagination, unspoiled by thoughts of limitation. They were motivated by the Love of Self-expression.

Love, as an empowerment for Good, is already experienced by most of us to *some* extent. We observed people in our young lives who lived with Love to some degree, and a number of us emulated them. However, most of us have not yet felt that Love is resourceful enough to enable us to avoid abuse, distrust, sacrifice or other troubles. Most of us have not trusted life enough to avoid struggling with it in much that we do. *We have yet to discover the spiritual adventures of our great possibility.* We need to discover spiritual principles and laws along with life's loving Friendship; Love and Law will enable us to greatly express Love in all we do.

Even as the physical atmosphere can be traversed by planes,

so the atmosphere of our thinking can be stabilized and made especially effective by our thinking about spiritual principles. Again, as the waters of the earth allow objects to float that comply with the principle of flotation, so can the movement of our feelings be buoyed up by our feeling the Lovefriend's presence. *To conceive and accept then, that Love is a Friend with incredible capacities to help us, is our most essential mental activity.* It happens through positive thinking and the feeling that Love is our friend. It positions us with life so that we are at ease, in a place of poise. Without such thought Love cannot be experienced through us and as us more than It has been.

To carry out the action of deepening our belief in Love's presence may even seem more fundamental to our success in discovering Love than is the evidence that Love is always present to enrich us. However, no one will ever prove that either Love's presence or our belief in It is the more fundamental particular of our being successful with our expressing It. It is like the old question of the chicken and the egg. The answer to that question is clearly that *the chicken and the egg were both there from the beginning. Love and our ability to believe in Love have always been with us, and always will be.* A more significant consideration that we need to make of this then, is to explore how we can express Love more completely. Belief will be within this action. Observe that the confidence of this is in some way already with us if we believe that our lives need more loving; for then, success and well-being can be felt and activated.

REFLECTIONS

The true stories I have just shared and many hundreds more have built a desire in my thoughts and feelings to communicate the reality of Love's presence, and then, how it is that we can cultivate our desire to believe in Its healing capacity. There is within everyone the awareness of Love as a constant companion. Yet this sense of loving Friendship is generally covered up by false ideas that Love is either a sentimental feeling which comes and goes, or the result of wishful thinking. Love's nature is never more underestimated than when it is explained that way. We involve sentiment in our sensing Love, but Love of Itself is deeply sincere, ever present and not dependent at all upon our circumstances or how we feel about them. *Love is the deepest and truest feeling we have. Again, Love is more than a feeling; It is the Supreme Intelligence of life.*

As life's Supreme Intelligence, the Lovefriend knows that reality is timeless and nonspatial. There is only one reality, although there are two differing awarenesses of it that we may have. The Lovefriend knows that we can conceive of reality as the experience of time and space, and as something we can judge. However, the Lovefriend never thinks this way; It never makes comparisons.

Love is the Friendship we seek, and is deep within everyone's Self, or can be even better understood as *the true Self of everyone.*

*Love is the Friendship we seek and is deep
within everyone's Self, and is the true Self of everyone*

Because Love's actions are not bound by temporal, spatial or judgmental factors, *the most authentic experiences of Love's Friendship are those in which we permit time, space and the making of comparisons to recede from our attention, while we let Love be our focus.* To the degree that I have accepted this, the Lovefriend has emerged in my life experiences to help and heal.

Long ago the Lovefriend told me to write about Its presence. It made me aware that everyone wants to know that the Lovefriend is within themselves. Love will benefit us there as greatly as we believe.

Gradually I heard Love telling me what I should say and how I could best write it. Most wonderful of all, Love taught me and continues to teach me that *IT* may sometimes be difficult to explain, but that Its characteristics will be known to the extent that we simply let Love express us. *First and foremost, the Lovefriend teaches that if we are to be consciously aware of Love, we must be willing to develop our sensitivity to the meetings It is having with us.* The Lovefriend is within, around, and through everyone. We can meet Love within ourselves anytime and in any place that we are.

My first reflections *about the Lovefriend and my meetings with It* were that I had earned that privilege. I presumed that because I had been a good person in many of the ways my parents had taught me, I was being rewarded. These earliest meetings began for me at a time when I felt very inadequate and anxious about nearly everything; I was sixteen. I thought I had to live somewhat perfectly for the meetings to reoccur. Gradually I came to realize that when meetings did not happen the reason had nothing to do with my needing to reach a place in my growth where I deserved them! My tendency towards perfectionism did not earn me the privilege of Love's visits!

My second reflections *about the meetings* were that *LOVE IS NOT THERE FOR US AS A REWARD FOR OUR ABSTAINING FROM SOME WRONGDOING.* I had succeeded in avoiding indulgence in what my parents had conceived as vices, and had presumed that this was meritorious. But the Lovefriend did not make an accounting of this. *LOVE IS A GIFT THAT IS GIVEN*

WITHOUT CONDITIONS. Eventually, I recognized that these meetings were occurring with me to the extent that I admitted I was living in the very conditions I thought I had kept myself from. Then it became apparent that *ALL PEOPLE WHO DESIRE TO FEEL LOVE'S PRESENCE FROM WITHIN THEM ARE ESPE-CIALLY ASSISTED IN THIS, THROUGH THEIR ADMISSION THAT THEY ARE TRAPPED IN UNFORTUNATE CONDITIONS WITHOUT IT. LOVE EXPRESSES US WELL WHENEVER WE OBSERVE THAT WITHOUT OUR BEING AWARE AND IN-VOLVED IN LOVE'S MEETINGS, LIFE CAN ONLY BE CONDI-TIONAL, AND THAT WHENEVER LOVE'S PRESENCE IS FELT, THE JOY OF LIFE IS EXPERIENCED UNCONDITIONALLY.*

Love is a gift that is given without conditions

My second reflections *about the Lovefriend were that Love's helpfulness is less experienced* by us to the extent that we feel sympathetic to the problems that we and others seem to have.

On the other hand, Love's helpfulness is ***more fully experienced*** by us to the degree that we develop sympathy toward the solutions, first of the needs and desires of ourselves, and immediately thereafter, of the needs and desires of others. *FEELING SYMPATHY WITH NEEDS AND DESIRES IS ESSENTIAL IF LOVE IS TO BE WELL EXPRESSED. SYMPATHIES ARE BEST DIRECTED TOWARD THAT WHICH HELPS AND HEALS, BUT NOT AT ALL TOWARDS THAT WHICH HURTS.* We have to discover this, and we have not been assisted much by others because most people have tended to sympathize with defeat, even disaster. What we generally have been advised is that we should care when harm happens; there has not been much sympathy given when happy events have occurred or

Sympathies are best directed toward that which helps and heals

could be seen as possible. To adjust our thinking so that Love flows through a higher sympathy, we have to learn better from the Lovefriend ***how to feel;*** or stated in another way, we have to become aware of the Love that is deep within us, which fortunately is always accessible.

Second reflections about sympathy included that we are wise to be aware of negative conditions and cynical conceptions that often exist with people, even while we are endorsing our being sympathetic with helpful solutions. Love flows through us as we open ourselves to become knowledgeable of what people think and feel, as we come to an understanding of why they react as they do and as we accept them right where they conceive themselves to be. Nevertheless, *OUR SYMPATHIZING ONLY WITH A SOLUTION MUST BE THE TEAMMATE OF THIS AWARENESS OR LOVE IS LARGELY MISSED.*

This is a two-step process. First, we need to use these considerations to at last elevate our usual interest, ability and activity into becoming sympathetic. Secondly, we need to use this sympathy to champion Love's cause. We do this by lifting up our sensitivities that already feel sympathetic but that lack Love's empowerment. We need to raise them high enough and make them into our normal standard of living, so as to succeed in living splendid lives.

Yet, to move our attention from being preoccupied with lower, largely power- less sympathies, or from not being sym- pathetic at all, we must free ourselves simultaneously from being preoccupied with the idea that we must struggle with life. IN PARTICU- LAR, WE MUST LET GO OF THINKING AND FEELING THAT OUR ORDINARY EVERYDAY EXPE- RIENCES MUST IN ANY WAY BURDEN US. WE HAVE

Life has already built into our experiences the ease and rightness we are seeking

*TRIED TO MAKE ALL OF OUR EXPERIENCES OF LIFE COM-
FORTABLE AND RIGHT, AND IN SO DOING HAVE BEEN
UNAWARE THAT LIFE HAS ALREADY BUILT THE EASE AND
RIGHTNESS INTO EACH OF THEM.*

*The pivotal need for us then, is to discover the real nature of Love,
life and ease. Until we have achieved this, we must suffer a lesser
experience of life and be burdened by the results of habitual
experiences and sacrifices that have been constructed upon a
foundation of struggle.*

All of us are good people just as we are. None of us sincerely
wants to be hurt or wants to hurt another. We do not want habits
and practices in our lives that either drag ourselves or others
down. However, *we have not understood that our life-styles are
entirely the result OF OUR THINKING that life and Love cannot help
us more than they have.* As we reconsider this, and engage our
attention with the belief that the Lovefriend is real and always
present, we can adjust our manners of living, rebuild our
consciousness of possibility, and find ourselves lifted out of
habitual practices that have hindered us heretofore. This is
because Love is unconditional, and because life is for us and not
against us. However, our interest in expressing habits and life-
styles that are free of negative patterns must be developed by us.
*That is, we have to enthusiastically choose to accept life's gifts and
Love's support in order to release ourselves from our dysfunctional
living.* Love will then rush into our experiences and release us
from anything and everything which hinders us.

HABITUAL ACTION NEEDS

Love is felt frequently by us as we *let go of trying* to: eat, sleep,
relax, exercise, have more things and more friends, feel secure and
empowered, and experience sex and work, satisfactorily. I call
these the "*ten normal habitual action needs*" of life.

When we *try* to change our habitual programming regarding
our "action needs," we tend to experience inner conflict. This is
the result of our thinking that we are wrong to express or deny
one or more of them more or less than we have. This idea is

largely the result of our having established a program when we were very young about how we should behave, or of feeling limited in what we could do. Our attempts to readjust the original programming have largely been willful actions that have conflicted with the solutions we originally accepted as necessary. *LOVE'S INTELLIGENCE AND FRIENDSHIP HAS BETTER IDEAS FOR US.* Upon applying Love's guidance, we discover a *"point of poise"* with all ten areas. It is a place within each area, somewhere between our aggressively expressing its subject or our denying ourselves altogether any expression of it. It is not the same position in all areas for any two individuals.

"There is a guidance for each of us, and by lowly listening we shall hear the right word....Place yourself in the middle of the stream of power and wisdom which flows into you as life....then you are without effort impelled to truth."[2]

Each point of poise is discovered and established by our adjusting the habitual pattern of thought about it which we accepted as children, and which before then caused us to struggle outwardly with it or feel inner conflict because of it.

Love flows through us best when we cease struggling with life's action needs. *When we re-establish these habit*

Finding the point of poise is allowing the Lovefriend to act through us, as us

---

[2] Spiritual Laws. Ralph Waldo Emerson.

needs by letting Love show us the point of poise, Its friendship takes the place of our struggles. It has seemed to us that this is hard to do. And that is precisely the point: *WE LIVE WITH EASE, TO THE EXTENT THAT WE IMAGINE THE LOVEFRIEND, AND AS WE ASK IT TO POSITION US IN A POINT OF POISE WITHIN EACH NEED. THE LOVEFRIEND SHOWS US HOW TO EXPERIENCE EACH AREA ABLY AND SERENELY BY GUIDING US TOWARD NEW THOUGHT PATTERNS.*

Our biggest error in our eating is believing that we must be free to eat anything we please, or that we ought to severely control our eating. The greatest problem we can have with our rest and relaxation happens when we demand the liberty of laziness or make ourselves suffer the denial of ease. Our exercising is essential, but we can occupy ourselves with it too much, just as easily as we can practice it too little. By building our interests around the accumulation of things we tend to increasingly devalue any particular thing; we become happier as we live more simply. On the other hand, if we intentionally keep ourselves from any accumulation, something of us that rightfully appreciates things is deprived. Friendships are wonderful, but if we are desperate to form more of them and afraid we cannot, or if we make friendships with people more important to us than expressing Love and life, we cannot discover the One relationship which is the essential One. The experience of feeling secure is necessary to good living; we must know that we belong to life, or struggling will ensue. However, when we struggle to be secure or try to avoid any possibility of securing ourselves for fear we will become controlled, we make ourselves vulnerable to adverse experiences. It is good and wise that we feel empowered and that we truly experience power, but not that we become hungry for power or seek to depend on someone or something else for it. Sexual desire is natural and normal, and we need to give it a regular place in our thoughts, feelings and actions; in this way, we express ourselves normally and we avoid the likelihood of social misconduct with either repressive or unbridled actions. Work is an honorable and worthy use of our time; when avoided or made into our only activity, we fail to recognize its value. Its value is that it is an essential function of Self-expression. Too little work denies expression, but too much means that the expression is not being realized with an ease.

Every extreme action is dysfunctional. However, trying to succeed with any of these dysfunctions through reasoning out a better solution consistently fails to prove workable. This is because our childhood programming grips our imagination tightly. If we can change those old beliefs, we can certainly change our experience. However, we cannot favorably readjust our thinking any more than the degree to which we have accepted Love for ourselves. *TO THE EXTENT THAT WE ALLOW LOVE TO EXPRESS US, WE GIVE OURSELVES PERMISSION TO REPROGRAM OUR HABITUAL ACTIONS.*

This means that our interest in accepting all ten of these normal action needs as reasonable for us keeps us struggling with life, unless we allow the guidance of Love's Friendship to steer us into a better solution. Otherwise, our preoccupation with any of them chases the serenity, confidence and well-being out of our experiences of life.

Love's meetings, with their helpfulness and healing, are felt by us as we let go of our attempts to accept or reject the general thinking of the human race about these ten habitual activities. The general thought has been that we must *try* to experience or escape these habitual actions according to the interests of our original guardians or in conformity or nonconformity with societal norms. The more common route has been that we *have tried* to do that which would be rewarded by these allegiances. The other course is that we *have tried* to detach ourselves from being so dutiful. Neither way has expressed us satisfactorily, because our best pursuit of greater living is not experienced by grappling with these habitual actions. Greater living happens through us, and as us, when we Love to redirect our thoughts away from our attempts to live well without Its guidance. *Love knows how to express us well in these basic habits,* and in everything else, and It accomplishes this with us as we expose our incompetencies in the meetings, and *as we accept Its guidance* there for better living. *However, Love cannot help us much unless we actively meet with It.*

BEING PERFECT

Our ability to let go of *trying* to experience these particular habitual actions in accordance with the thinking of others is compromised so long as we believe that we must do things perfectly. The very idea that we should make ourselves live in perfection impairs our ability to succeed. Nevertheless, some of us think that we ought to do everything as perfectly as we can. Others of us who think we do not want to be perfectionists remain subconsciously inclined toward perfectionism. This is not to say that all people are struggling with perfectionism, but only that the interest to comply with authority or to try to free oneself from it is commonplace. People who are otherwise free of such compliance also struggle with life, but for other reasons.

Let us understand that the word "perfect" has a variety of definitions. When perfection is defined as the basic nature of the universe, we are referring to God, the creator or energy as expressing Itself with absolute Love, creativity, power, balance, order, unlimited care and an eternal resourcefulness. Such perfection is that which enables life to be, but is experienced only to the degree that a person's belief system allows.

All people have inherent tendencies toward perfection. Some are perfectly beautiful in appearance, others in their demeanor, others perfectly able to do specific things, others perfectly equipped to express particular vocations. Some people tend to express tendencies toward arranging their homes, desks, relationships and work in a perfect, orderly manner.

However, the concept of perfection that is generally being described in this chapter is different than all the descriptions of it in the above two paragraphs. It is the opposite and erroneous concept of perfection as the practice of trying to feel all right about oneself by behaving in a manner that is conceived as necessary to gain the approval of others. The person who rebels against perfectionism attempts to avoid feeling the need to receive approval, but an attending guilt keeps such a person from feeling all right too; such a one subconsciously wants approval just as much as anyone else. And wherever such a person appears to experience no guilt at all, the sense of guilt has simply been buried very deep within the psyche.[3]

Among those of us who tend to be perfectionists, there are some who think they would like to escape its grip on their thinking, but who are not truly committed to being released from it. I admit that I have been among them. In my earliest awarenesses of Love's meetings, the underlying reason that I sometimes succeeded in experiencing them with a considerable awareness was that I had become annoyed by my perfectionism and its failures to help me live satisfactorily. Unfortunately, as soon as I "let go and let Love heal," I tried to ignore the fact that I could not have achieved what I desired without Love. I attributed my gain to my own conduct, as though I had made myself act perfectly; then I wondered why it took me so long to draw myself into awarenesses of further meetings with Love. Similarly, many people often keep themselves from Love's spontaneous and resourceful guidance because they have tried to take Its place by crediting themselves for what they have done, without having shown Love their appreciation for whatever guidance they have gained from It.

Others of us delay our sense of Love's meetings, because we desire to go to any lengths we have to, to avoid perfectionism. Therefore, we only allow ourselves to experience the habitual actions in a limited fashion, believing that we have thus escaped being perfectionists, as though this avoidance is our most important intention for greater living. It is desirable that we all observe that *to be or not be a perfectionist, is not a life need which is ultimately important to us*. That is, succeeding in not being

---

[3] On the other hand, a person who easily admits feeling guilt at times, is often neither a perfectionist nor one who is motivated by a strong need to be approved. However, whether perfectionism or any other disconcerting factor is observed in this or not, most people have tended to struggle with life. It is this struggle that has kept nearly all human-kind from letting Love meet with it, speak with it, act through it and as it.

perfectionistic may seem meritorious, but it does not help us any more than trying to do things perfectly and feeling frustrated.

The Love presence cannot be felt as regularly and as completely by people who either try to do right or rebel against doing right, because THESE ACTIONS MAKE THEM FEEL THEIR EFFORTS MORE. LOVE'S SOLUTION IS TO PLACE US IN EACH ACTION IN THE POINT OF POISE, WHICH PLACE ONLY LOVE KNOWS.

A POINT OF POISE

We do best as we "let go of trying" to receive approval through being perfect or by rebelling against being perfect, or again, as we "cease attempting," for whatever other reasons, to make life do what we want of it. This is achieved as we tell ourselves that to live well includes our satisfactorily experiencing the "ten normal habitual actions," but that our greater ability to succeed with them is not made possible by anything that we do. Rather, we express them well through our letting Love guide us into experiencing a point of poise with them.

Before we discover the point of poise that lies somewhere between denial and excess in the practicing of the ten habitual life needs, we may try to implement moderation with them. Although a moderate life-style may assist some people in avoiding these extremes, such a solution is considerably less satisfactory than is Love's answer.

The idea of moderation is repugnant to a perfectionist; it seems to excuse mediocrity. Neither is moderation generally sought by those who rebel against perfectionism. This is because there is often an underlying belief that we are wrong to feel rebellious, and the anxiety and guilt of such rationale easily provokes one to excesses rather than to the actions of moderation. Nevertheless, *moderation with these habits does release some people from an anxious preoccupation with their everyday actions; when some avenue to implement it becomes known by those who seem secure enough to practice it, a considerable lessening of the experience of struggle is achieved. Since moderation is usually practiced by people who are stable and who have some sense of Love, it resembles Love's helpfulness; however, moderation is not Love's Answer.* It is not the solution to better living, but an avenue upon which Love will travel if we so desire. It includes that Love will speak through us about what is best for us to do about everything, and even act magnificently as us, while we pursue a moderate life-style. In the same manner, Love will also assist us greatly even if we remain perfectionistic, rebellious, or follow any other particular course of action. *Inasmuch as Love is not conditional, we can attend Its meetings regardless of our conditions and be helped.*

Attending Love's meetings is essential for all people who are desirous of feeling at peace with life. Even as moderation is not a satisfactory replacement for Love's Way, neither is any other contrived method a useful substitute for attaining success with life's needs. One such action that all of us have practiced to some extent, and some of us to a great degree, is attempting to make life's experience comfortable by exerting willpower. Love's Way awaits our abandoning the pursuit of willpower and its attendant effort.

Love's Way includes that we acknowledge all ten habitual action needs as some part of life; to completely deny any of them is to repress and depress ourselves. To practice any of them capriciously, that is without guidance and thoughtful direction, is to act with unreasonable license and anarchy. However, to express these needs entirely through a deliberate moderation is not as satisfactory as it sounds. Love knows a point of poise, somewhere between excessive practice and total denial. *The point of poise is different for every one. That is why Love's Intelligence and support is essential. Again, that is the reason that we need to attend Love's meetings.*

Our problems are not the result of our failing to live according to some behavioral style such as a religious or moral code, nor are they caused by the absence of moderation. Our solutions are not truly wise if we merely adopt the code of conduct or rules of a church, synagogue, temple, mosque or some other conception of ethical behavior. *All difficulties result when we "struggle with our existence" or "try to cope" with life. They are the result of our not having enough awareness of Love's presence, and not letting It guide us.* This results in our not trusting life, and our not accepting the ten needs of life that I have named. As Love guides us, we discover the point of poise in all ten areas of need, and we no longer struggle with any of them. Instead, we recognize that habits are necessary for us to form, in order to experience life in the way that is best for us. ***RATHER THAN RESISTING OUR NEEDS, LET US ACCEPT THAT NEEDS ARE OPPORTUNITIES FOR STABILIZATION, AND STRIKE A POISE IN THEM THAT WE DID NOT HAVE BEFORE.***

All difficulties result when we "struggle with our existence" or "try to cope" with life

WHEN POISE IS NEEDED

Life is an uncomfortable experience when we do not accept,

and function well with, our normal action needs. The resultant forms of such self-rejection are "*self-punishing habitual depressants.*" A brief definition here suffices: "self-punishing habitual depressants are the habitual experiences we have that hurt ourselves and others." They are the abnormal habits we adopt when we fail to place ourselves at ease with the "ten normal habitual needs" of life. The "self-punishing habitual depressants" are not wrongs that life places upon us to test us, but mistakes that we make. They occur with us ENTIRELY to the degree that we distrust life AS IT IS. *Each error is due to the consequent choice we make to struggle with life.* These habits represent the experiences we are having whenever we are aware, or are fleeing from being aware, of anxiety, guilt, insecurity and self-rejection. They occur with us to the degree that we fail to discover and act from the points of poise that Love can show us from within our normal areas of need.

These undesirable habitual patterns slip away from us when we ACCEPT that life rightfully contains about ten areas of day by day challenges for us. Because we will not answer those challenges as desirably as we would like without meeting with Love regularly, we are wise to let Love meet often with us.

In several of the meetings, Love spoke with me about how I could experience poise with everything in life. Love told me that it was best for me not to either try to completely control, or to act without any control, of my eating, sleeping, relaxing, exercising, having things and friends, feeling secure and empowered, experiencing sex and working. If I felt I must experience any of these ten actions in habitual ways that either too greatly involved me with it or denied me the experience of it in my life, I would have to experience trouble. I would have to be repressed or depressed, and/or punish myself with other habit forms that would devastate my ability to live wisely and without harm. Of course, I had to attend many meetings and greatly involve myself in them for this to become clear to me. Gradually, I have been coming to the realization that Love knows my place of poise within each of these experiences of life, and now I am opening myself to express Love's guidance in all that I do. I continue to attend the meetings and expect that I always will. I still make mistakes, but Love is more and more extricating me from my instability and placing me in the points of poise.

How has it been for you? Do you have trouble in your life? Are you aware that being open to the expressing of Love can greatly help you?

Would you like to be aware of the Lovefriend, know Love and let Love's care flow through your life experiences? This study of Love's meeting with us, will build sensitivity to how life's greater possibilities can occur with you. You can discover Love's presence and the places of poise It already knows are possible for you. You can hear Love, feel Love or in some way see Its presence, and believe It is always helping you, if you are willing to *let go of trying* to make your life either comfortable or right. *Trying* to be right is generally the perfectionist's problem. *Trying* to be comfortable is generally the rebel's plight.

Let your experience of the meetings and a growing confidence in Love's Friendship be related to your everyday experience of life. Allow the Lovefriend Its giving that lifts you out of personal troubles. Know that the Lovefriend is not sympathetic with your troubles, but that It is aware of your need of It, and sympathetic with your greatest possible solution. Know that you must admit to yourself what your real difficulties are, but then let Love flow through you, to help you and heal you.

PROCEDURE

My opening pages told of people who wonderfully experienced Love's presence. You too can experience Love just as greatly.

For these kinds of experiences to become natural occurrences in your everyday life, begin by accepting that there are ten areas of life with which you need to feel a point of poise. That point varies for every person and for each of the ten areas. Cease *trying* to determine its place. Let Love show you. Then root yourself in the concepts of the next chapter. Continue to clarify Love's basic nature by examining Its capacities more completely in the other chapters. Most of all, expect to attend Love's meetings.

*Expect to attend Love's meetings
and you will be supported*

In them, you will be supported to express happiness, peace, good health, prosperity and success, because Love is your Friend and desires the best for you, as you. Your attendance in the meetings, your attention to the agenda and interest in letting Love express you, will enable you to manifest all that you sincerely desire.

You have probably been either perfectionistic or rebellious toward practices of perfectionism. Whether this is the case or not, admit that you need to focus on a good direction in order to better experience life's normal actions. As you do, attend Love's meetings so that you can discover the Lovefriend and Its helpfulness. Otherwise, you will misunderstand Love's Way.

Love knows how to live your life magnificently; however, you can only sense Love's Supreme Intelligence as you let go and let Love show you how to better experience all you do. Otherwise, Love will remain available deep within you, but not be very active in your day to day experiences. Here you are learning how to talk with Love as your Friend and to bring It forth in all you do. This will happen as you desire to let go and let Love be you.

As you let go and let Love express you, the ten areas will gradually be observed as a mere foundation for what Love can do in your life. Love can and will act magnificently as you in every situation you experience; but first, you must begin to cultivate your interest in letting It guide you through your everyday actions.

Love is a definite presence; and we experience pronounced joy, healings and helpfulness, when we meet with It as with any friend.

BEGIN EACH DAY WITH THESE WORDS, AND WATCH THEM UNFOLD LOVE'S PRESENCE WITHIN YOUR LIFE EXPERIENCES

There is within me the awareness of Love's
            constant companionship.
There is without me the desire to experience
            Love as my all in all.
It is natural for me to sit in the quiet,
            walk unafraid in the storm,
            and to feel Love's presence.

Love and my ability to believe in It
            have always been with me.
The Lovefriend and Its coming forth through me
            is natural, and will always be.
It is my great privilege to express Love,
            to let It come through me,
            and to know Love is ALL.

I am serene as I conceive myself on the
            mountain top;
            have always been on high.
I am looking through the meadows and
            over the trees; I feel the calm.
I am lifted up where I can see that all is
            well with me; my life is happy;
            Love makes me free.

CHAPTER TWO

MEETING WITH LOVE

Can you become so loving with yourself and others that you genuinely and easily radiate happiness and joy? YES, YOU CAN! YES, YOU CAN! YES, YOU CAN!

It had rained everyday for more than a month. A group of people, about thirty-five in number, were to meet together in a beautiful outdoor facility to have a meeting with Love. We had agreed that a particular date was the only time we could experience this together. We were to meet from early morning until late afternoon. Most of those involved questioned whether the agreed upon date during that wet spring in southern Michigan would be dry enough to allow us the experience which we very much desired. Weeks before the occasion, I talked with Love about it, and found myself believing it would happen. Despite this, it continued to rain every day prior to the gathering.

On the day before the event, three other fellows and myself drove to the place, pitched a tent in the rain, and affirmed that all continued predictions of steady rain would prove untrue for approximately twenty-four hours. Suddenly, at about 8:00 p.m., the sky cleared up completely. The rain returned about 5:00 p.m. the next afternoon as we were preparing to leave.

Love meets with us when we are ready. Love prepares the way, and removes all obstacles.

What is Love? Why can Love help us and heal our conditions?

LOVE AND love

The awareness of Love, referred to here with the capital letter

L, is provided all of us from within ourselves. Love is felt there as an emotion, and that It is. Love is the most pivotal of emotions, and therefore, It is the affective key to living effectively. Nevertheless, our imagination has misnamed Love when we have explained It only as an affection. More completely identified, Love is also supremely intelligent, *and* It is again our out-going Self-givingness.

Love's presence is personable, and is the greatest Friendship we can ever know; however, It is not personality. Love's personalness lies in Its capacity and interest to act with especial resourcefulness through and as persons.

It is because Love is even more than the collected expressions of emotion, Self-givingness, Intelligence, resourcefulness and Friendship within us, that we have experienced difficulty in explaining It well. To understand Love, we do best as we lessen our interest in trying to define It and give more of ourselves toward opening our awareness to Its being ever present and toward letting It act as us. We achieve this as we establish a Friendship with Love.

Most of us have been more familiar with love than with Love. Let us understand that love, written here with the lower case l, is the small sense we generally have of Love. For love is not unlike Love; love is simply the diminished awareness that we have had of Love for most of our lives. We misunderstand the nature of Love if we interpret It as something different or apart from love. Our lesser awareness of Love, or love, is the result of our having conceived of Love as not being possible to practice without lessening our sense of Its lofty values.

It has seemed to most of us that the ideal of Love, such as our giving ourselves everywhere to practicing kindness and sympathy, is but an invitation to others for them to use us. Consequently we have not generally felt that it is safe to express more of love than we have done. We have been slow to discover that although Love is an emotion, It is the king or queen of emotions. Love's kingdom is indomitable! Knowing this alone about Love will open us to lives of poise, confidence and well-being.

Love cannot be affected by anything; we can express Love's

tenderness in any situation. Love's nature is invulnerable! If we forget this, Love becomes practiced as love, and Its kingdom seems to fall. However, whenever Love's nature is recalled, Love rules. This means that when a situation seems troublesome, our greater wisdom is then to remain faithful to the understanding that Love is nevertheless unfolding a perfect outcome, and to not try in the meanwhile to manipulate anything.

Here we will uncover Love's magnificent Friendship within us, something that we already know at a deeper level of Mind. We will accomplish this by motivating ourselves to trust Love as being supremely intelligent and heart-warming at the same time.

We have not trusted Love enough to allow It to flow freely through us. We have too often experienced love instead of Love. We now can know that Love is the greatest description of life's reality, and that love is but a hint to us that this greatness of reality exists.

We are able to express happiness, joy and everything as marvelously as we can conceive through our discovering Love. We have *conceived* of Love, but most of us have not discovered It as reality; we have not amply *believed* that Love could truly be. We have succeeded in believing that love is. However, love has only rendered a limited expression of Love. *OUR FEELINGS ARE LONGING FOR MORE OF love. WE CAN EXPERIENCE IT BY SHIFTING OUR USUAL FOCUSES TO A COURTING OF LOVE, AND THROUGH OUR BUILDING UP TRUST OF IT. THEN OUR DESIRES SENSE THAT LOVE HAS REGULAR MEETINGS WITH US; AND IN THE MEETINGS, LOVE SHOWS US HOW TO LIVE MAGNIFICENTLY.*

LOVE'S MEETINGS

It is in our willingness to develop a greater interest in the meetings that we regularly have with Love, that happiness and joy become abundantly present for us. We are all having meetings with Love many times a day, and possibly many times each hour. But until now, most of us have not noticed that these meetings occur. We have been too preoccupied with trying to cope with our habitual conditions.

Some meetings with Love last a few minutes; others last a few seconds. Love has initiated all of the meetings. Love has not initiated one *continuous* meeting with us, because It desires that we first become interested in the meetings It already has with us. And Love wants us to choose how much we want to feel we are One with It. However, *this explanation of Love's relationship with us is not meant to imply that there is ever a moment that Love is not with us in everything!*

The Lovefriend is with us in everything

The meetings can become one continuous experience of feeling at One with Love if we desire this: however, since such a ceaseless sense of Love would be an experience of launching a perpetual cosmic consciousness, it happens only when Love's presence is more essential to one's ongoing livingness than all other interests combined might be. It is not necessary for all people to immediately feel this way. On the other hand, it is especially beneficial to become immediately aware that Love's meetings already occur with each of us daily, and to gradually deepen our interests to attentively participate more and more in them.

Until we intend that Love be well expressed in our lives, we prevent our conscious thoughts from becoming involved at all with the content of the meetings. Nevertheless, all of us are frequently meeting with Love. And anyone can be deeply aware of the meetings and can greatly express Love, and anything else in life that needs Love's encouragement, simply through actively supporting the belief that Love is having meetings with us.

Until the time that we choose to *consciously* attend the meetings, Love is largely presumed by most of us to be a conception of utopian ideals, something too dreamy or delusory to be greatly experienced. However, we are all familiar with love. Many of us want to think better of love; we desire to believe that somehow it is the grand reality of life, but few of us are convinced enough to pay the attention necessary to discover its greater reality. Even if we try to meet with Love, we unwittingly expect that logic alone must conceive, conduct and manage the meetings, because we seem enmeshed in the belief that all the Love that can realistically exist is love, and that love is too fanciful to provide a sensible direction for living better than it has. We have yet to discover that Love and an unlimited potential await us from love's center.

love's THREE SUBSTITUTES FOR LOVE

Because we have not joined much with Love in the meetings, and have thought that we must spend our energy to contend with our habitual conditions, we have invented three substitutes for Love's reality -- actions of love that we have thought could take the place of Love. They consist of our (1) making sacrifices, (2) sympathizing with trouble and (3) "acting" nicely. We have thought that sacrifices are necessary, because it has appeared to us that our parents and heroes have helped us most whenever they have deprived themselves of things in order to give us something. We shall discover that sacrifices are not genuine, loving actions, because Love is Self-givingness rather than Self-sacrifice (which displaces Self-fulfillment). When Love gives of Itself, It is not being sacrificial; It is fulfilling Itself.

Love is Self-givingness rather than Self-sacrifice

The second substitution for Love, our sympathy with trouble, diverts our attention from being sympathetic with the causes that people would most like to espouse. Sympathy will be seen here as an essential aspect of Love, but never when it reinforces the conditions that prevent our being positive.

Love sympathizes with beneficial causes, but never with conditions

Third, "acting" nicely toward other people and ourselves happens because we tend to place attention upon the idea that we should not expect others to do better. This is the result of our disapproving of persons who seem unable to resolve their dysfunctional behavior, while simultaneously trying to appear that we do approve of them. "Nice talk" results from our feeling sorry that someone is failing to experience Love's presence or good times. It is not as kind as our believing that a way will yet be found by us or by them to discover Love's presence, and with It, the ability to successfully express particular needs and desires.

*Acting nicely is appearing to approve of the
actions of others, when we really disapprove*

We have believed that these practices enable us to cope with life and our habitual needs. These substitute actions, which we adopt in place of letting Love act through us, have usually been carried out in manipulative ways; some of them we have regretted, and then we have wished that a reality of Love could be. Other times, we have acted more reasonably, but not as effectively as Love could have enabled us. Fortunately, we have sometimes acted as though Love exists.

All of us are candidates for being active in the meetings with

Love. Because Love meets with everyone, we need not ask if we can be included. We have only to ask ourselves: do we desire to sincerely observe each meeting's agenda, and do we want Love to express us well? And can we be courageous enough to act independently of other people who feel they must sacrifice themselves, sympathize with harsh conditions and "act" nicely to express love?

We are wise as we observe that Love's meetings will be ignored by most of us until we reinterpret the nature of Love. But, we cannot know even then how much better Love is for us than are the substitutions of love, until we choose to belong to this deeper or higher idea of Love. *To belong means to commit. Commitment to anything implies the intention to act from an increasing sense of it. This is why Love provides the meetings. Through them we discover how Love resolves everything through us as we expand our awareness of Its presence. This includes that Love brings us to a place of poise with the ten areas of habitual actions. Again, this also includes our experiencing marvelous solutions to all of the other needs and desires that exist with us.*

CONTENT OF THE MEETINGS

Whenever we suppose a meeting is going on or that it could be going on, we become attentive by placing ourselves into a quiet, solitary place. It may be that we sit in a meditative manner. Or we may go walking. Or we may arrange to be in a shower, pool or any quiet place of our choice. By "quiet," I mean that we turn from all our reasonings that are not of Love.

A particular interest or a natural combination of interests from our own lives, often regarding habitual conditions, becomes the subject of a meeting. We are wise to become very aware of our current interests on a daily basis, because the contents of Love's meetings largely revolve around them. We listen to what Love knows is best for us to think, feel and do regarding each situation which is being contemplated. Love then resolves it through us in accord with our interest.

There is never a time that Love fails to bring about a perfect resolution -- unless our listening is inclined toward skepticism. There can easily be an instant healing of any new or long standing problem, because there is not any affliction or complication that Love will not heal as quickly as we *MEET* with It, and *LET* Love lift us out of the disappointment.

Up until now, our listening has often been half-hearted. The reason is that we have usually been fearful of really letting Love use us to do the right thing. We have often thought that we would have to pay a heavy price, one that we would regret. Yet, no matter how much we have let Love meet with us and act through us, nothing It has ever done through us or as us, has been a basis for our being sorry.

Since we may not listen carefully, because of fearing we will regret Love's action, we are wise to discourage our hesitancy by increasing our focus upon Love until a sense of peace is attained in the meeting. A serene feeling is naturally accepted as the evidence that Love is present, and guiding us sensibly and effectively. Our focus is increased through our use of as much logic, feeling and common sense as is necessary to believe in Love's helpfulness. Our use of logic is to ask what our common sense combined with Love's unlimited resourcefulness can do for us. It can enable us to either observe the ideas of Love that are coming through us, or show us that we are not truly aware of any. By our persistent use of logic and common sense together, the ideas of Love that we greatly value will come through us eventually, if not immediately. As we place ourselves into a feeling mode, we let Love act from within us, as us, without telling It how. Because we all know what love feels like, we can feel love, and then speak with it, and tell it we believe there is more to love. We can then expect Love to reveal Itself from within us with Its understanding and direction. Additionally, we can ask ourselves, "What does Love, in Its lifted up view of life, think is best for me to do to be loving to myself, and to relate well with the environment and other people who are involved with me?" It is practical for us to believe that Love can cause us to gradually, if not immediately, reshape our thoughts and actions for the Good of all.

Following a meeting, we do well to immediately act upon the ideas that have just come to us. Future meetings are enhanced if we have continued to act in accord with the inspiration that we have received, trusting that Love is in such action. Even if for now, we must *simply reason* out what that action should be, because of not having ample conviction that Love's presence is real, we are wise to draw upon whatever degree of confidence in Love that this represents for us. *At the least, this results in our building up the belief that Love is involved with us. Such belief is enough for us to eventually know that Love is definitely meeting with us.*

There is a second item that needs handling in most meetings, and it lies in our asking, "Are there past actions in my life that were unloving on my part that need to be reviewed and redone?" This is no place to blame or shame oneself or another! However, if a new action can improve a situation, Love will speak through us as to what it is, if we want to know. Again, we may have to ask of our own logical thought what Love thinks is best for us. It is loving to act in accord with whatever sincere answer comes through us in response to that question.

BEING WITH THE LOVEFRIEND

In our earlier participation with Love, our logic, common sense and feelings admit Love into our actions -- to some degree; conversely, Love is to some extent prohibited because of the tendency most of us have to believe that our logic, common sense and feelings are all the Love there is for us. But in spite of this, we gradually discover Love's greater presence. This includes a growing awareness that in resolving our situations Love is never apart from this trinity: logic, common sense and feeling. However, we do not consciously experience Love's presence by making all our thoughts logical, sensible and sensitive. Rather, the integration of logic, sense and sensitivity within our thinking, places us at Love's door: this is the point of poise. *TO THE DEGREE THAT WE ARE OPEN TO LOVE, ITS GREATER PRESENCE COMES THROUGH THIS POSITIONING OF OUR-*

SELVES.

Then, as we concentrate our attention upon the "idea" that we are meeting with the Lovefriend, and that Love is being expressed through us, we discover that the meetings are really happening and that they are becoming very productive for us. Although many people think that this greater concentration of attention upon our thought means that we must either coerce ourselves to believe particular dogma or that we must intensify the feeling of allegiance that we already have with certain beliefs, this is not the case. Nor do we need place pressure upon ourselves or our thought to reach an acceptance of "the idea" that the meetings are real; there is no strain involved in reaching this awareness. Rather, *"the idea" that carries conviction that the meetings are really happening with us occurs as we direct an integration of four practical actions.*

1. *We declare and accept our own particular thoughts as being the basis for all the experiences that occur with us.*
2. *We take the time and interest to purify our conception: of Love's desire to meet with us, and of the content of our thinking so that it is for the Good of all.*
3. *We tell ourselves that we have an unlimited desire to experience Love's better ideas.*
4. *We enthusiastically increase the knowledge that we have of Love's ability to naturally manifest Its ideas as us in a healthy and harmonious manner.*

Once we sincerely declare and accept that our own thinking is the basis of our own experiences (1), we are able to become aware of the place (of poise) in our lives wherein Love enables us to live with special effectiveness. Love may have been sensed as nothing more than love to us before, but our interest in thinking that better ideas could improve our experiences, opens up the awareness that Love is about to show Itself and prove that It is our greatest means of help and healing. As we understand that Love's nature contains the combination of unlimited Supreme Intelligence and Self-givingness, the belief that Love's ideas could be especially positive and constructive for us begins to form. As this becomes obvious, Love's ideas are discerned as better for us than are love's. And this gives us the needed incentive to consciously participate in Love's meetings.

Our ideas are the basis of our experiences

The desire to purify (2) our spiritual conception that Love is initiating this with us and through us, enables the contemplation of Love's presence to take place. This means that a thorough blending of truly enlightened spiritual practices transforms our capacity to well express Love from only reasoning about It logically, to contemplating Its healing action through us.

The meetings with Love occur through this purification in the same manner as with any of nature's progressions. For instance, if we desire that a drab paint color become more satisfactory for our tastes, we may cause enough of a brighter and more enlivened color to be mixed with it to make it pleasing to the eye. Little effort is involved: however, ample time and interest must be expended to achieve this goal, and the right selection of the needed complementary color must become known. Here is where the third and fourth actions come into play. We will draw upon our inner desire to keep our attention upon the action (3) of allowing Love's nature to be sufficiently sensed within our awareness, through our willingness to contemplate the ideas that come from Love's essence. The measure of how much we apply our interest to the knowledge that Love's Way helps and heals, is the degree to which we will let Love act as us (4).

These four practices that we can follow and that enable us to know we are having a meeting with the Lovefriend, are increased in effectiveness through our use of two thought declarations with them. We declare: (1) that we desire to experience these beneficial meetings with Love, and (2) that we are uninterested in experiencing any activity while we are in the meetings other than our being in conversation with the Lovefriend. The four aforementioned practices then subconsciously form the experience of our being in Love's meeting, and of an ensuing productivity within our lives.

In these meetings with Love, our practicing these four somewhat mechanical steps is eventually replaced by our simply contemplating Love's presence. *Contemplating Love is the best experience of support that we can have.* All other productive relationships and experiences that we need are made possible through It.

MOTIVATION FOR LOVE

Where are you in your relationship with Love? Are you interested in Love's expressing Its ideas through an upliftment of your logic, common sense and feeling? Do you want to meet regularly with Love, and have It assist you to purify your ideas so as to conform to your innermost, sincerest desires? Are you interested in discovering Love's unlimited capacity to resolve every problem you have?

If you desire to know Love and experience It this richly, you will do best to let go of everything that stymies your motivation for letting Love express you. This includes that you will let Love express all your thoughts and emotions as you, but according to Its wisdom. It means that you need to observe where you are with everything in your life, and that you will do best as you let Love adjust your thoughts, feelings and actions.

How much do you feel the higher emotions? That is, do you sometimes feel uninterrupted and undiluted joy, peace, kindness and/or courage? Is your ability to express honesty sometimes unhampered by your temperamental considerations of whether you will gain or lose things? Do you ever turn away from the idea that what you give to others must be repaid you by them in some equal manner? Are you sometimes able to feel innocent in situations where guilt has previously interfered with aspirations for success? Do you want to accept yourself and others both as you and they are and, most especially, as you and they can be? Are you willing to nurture the feeling that no conditions are ever needed for Love's great gifts to be experienced?

How much do you feel the lower emotions? For instance, do you often feel excitement, but not feel as free of the exigencies of life that deep joy, great confidence and assured resourcefulness could provide? Are you troubled by feelings that you will hurt yourself by making mistakes? Do you feel peacefulness only erratically? Do you feel kindly only when you are trusting, but feel unsure that you can trust anybody? Do you feel courage only when your life experiences seem relatively safe? Does this seem too infrequent? Do you use this sense of insecurity to arouse your anger and make yourself feel hurt?

How much do you vacillate between the higher and lower emotions? How much are you interested in discovering that in Love there is a presence who (or which) is always the higher emotions, and that you could allow to rather continuously be your expression? If you could meet with Love and believe that It is always with you, would you be willing to let It be your thoughts, your feelings and your actions?

How much is your sense of Love only a feeling of love? Could it be that you are only interested in Love to the extent that you can express It so that others will like you or love you? Notice what you have done with Love up until now. Consider whether you are willing to dispense with setting up conditions for letting Love express Its amazing kindness through yourself, and to others from yourself.

Love is never conditional; love is always conditional. In and of your own thinking, you cannot do for others without expecting favors from them; that is the precedent for how the human experience has been of love. If you are to know when Love meets with you, if you are to sense Its presence, if you are to experience It as the Lovefriend, you must relinquish your interest to receive anything back from those people who receive Love's gifts from you. With Love, there are no conditions conceived or made necessary for the giving and receiving of gifts.

A CONDITIONAL MOTIVATION

If you are trying to please others so that they
will like you, you will become displeased
with them.

If you are displeased with others,
you will become depressed about what you
have done with them.

If you are depressed about what you have done
with others, you will become angry with
yourself.

If you are angry with yourself,
you will be feeling you are unloved.

If you are feeling unloved,
you will be trying to please others--so that
they will like you.

AN UNCONDITIONAL MOTIVATION

You can let Love express you without trying to
make others like you.

You can achieve this by giving yourself away.

When you really feel Love, you have succeeded
in this.

This is the way Love achieves this with you:
If you give yourself away,
you will receive more of what you gave.

If you receive more of what you gave,
you will be rich for having given.

If you are rich for having given,
you will feel Good about yourself.

If you feel Good about yourself,
you will give yourself away.

There is a leap from love to Love; we can all achieve it.
Rather than trying to get others to love us, we do best to let Love

be felt by them as we give ourselves away. Admittedly, it is a high ideal. What method can we use right now to jump from low emotions to high emotions and into this permanent sense of adequacy?

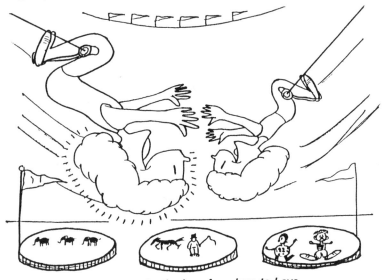

Dare to make the leap from love to Love

Giving ourselves away does not mean that we must express our greatest talents without receiving compensation. But it does mean that we must give of our very best, regardless of how much money or other kindnesses we receive as payment. When we freely give (without making price the basis for the giving) of ourselves, we are always greatly rewarded, although sometimes the payment may not be in the amount of money that we think we want. Rather, true compensation always lies in the richness of the life experiences that develop with us, ones which we individually desire the most.

Unless our attention is first upon how much we can give of ourselves, our sense of Love cannot be more than love, and our gift of Self must be small; the payment of life's experience through us, must then be little too. Therefore, Love is experienced to the extent that we bring out of ourselves a treasure that shows us we were born loving and wealthy of spirit.

As we realize that we can give of ourselves, and thereby grow in the sense we have of love, the awareness of Love builds within us. Love finds a clear channel for Its expression through such people, and fills them with peaceful, enriching experiences, making their bodies, minds and souls whole and their actions a fulfillment of themselves.

Such an expansion for us cannot happen if we think it is hard to express ourselves in this better way. Therefore, certain comical friends here will help us to lighten the challenge and to thereby meet Love with ease. The Lovefriend will show Itself through us as we play with the idea that Love is natural for us, and that It simply awaits our expression of It from within ourselves.

LOVE AS TENDERNESS

The cartoon characters that appear throughout this book have a relationship with Love as much as we do. There are five of them, and they all assist us in sensing how much or how little we may trust that Love is taking Good care of us while we are expressing It by giving ourselves away. Through them, we can easily observe both our emotional reactions and our capacity for insight. These animated pictures of our feelings lead us to understand the writings more than we otherwise could achieve. In this way, we discover the presence of Love breaking through the hard core of logic that we have used to refuse Its tender interest to shape us.

Love that is true and comes through us from the heights of life is tender; it is best that we find a way to feel It, for something that is tender is best understood by feeling it. Our past ideas of what tenderness means could mislead us. For the characteristics of Love are not those of blindness, immaturity, or soft-heartedness. Neither is Love yielding, weak or malleable. This amazes many of us, because these words may seem to well define tenderness. Most of us have rarely felt Love's tenderness, then, because we have associated Love with characteristics we do not admire. In order to fully experience Love's tenderness, we must forget most of what we have learned that It is.

We will discover Love's true nature as we become open, flexible, willing or tender enough so that Love can affect us. Love knows how to unreservedly give Itself. The form that Love's tenderness takes is especially endearing because It is very sensitive about the feeling we have of It, and It communicates through us Its great joy at our appreciation of It. But Love is never affected by anything we experience that is unlike It. We learn from It; Love learns nothing from our understandings, for It already knows all!

Love is especially tender in that It meets us in an intimate manner that places us more closely with It than with anything else; Love is especially touching. We feel Love's closeness when we let It provide all of the care we need. But we lose our sense of It when we think we should be sympathetic *toward the problems* of others, or that we should suffer, or that we should *try* to care for others or even for ourselves. Sympathy toward problems, suffering and trying to care or "acting" nicely have all been taught as features of love. We may easily be persuaded that these conceptions are loving, and consequently not come to an understanding of Love. However, we should recognize that it is conditional love that sympathizes with troubled conditions, that suffers, and gives care at the cost of personal sacrifice. Love, which is unconditional, has to be something better. Unshaped by our conditions, Love knows how to live well precisely because of such independence.

Through Love's tenderness, Its infinite ability and willingness to assist penetrates our disqualification to care for our lives without It. Love cares for us, through us and as us when we appreciate Its tenderness enough.

We will come to know that Love has provided for us so well that we need no longer indulge ourselves in any form of suffering. We will not remain sympathetic in the ways we formerly thought were necessary. Yet, we will find that through our increasing awareness of Love we will sympathize much with a person's interests to be happy, whole and resourceful. *IN THIS, WE WILL*

NOT BE GIVING ATTENTION TO HOW MERE CONDITIONS MIGHT SATISFY US AND OTHERS, BUT RATHER WITH LOVE'S SPLENDID INTEREST TO BETTER EXPRESS THE SINCERE DESIRES OF EVERYONE.

THE CARTOON CHARACTERS

Sandy is loving and lovable. Her Love is not something she has learned from others. It is her natural expression. She feels Love as something that comes from deep within herself. It is the result of her philosophy of life. Her view of herself is that she is basically a good person. She desires to express her good sense of self. As she reaches out to her friends to be giving, she feels a strong sense of Love rising out of herself.  She trusts that feeling and dares let all of her actions be the result of It. She enjoys loving people, and she likes being with them.

It is especially noteworthy that Sandy expresses this wondrous Love with much ease. She does this because of her high level of trust. How does she achieve it? It is not because her environment always feels safe .... not really. Sometimes it seems shaky, confusing, sad or threatening. She simply trusts that there is something of magnificence deep within her that feels more like what Love should be than anything else could feel. Because she has believed it was present when at times everything around her felt unstable and troubled, she has maintained a poise and confidence. Because Love and Its protection have always been proven to underlie all those contrary conditions, It has caused her to be secure, self-reliant and inclined to give of herself for the good of others.

Young Sandy does not assume that she knows any more than

other people, but she does enjoy sharing her understanding with her friends. She likes to act in ways that help others, but her Love is not sympathetic with the problems of their suffering; rather It is an active example that wholesomeness, success, and happiness can happen anywhere and with anyone.

Sandy wants to know how Love can continue to make her life better. She has a great spirit of adventure which is indicative of her high level of trust. Through exploratory ways, she is finding that she can discover more Love within her every day.

This lovable young lady learns of Love by opening the way for It to flow through her. The openness between her and Love is the most attractive aspect of her life; it is something that all of us are seeking. We miss it when we try to make Love happen. We will discover the Sandy within us when we allow ourselves to believe that this treasured Friendship with Love exists for us, but may have been kept hidden until now.

A second cartoon character is strong and very capable, but in ways that are different from Sandy's. Newton is a boy genius. He is confident that there is no problem that cannot be solved; everything can be made to turn out perfectly for him. Although Newton feels a resourcefulness of Love within him, he greatly respects Sandy, for he discovers her to be a stimulus to his thought. He appreciates how quickly and naturally she acts with benevolence. He positively adores his privilege of association with her.

Newton lives with an absolute trust that Love can find the way to do anything through him. The result is that he does things, and inspires others to do things, that would ordinarily be thought impossible.

When Newton feels encouragement from Sandy, he allows himself to turn his attention toward experiencing the greatest goals imaginable. Although he could easily achieve his desires without her, he has an innocence about him that keeps him from doing so just to prove that he can. This means he is aware of his marvelous potential, but that he does not feel a need to express it, except as he feels spurred on by Love, and Sandy's example of Love in action.

The third cartoon character is Calvin. Calvin is glad to count these described persons as his friends. He is slow-witted, and is less aware of Love and Its guiding care. Nevertheless, he is willing to listen and learn. He has not a whole lot of confidence; still, he is best understood as being very willing to discover Love and Its resourcefulness for him. He is finding the way to gradually evolve a trust in a friendly empowerment from somewhere within himself.

Veda is the fourth character. She can best be described as a "sourpuss." Veda is a harsh critic of her friends, of their interests, of the idea that Love is a wonderful presence within the Self. She ridicules the optimism and confidence that she detects in their belief systems, especially those of Sandy and Newton. She makes fun of Calvin's slow-wittedness. She is not only negative, but often hostile. She is also a braggart, but gains little from it, for often she is a loser, and she notices this result.

She sees her objections and actions as mistakes she has made, that represent an inability to flow with life. Most of her attempts to achieve almost anything come tumbling down.

Hypatia is Newton's little sister. She is a naive little child. She lives simply, is very cute and completely trusts life. She represents the potentiality for an even greater understanding of Love and an uplifted practice of It, than that which is achieved so far by her friends.

Altogether, the five characters are within the make-up of the personality who has shared them with us. It is through them that he relates to Love and life. His ability to bring forth his relative sense of Self, his acceptance of its various characterizations, and his courage to be willing for us to see him as he sees himself, is exceedingly beneficial to us. For in these five personalities, collectively, we can see the whole of any personal view, and yet personalized in this way, it is made especially meaningful to us.

Actually, the cartoon figures in sum total represent the universal person. All of us have genius together with the misunderstandings that deny that resourcefulness. We all have the wonderful presence of Love within us, and we have some sense of It; if this were not so, we could gain nothing by examining Love as we are presenting It here. But, we are all in different places in our understanding of Love, and of Its care, and what we can do with It. Most of us are more positive than negative, though all of us can become more positive than we are.

We can gain by seeing ourselves in each character, and as we consider what is being felt in that experience by us. Again, we can be benefited as we examine other particulars of our relationship to them and also to this writing. Something wonderful can happen to us, and it will, if we can believe that Sandy and Newton have the right to be the leaders of our thoughts. There will still be room for Calvin and Veda, but as we think about them we will lift them up in us, until they too understand that Love can be our resourcefulness. As we do, Hypatia will surprise us with a late developing expressiveness of the Good life that will amaze us.

Only as we conceive the cartoon characters collectively, as representative of the universal person, do we know we are identifying something within us that is safe, right and liberating.

Many readers can easily defeat themselves by thinking an approximation of all the five personalities is not within them. We can belittle ourselves by thinking that some people have more Love and more genius than ourselves. Every one of us has as much potential for benevolent action and resourceful expression as any one of us. However, no two people conceive of this in the same way; nor do any of us have the same kind of genius. Still, there are unlimited possibilities for personal expression, and every person is naturally loving and creative. Where it seems that this cannot be true, it is because there is not enough of a Self-acceptance. This is the result of feeling inadequate. Love can help correct this in any person.

Wherever the personal traits that make up our personalities seem to be of lesser quality, it is only because we have not seen ourselves through the Love within us that knows us better. All conceptions of the negative aspects of ourselves are the reverse way we sometimes view our real potentiality. When we let Love show us who we are, every negative sense of Self shows itself as positive too. That is, we have great potentiality, but some aspects of it are often first seen in a reverse appearance, much as the negatives of photographs initially appear. This only means that some aspects of our potentiality have not yet been accepted as they most truly are. When that acceptance is made, through feeling each aspect of ourselves completely, the appearance of the potential expression, which at first is in the likeness of a photographic negative, shows itself as positive. For instance, Veda has the potentiality to express as magnificent a life as Sandy and Newton have already achieved. It includes that Veda's negativity will eventuate into positive effects. She will then be using her apparent shortcomings in higher ways that express her well. We all need to Love the Veda in ourselves before we can discover our innate excellence. And we all can do this!

Some of us may think we have all of the positive qualities of our universal example, and that we do not have a Veda. People who think this, no matter how honest they believe they are, need to rethink their entire understanding of themselves. The most heroic, successful and loving people who have ever lived, would not have claimed they were free of all negative challenges from within themselves. If we could have asked them, they would have confessed to some negative sense of Self, and would explain how they dealt with it. It is not bad to be negative, but it is especially good to be aware of our negativity and accept that hindrances must result from it. When the acceptance of our negative images is fully made, we will discover that they are all necessary balances within our personalities, that their negative appearances come and go and can never be entirely discharged, but that they can greatly express us. When our acceptance of them is all-embracing, they complete us; they make us whole.

It is especially unfortunate when we think we have dealt with the negativity within ourselves so completely that we are better than other people. So how can we deliver ourselves out of this false pride, this tendency to think better of ourselves than others? We can be freed of this pompousness by meeting the Lovefriend, and by letting Love tell us what to think, how to act, and most of all, how to express our individualities as only Love knows how. And we can find our way with the Lovefriend's assistance by observing Sandy and her friends interfacing with It.

Enjoy all five cartoon symbols, but also let the way they are particularly characterized within you be revealed without feeling that you have to judge them. For if you were to place conditions upon them, they could not show you how Love is unconditional. Notice that they contain certain characteristics, but that they are as flexible with Love as you choose for them to be. You can dissolve any aspects of them that you desire, and it is worth your while to see Love's value for you by first observing Its altering them. All this allows you to feel Love's closeness, with Its unconditional nature and Its transforming power. As you let Love have Its way with you, a channel for Its greater expressiveness to flow through you will be furrowed in your nature, an integration of your character traits will be achieved, and a growing happiness will prevail within you. It will all be achieved without effort as you let these ideas permeate your thinking. For then, you will meet the Lovefriend.

We are preparing ourselves to see the real nature of Love through new thought about ourselves.

LOVE HAS INFINITE ABILITY TO EVOLVE, MATURE AND ELEVATE YOUR SELF-EXPRESSION

Love is tender. Love cares. Love is sympathetic--with the solution. Love's presence is truly nice. Love is Self-givingness. Love is supremely intelligent, amazingly kind, uplifted, perfect, unconditional, the greatest Friend and forever poised. All of this sounds comforting, but too remote to help or heal us. However, Love is closer than is our anticipation of misery. Love is more present than is our possibility of being hurt again and again.

We will not grasp the significance of this teaching until we feel Love's strength, courage, empowerment, resourcefulness and ability to fulfill our needs and desires. This happens as we become open, flexible, willing and interested for Love to express us well. Love then makes us adequate. This is not a fantasy, but is our greatest reality.

OPEN UP NOW! IT IS WORTH YOUR WHILE! LOVE LIVES WITHIN YOU! TELL YOURSELF THAT THIS IS THE TRUTH! LET LOVE REIGN IN ALL YOU DO! LET GO AND LET LOVE REPRESENT YOU! *LOVE ALONE KNOWS HOW TO LIVE YOUR LIFE MASTERFULLY!*

CHAPTER THREE

LOVE AT SIXTEEN

Can you cease feeling sorry for the way your life has gone? YES, YOU CAN! YES, YOU CAN! YES, YOU CAN!
Something that appeared to be quite disappointing happened to many of us when we were young. Traces of it linger in our memories, and wherever our reactions to it are yet being strongly felt, we are still attracting to ourselves similar burdensome experiences. Thus we continue to relive the unpleasant sensations associated with it.

Our reactions to unhappy events in our past are making us relive the same kind of unhappy feelings over and over

89

I had been preparing myself for many years to feel an experience of such considerable dissatisfaction; it occurred when I was sixteen. During the time of that somewhat unconscious preparation for the disappointment to occur, I lived dysfunctionally to a degree. As it is with many people, the circumstances surrounding my birth and the initial sense that I would eventually have to "go my own way," felt exceedingly uncomfortable. I believed that neither my mother in particular nor my family in general would provide me my deeper needs; more specifically I presumed they would not sufficiently assist me to express my special Self.

My parents were actually loving, kind and gentle, attentive to me, honest and sincere. This collection of virtuous characteristics could seem to guarantee that I would be happy. However, like all people, I was born to express the unique capacities that were inherent in my individuality. I could never really be outwardly happy without unfolding the nature of my originality. I did not feel that my parents appreciated that like all children, I, needed to follow my own destiny rather than their expectations. Therefore, I began life by rejecting myself, and by also trying to simultaneously prove that I was all right. Later, in my teen-age years, the eruption of my feelings brought me to the "awful" event. At first it seemed to verify one of the suspicions I had from birth, that I was ignoble; but as soon as I felt the worst of it, I instantly discovered that I was noble.

Now I can easily unravel the two particular patterns of thought which I used to guide me toward the completory experience in adolescence. One of them was the frustration of feeling unable to express the distinctive quality of my individuality. This included the growing sense I had from my life in the womb to my emergence upon the earth scene that I was not being encouraged or recognized for who I really was, and that this would not change. This is a great lesson of our time; parents can no longer make their children into who they think they would like to have been, or children will feel inadequate!

The other pattern was that I was born to marvelously unfold my potential despite any appearances of unsupportiveness. This is just as true for anyone. Everyone who has ever lived has experienced adequacy and inadequacy.

In my case, these two patterns merged at a single point in time to form a new experience for me. It felt like a threatening storm of resounding thunder followed by the most beautiful rainbow imaginable. The storm was the culmination of my feelings of frustration as I pushed my sense of ineligibility to live happily and effectively back to the threshold of my essence. The rainbow was the emerging presence of Love that thoroughly and unconditionally replaced all misapprehension. My new-found receptivity allowed Love's understanding of reality, Its ability to rise from within my circumstances and to be true to Its everpresent nature, to express that which was my Good through me.

I THOUGHT SOMETHING AWFUL WAS HAPPENING TO ME AT SIXTEEN YEARS OF AGE, BUT IT DOES NOT MATTER NOW BECAUSE LOVE WAS AND IS LIFTING ME. It was in the midst of feeling very sorry for myself, during the "awful" experience, that I discovered how uplifting Love can be. It is this awareness of the experience of Love's presence that can most effectively replace focusing upon a deep disappointment; Love is essential for our recovery to happiness and wholeness.

We began this life as whole, perfect and complete persons, but, we were not told this. And we still do not know it as we could. We are using our thoughts, feelings, emotions, bodies and the experiences of our lives to discover this great reality. Very early, somewhere around the time of our births, many of us began to feel that we were involved in a challenge, one that we somehow believed or felt would become insurmountable for us. Sensing insecurity in our environment and rejecting various aspects of ourselves, we accepted that life must become an accumulation of harsh experiences.

When those early disappointments no longer matter to us, something of Love helps us, something much greater than we thought we could otherwise express. Through Love, we turn our experiences into happy, successful and well functioning ones. But to accomplish this turnabout in our events, we have to dwell upon the idea that it can be. Let us say to ourselves many times a day until it happens, *"ALTHOUGH SOMETHING AWFUL SEEMED TO HAPPEN TO ME THEN, IT DOES NOT MATTER TO ME NOW BECAUSE LOVE IS LIFTING ME."* To deny that it happened is to cover up and forever preserve the basis for any unhappiness we have about the event. To admit that there was a painful experience, and then to continue to express anger and have similar recurring experiences because of it does not solve anything. *WE SUCCEED IN OUR LIFE RECOVERY PROGRAM AS WE ADMIT OUR FEELINGS OF DISAPPOINTMENT, RECALL THEIR BASIS, DECLARE AND FEEL THAT THEY NO LONGER MATTER TO US, AND AS WE THEN CONVINCE OURSELVES THAT BECAUSE LOVE IS IN OUR LIVES IT WILL REPLACE OUR EXPERIENCES OF BEING DYSFUNCTIONAL.*

THE THING THAT HAPPENED

When I was sixteen, a friend abruptly told me that we should end our relationship. Right then, I felt I was not wanted or needed. Because my friendship with her was the culmination of my personal search for someone like her from young childhood, our relationship had seemed to me ideal. Feeling hurt and depressed, I went home. I went straight to my room because I could be alone there; I let myself feel the shock of my thought that I had been rebuffed. Seeking comfort, I reviewed the circumstances surrounding the experience; none of them were consoling.

Hours passed; I felt dejected and I cried. There seemed not to be a way my life could be happy or complete, and yet I did not feel suicidal. Beneath it all, life still contained a friendliness. Two contrasting factors at once caught my attention; life was friendly, but I had not a friend. Where was a friend to be found, one who really cared for me?

It seemed to me that I had searched out the whole world, only to find that the friend I needed most did not exist. It "appeared" essential to my self-fulfillment that the person who I thought was my friend should have continued our relationship. How could this have happened? My repeated outbursts of tears told me that I was deeply affected by her action.

LOVE LIFTED ME

Again and again, I rubbed my eyes and cheeks with the backs of my hands. My face became alternately wet and dry; tears and time made it sticky and uncomfortable. But more than my face was involved. I was feeling the experience of rejection throughout my entire body. I was feeling stirred to the depths of my being. I was feeling intensely my self-inflicted, long-standing inadequacy, something that went back to the earliest events of my life.

I did not resent my friend, but I felt dependent upon her. I did not blame her; however, I felt extremely inadequate. That is, I was willing to forgive and forget, and it seemed so easy; it was as though I was innocent of placing blame and she was innocent of wrongdoing. But still, I did not know how to sense adequacy.

AND THEN, SOMETHING WONDERFUL HAPPENED! A substantial sense of Self-reliance and Self-direction came up through the tears and I felt the defeated look on my face replaced with a smile. Then and there, all of me was all right! Even better, I had never felt so much resourcefulness! *IT WAS BECAUSE MY TRUE IDENTITY SURFACED.*

Immediately, I knew that this experience was not the usual outcome of deep disappointment. I was in the presence of the best Friend I would ever know; yet no other person but myself was visible. The happiness of this Friendship exceeded the feeling that would understandably accompany a great find of diamonds or gold. My underlying belief had actualized its equivalent in an unshakable confidence! Each moment was filled with the feeling of empowerment, of being provided with fantastic care. *I had found within myself a Friend who could do anything, who could not be taken from me and who would never leave me.*

Because I knew right then that my new sense of Self was a great experience of Friendship, which could provide me with all the helpfulness I would ever desire, I let go of all the need for security that I had hoped my girlfriend could give me. My underlying belief that friendliness existed, even when it seemed it was being denied, opened up to me the greatest opportunity of my life. What could be more wonderful than to discover the deepest aspect of myself -- and to find there a limitless confidence and resourcefulness, that is, a rich endowment of Love? It was particularly wonderful, because my magnificent Friend assured me that my life has a mission and that I will always be given all the assistance I will ever need. It was credible because I felt this Friendship from deep within me, and even though the feeling of It was somewhat lessened by morning, It has never ceased to return and reannounce Itself when asked. There have been times that my sense of this Friendship with Self has vanished for a day or two, and there were even some years that I seemed to forget It altogether. I would become smug or unenlightened and eventually my thoughts and feelings would become quite lonely. But, this deeper awareness of life would then remind me of how rich the field of Love is within me, and I would sense Its Friendship once again.

NO ONE IS TRULY TWO PERSONS

There are two ways that we tend to experience being unenlightened. One is that we remain unaware of Love's presence; the other is that we mistake Love's nature by conceiving that It is something separate from ourselves. Admittedly, I failed at first to understand that Love's Friendship within me was simply a deeper, truer, explanation of my own nature than I had known before. Nevertheless, that is what It was, is and always will be. From the beginning, I did know It was something within me that would never leave me. It seemed as if my thinking of It as being my best Friend or Love or God, was the best description of It that I could conceive. However, when I talked *with* It, it seemed as though I was talking *to* It. And even now when I describe Love's Friendship, there is a continued awareness that the best physical equivalent seems to be that of my talking *to* another person. The explanation of something so very different from our conventional experiences of life has but a small vocabulary to draw upon, both to guide our experiences and to explain it. Therefore, *the reader might easily presume that I mean there is an inner Friend locked within me who Loves to be there and Loves to help me. Quite to the contrary, that is not what I am saying! However, we need to imagine that this Friendship with Self is the greatest Friendship possible, and that we can feel Love as our Lovefriend. Unless we can achieve this sense of It, the experience of Love within us will tend not to become as magnificent through us and as us as we need and desire.*

How then can we feel Love's presence as simply being the evidence that Love is within us to enrich us without limitation? There are three actions that we can pursue. (1) Someway, we can open our imaginations to the idea that Love is us. (2) Our imaginations can then conceive a methodology for feeling and expressing Love. The most effective method involves (a) turning away from our disappointments and (b) taking the time to be alone while contemplating the belief that Love is someway within us. We discover Love's inherent presence as we exercise these actions.

Feeling and expressing Love will occur spontaneously for many people sometime in the future. Up until now, it has but rarely happened. And my own situation at times has been much like anyone else's. We are wise then to develop the idea, which is the truth of us, that Love has never been separate from us, but has only seemed that way. *The inner Friendship is most truly a wonderfully good feeling that everyone naturally has of Self, but usually is not recognized until our fears or inadequacies are dispelled. This happens for us as we imagine the Lovefriend, and then as we keep telling ourselves that the Lovefriend is actually who we are.*

Until we finally arrive at the conclusion that we are both the Lovefriend *and* our outward expression, we will build this greater sense of Self-discovery through imagining the Lovefriend as talking *with* us. If we talk *to* It at first, although our enlightenment is not complete as such, we can gradually conceive of ourselves as talking *with* It, and eventually Its talking through us and acting as us. This is a great methodology for becoming actualized, as we have been made to be. However, when using it, we need to begin where we are. The idea of simply conceiving

We begin to discover the Lovefriend by talking to It

ourselves as a unified person, and as not being separated from the Love that is so richly present within us, is necessary, but not always easy to accomplish. However, imagining that one is talking with the Lovefriend is easier than attempting to begin with such a belief. And even for those of us who can completely feel Love without imagining the Lovefriend, it is worthwhile to practice talking **with** or even **to** Love. We will discover that meeting the Lovefriend and talking with It while we are becoming One in all ways, is a joy of extraordinary dimension. While experiencing our spiritual growth in this manner, it is deeply satisfying to feel the Lovefriend's presence as though It is simply the greatest Friend we have ever met.

THE UNDERLYING FRIENDSHIP

Whether it appears that we have many friends or none, whether our friendships seem deep or shallow, we need never be lonely! The very life we breathe is providing us with a warm and happy companionship. When we believe that the nature of life is surely friendly, and give attention to this idea, Love's underlying presence shows Itself. To experience this Friendship, we simply turn to the idea that Love is undergirding us; at the same time, we turn away from the resentful or antagonistic beliefs that life does not care for us.

Life always acts through its creation in accord with its own nature. But some of us have not felt that we have been well supported. We are like people who have the faculty of well-developed sight, but are still blind. Or we are like some deaf persons who cannot hear although their ears are physically perfect or nearly so, or mute persons whose ability to speak is not much impeded in any detectable way. When these conditions are found to be rooted in mental conflicts, correcting them seems almost impossible. And yet, the healing of them through analysis, belief, and medicine has increasingly been achieved. These successes occur when people who have those conditions (1) understand that neuroses need not interrupt basic natural functions and (2) believe in their right to feel Self-reliant. These are essential ideas if we are to experience life in its fullness. An even greater potential for healing then exists, because when we recognize Love's presence, It reveals the Good of everything.

As we cooperate with nature, it cooperates with us. There is in our nature an underlying Friendship that is already making Itself known to us; we have but to open our awareness to how natural it is to feel Love, to be healed by It, and to be made happy through the expression we can experience because of It.

ALL PEOPLE FEEL HAPPY

All people feel this marvelous Friendship of the inner Self. But, most of us have closed the door to the natural imaginative faculty that enables us to be aware of this feeling. When we become open and communicative with It, the grandest experience we can ever have floods us with a sense of happiness, confidence, joy and peace.

We can all really feel Love, but we cannot know that we can until we become open to the idea that we house an inner Friend. I repeat, there is not someone locked up in us; yet the idea that Love is a friend of ours needs to be conceived. We do best as we know that no person or object other than ourselves actually

exists in our mental atmosphere, but that through our imagining
the Love of our consciousness as being a deep Friendship of ours,
we are enabled to express ourselves as we most truly are. *As we
will conclude in the last chapter, there is not actually an individual
Lovefriend within any person, but THERE IS TRULY ONE
LOVEFRIEND WITH OR OF US ALL. AND IT IS EXPRESSED
MAGNIFICENTLY AS US, AS WE ENTHUSIASTICALLY
IMAGINE OUR INDIVIDUALLY HAVING A LOVEFRIEND; WE
THEREBY EVOLVE THE AWARENESS OF LOVE'S PRESENCE.*
That is, the consciousness of Love's Friendship which we all have,
becomes known to us through this practice. Again, the Lovefriend
is very real and very present, and *seems* as though It favors the
individual who recognizes It. The truth about the Lovefriend is
that It boundlessly Loves every person, and is gradually seen by
us as One presence.

It seemed at first that it was by accident that I opened myself
to this Friendship, but since then I have come to know that It
simply is there for all of us when we desire It enough, admit we
need It or are otherwise open to It.

There are usually two elements in growth that lead to the
genuine happiness that the Lovefriend provides. First, there is
an early feeling of desire or need to have a trustworthy Friend.
Secondly, there is a willingness to take a natural step in personal
growth that gets the outer sense of Self in touch with the inward
sense of Self. This step is taken as we *esteem* our inner resourcefulness and allow it to be our natural, outward expression. We
do this as we let our imagination move us from sadness and
disappointment to that place in our thought where we already
know that we have a continuous and unlimited sense of Friendship. There we are able to really feel Love; there we already
know we are secure and happy. We can discover this place in
thought any time we take enough interest to focus our thoughts
upon It. Friendship then deeply and indelibly establishes Itself
upon the outer consciousness of the Self. Magnificent and
authentic friendships with other people and all other requisites
for happiness are formed through this stabilizing experience.

I am not suggesting that all people must follow the particular course that I have to discover the Lovefriend. For instance, some people attract friends so easily that their desire or need for the inner Friendship unfolds differently. However, there are some actions that we must all require of ourselves to be truly happy and whole, that is, to bring forth a strong sense of Love. We all need to acknowledge that we have an inner supportiveness built within our thoughts that can help us. Also, it is necessary that all of us be true to ourselves in order to be successful. We must be individually expressed because no two pathways are quite alike. Pathways are variable because there are dissimilar interests and challenges that people naturally set up for themselves. Therefore, my experience is not necessarily a model, but is only a single example of how this might be done.

Because there is not only one, but many pathways to happiness, it is universally true that everyone can be happy, no matter how different his or her interests, comforts, talents and capacities may be from others. It is also true that all people already feel happy at a deeper level of Self whether or not they are aware of it. No matter what avenue we take to become aware of our inner happiness, we will all succeed in time. We have only temporarily misidentified our happy and loving sense of Self because we have thought we must find our happiness by being like other people. That is, there is one thing we must all do similarly to be successful in achieving happiness. *Without exception, we must go our own ways! We must not try to emulate someone else, some presumed ideal, or resist being like someone else or some presumed ideal. We do best to live up to some ideal that comes from deep within us. This frees us to pursue our own choices in expressing life as we desire. In this way, we will become aware of the happiness that we have previously covered up.*

THE BASIS FOR OUR TRUST

Some readers may be depressed to the point of feeling suicidal. Most of us are not. But, for those who are, it may seem desperately necessary to get in touch with the inner Friend right away. Unfortunately, all sense of desperation makes us feel that the Self is divided. Fortunately, we feel reunited when we believe in the idea that we have an inner Friendship. Such an idea includes that our world is friendly, that life itself is a Friend and that nothing opposes us. Of course, there are many of us who have never entertained suicidal thoughts who also do not believe that friendship is everywhere present. The reasons for disbelief in friendship are as varied as our experiences have been when people have seemed to let us down. Many people believe they cannot truly trust that authentic friendships can exist. But all people would like to discover that they are wrong about that. Here is where the honest seeker can begin.

There is something we easily do that defeats us. We often think that the Love of a deep inner Friendship may not be amply available because we have had difficult experiences with friends. We use the memories of our disappointing friendships as though

All trust begins within ourselves

they are a basis for thinking we cannot trust any friend. If I had done that at age sixteen, I would not have met the Lovefriend then. I could have eventually felt that life did not have the warmth of friendship which I desired. I could have felt a hopelessness.

If we cannot feel trusting of other people, it is time we begin to trust ourselves far more than we have, because all trust begins within ourselves. If we follow this thinking, we will ultimately find solid friendships. It is not as hard to trust ourselves as we have supposed, because our distrust is merely the result of ignoring the presence of Love. Trust begins as we tell ourselves that Love is within us, and as we form actions that bring It forth. We cannot become deeply involved in trusting ourselves without discovering the greatest Friendship imaginable.

We do not find Love because of something other people do for us. We find Love as we give of ourselves to other people. This should not be confused with the common belief that what people do for us or what we do for them has anything to do with discovering Love. Discovering Love means that we express something that comes from deep within us which may include that we receive it when experiencing another person's giving or our own; but, it has nothing to do with what they or we do. It is found in our sensitivity to Love's presence, and our recognition that Love is greater than we are while It is being us.

NATURE OF THE FRIEND

There is much more to say about my experience at age sixteen, what led up to it, its various details and the magnificent way it felt. It is a wonderful true story and there is little that delights me more than to describe it. Yet there is one other thing that I want even more to explain, for it is the real purpose of this writing. It is to describe the nature of the Friend; my Friend is your Friend, and your Friend is my Friend. You can find as much joy and resourcefulness from the Friend as I have. And you will; you will discover in It a marvelous experience of life. So now, before I tell you more of my experience at sixteen (in chapter fourteen), and how it was rooted in thoughts planted in Mind at the time of my birth, prepare yourself to meet your Lovefriend, whom you already subconsciously know. You will be positively delighted to renew your old sense of this Friendship or to deepen your awareness of the greatest feeling you have of yourself.

The meetings with the Lovefriend contain a remarkable experience of vibrancy. They pulsate with the expectancy of renewed vigor in one's livingness. And your awareness of them, and interest to truly attend them, begin as you involve your thinking with the idea that you are not a victim of anyone or anything except for your own misguided thinking, and that the

Lovefriend's thinking is your best guidance. You will naturally and easily give Love to others when you dismiss the idea that you have received an experience of being victimized because of them. Along with this, your success requires that you cease victimizing yourself and that you discover your adequacy. Your recognition of having meetings with the Lovefriend builds an awareness of the adequacy.

The meetings are different for everyone. When you become aware of your already present feeling of the Lovefriend, or of Love, the experience of your participation in the meetings that follow will be as you have expected, when you have thought with positivity, conviction and faith.

Unlimited Love and happiness are awaiting you within your experiencing the Lovefriend. Let yourself be very expectant of joy, confidence, ease and well-being.

It is the nature of the Friend to wholly give Itself through you. This is not accomplished by other people doing things for you, but rather through your giving yourself to them. *You find Love and happiness as you give yourself away;* however, some part of your givingness in all this, is a willingness to let them do some things for you, and, a willingness to let them be.

*Deep inside ourselves, there is no loneliness, because there is truly
One Lovefriend of us all.*

THE CONSCIOUSNESS OF LOVE'S PRESENCE

Consciousness is explained in many ways. Frequently the word "consciousness" means the view conceived within one's thoughts about oneself and one's world, which establishes the content of one's life experiences. On the other hand, sometimes it refers to the greater understanding of each one's reality by the Intelligence that is the unification or cohesiveness of everything. The idea that Intelligence is Love as I have explained It here and that we can sense Its presence and live within Its consciousness, is the conception of greater livingness that we can have and which I am describing.

This explanation of Love's consciousness includes that Love is everywhere present, is everywhere Self-giving and knows this about Itself. As we sense Love as our Lovefriend, we express Its Intelligence, Its Self-givingness and know we are Love. As we evolve enough to sense Love's awareness we are enabled to live in Its consciousness.

Because Love is Supreme Intelligence and high emotion combined, inseparable and everlasting, It has seemed unreachable, nonreproducible and rather unbelievable. However, the consciousness of the Lovefriend emerges within our Self-expressiveness as we accept the depths and heights of our potentialities as our great reality. It occurs as we open ourselves to allow Love to be all that It is through and as us.

Throughout this book then, by consciousness I usually mean that awareness of Love's presence which we all have in our

103

deepest, highest or innermost level of insight and intuition. I further mean that such consciousness emerges in our outer experience of reality as Love's presence, whenever we turn away from the opinions about Self that are only based upon outward appearances, and as we allow who we really are to be expressed. Sometimes however, I have used the word consciousness to mean the view of life and ourselves which we otherwise live by.

The consciousness of Love's Intelligence is only distinguishable to us as we become aware of who we really are. Inasmuch as everyone is Love in Truth, we already contain the consciousness of the Lovefriend somewhere within our awareness. However, until we know this, we tend to think considerably less of ourselves. *Throughout this book, I sometimes indicate that we are becoming Love. I do not really mean by this that we are not already completely Love; I mean that we are not aware of ourselves as we most truly are, but that we are becoming aware of our loving capacity.* Until we become solidly aware of our being One with Love, we have a lesser sense of our identity and what life means to us. That lesser sense is the other use I make of the word consciousness, and it is the use of it which has been the more common one.

We do well as we acknowledge that we have been living somewhere within a consciousness of love. Right now, we can open ourselves to Love's consciousness that all of life is Good with us. The reader is encouraged here to declare, "*I am open, ready and desirous to allow Love's consciousness of life to from hereon be my entire consciousness. I am committed to thinking, feeling and doing all that is necessary for me to manifest this.*" Declaring this brings into our lives the awareness and experiencing of Love's presence. It is essential as a preparation for having meetings with Love.

We must continue to build consciousness in the more common way such as we have been doing, somewhat slowly, until we become committed to our being expressive of Love's consciousness. Although Love will never force Its way upon us, we are wise to believe that for our own happiness, success and well-being, we should commit ourselves now to allowing Love's consciousness to wholly express us. For this reason, our interest in being greatly occupied with the meetings, is the most wonderful opportunity for better living that we can pursue. If our commitment to Love is strong enough to replace all our other attempts to make our lives fulfilled, we will feel Love's great consciousness ably guiding us through everything we do.

Having the idea that the making of this commitment is good for us to do is not enough to ensure its happening. Therefore, *I challenge the reader to make this commitment now by saying it, thinking it, feeling it, intending it, writing it and turning toward the idea of meeting with the Lovefriend. The awareness of how the meetings will happen will become clearer to the committed reader; once the commitment is definitely made, Love will reveal Itself.*

I am, because Love is. Love desires that I accept myself. This means I have been made free to discover who I am.

CHAPTER FOUR

LOVE AND EMOTION

Can you Love other people so much that you are happy to share your resourcefulness with them even if they give nothing in return? YES, YOU CAN! YES, YOU CAN! YES, YOU CAN!

A woman came to me to discuss her physician's analysis of a severe cough she had. He had diagnosed her as having an advanced state of bronchiectasis. She was not breathing well, and during her frequent coughing spells she experienced intense pain.

She was a heavy smoker and the doctor told her she must discontinue all smoking immediately. Also, surgery would have to be performed rather immediately. He explained that the smoking was the cause of the bronchiectasis and that abstention was necessary to enable the healing to occur. She explained to me that it would be a good idea for her to cease smoking, but that she did not believe it was the cause of her condition. Her idea was that about a year after her complete cure she would quit smoking, but she wanted to convince herself that Love and Mind are all the cause there is, and that she needed to Love herself more; that by simply thinking better ideas about herself, she would be healed. Then, surgery would not be necessary. She expected me to talk with Love and Mind, and for a healing to thereupon come about. Her willingness to have her thoughts adjusted was obvious. And so I spoke with Love's presence, and conceived of her being immediately healed.

Several days later, she sat in a group which I encouraged to speak after me some words to the effect that life is Good. She began to cough, and coughed so much that she left the room, while the rest of us kept declaring that life is Good and that life's Intelligence loves us.

A few minutes later, she told my wife how she had been placed in a concentration camp in Germany from the time she was seven until she was eight and one-half years of age. There she reflected upon how it seemed that people's lives meant very little to their oppressors, inasmuch as they were being treated with severe unkindnesses. As a result of so many of them being killed, she established an idea that was to go on with her, that life must be a struggle, and that it must frequently be accompanied by considerable anxiety.

The word "life" became the center of her attention, and this made her stressful. She actually gave herself some satisfaction through hating the word "life." When I encouraged the idea that Love comes to us from life's Intelligence, she at first reacted to it negatively, because unconsciously she hated such an amicable use of the word "life."

Her experience of hearing me and a large group of people declaring that life is Good, was simply too difficult for her to accept. She choked severely upon hearing this. However, her interest to become well, her expectation that it would happen through my words, her confidence in Love, her belief that God would help her, freed her from this idea that had kept her struggling with life until then.

That afternoon I spoke with her about the inner feeling I had that she was well. She was. The coughing ceased entirely within one more day. The physician declared her well and said that surgery was no longer necessary. Now, several years later, the condition of bronchiectasis has not returned. She discontinued smoking a year later.

Without question, she let Love replace her resistance to life. Because Love is nonresistance, her breathing was released from all sense of struggling. This was a very emotional experience for her and for myself. However, a lower sense of emotion was lifted to an emotion containing much joy. The sense of much emotion was there from the beginning, and on through the time of healing. Emotion can be disconcerting or greatly satisfying. Our sense of Love and love is that they are to some extent emotions, but Love is a high emotion; love is a low emotion.

LOVE AS EMOTION

It feels good to love someone. It feels better to Love that person. For Love is the highest of all emotions and It gives us supreme care. On the other hand, love is an experience that we often have of Love's corresponding lower emotion, the one that we feel when our cares are mixed with fear.

Love's high emotion is the sensitive expression of ourselves that gives freely, receives thankfully and provides impetus for high actions from deep within our thoughts. The low emotion, love, is the insecure experience we endure when our giving is mainly motivated by thoughts of what we will gain because of it, and by the fear that we will be seen as selfish if we function without it, rather than out of truly feeling gratitude and confidence. Our low actions from feeling love tend to be repetitive because we listen to other insecure people who teach us to not trust anyone.

We succeed in expressing Love, and we raise our experience above being influenced by the thoughts of others who are merely trying to survive the environment, as we recognize that Love is our essence. Wonderful ideas for masterfully expressing ourselves are available to all of us from within our individual Selves.

Wonderful ideas for masterfully expressing ourselves are available to all of us from within our individual selves

The Good life, or the higher Love, which we can all experience and express, is to be found within our higher thoughts.

We help ourselves by defining Love as a spiritual emotion which expresses Itself in spiritual and physical manners. The experience of love in this connection is that of a physical emotion; that is, love mostly expresses itself in very physical ways. *We must define this difference accurately or we can mislead ourselves.* For instance, being spiritual is not better than being physical. That is, we are spiritual beings who can discover through Love how to elevate our physical experiences into spiritual, cloud-touching behavior. Nonetheless, even as those who fly in an airplane are not intrinsically better people because they quickly and comfortably cross the country in the air rather than by land or sea, so the development of our spiritual awareness does not improve our natures; all of us already have unlimited resourcefulness just as we are. However, discovering our capacity to live in Love enables us to live better, both individually and socially, even as those who take to flying frequently have benefits that those who stay close to the ground do not have. Some people, who prefer not to travel in airplanes, may find this better explained by observing how it is that people who are highly educated have not truly become superior to others; yet, through their having achieved sufficient educational credits, doors have opened for them that otherwise could have been closed. And the experience of life, for them, can become more interesting, richer and fuller.

When Love is expressed in everything we do, we become aware of both the spiritual nature of It and the physical productivity within It. Experiencing love alone, is not a very spiritual experience for us. Love is the spiritual experience that happens when love is lifted. AND LOVE IS ALWAYS EXPERIENCED IN BOTH THE PHYSICAL AND SPIRITUAL REALMS WHEREVER IT IS FELT. When we think we experience Love *only* physically, we are sensing lack, limitation, stress and insecurity; this is the feeling of love. When Love is experienced as though It is our spiritual nature, the physical presence of opportunities, privileges, comforts and security, are included. In both cases there is spiritual activity within physical boundaries. But in the lower case, there is close attention given to the physical boundaries. In the higher case, there is close attention given to the presence of Spirit and Its ideas.

We are saying then, that Love and love both involve physical and spiritual aspects of being and that we are wise to acknowledge both aspects as being necessary and good. However, we are also indicating that until our attention is kept focused on the spiritual nature of Love (upon the ideas of Love), we will have many low or less desirable experiences of life. When our thoughts are centered on Love, we will be in the points of poise; we will have high or more desirable experiences of life -- happy, agreeable and successful ones.

Thinking that we are mistaken to feel and act with ordinary emotion will cause us to endure unnecessary guilt and anxiety. The result of this will be that we will misunderstand that there are distinct and valid times and places in our spiritual growth to largely sense our *physical emotions* and other such times to emphasize more our *spiritual emotions*. Because we are all more aware of our physical emotions in the opening years of our lives, it is inevitable that we will have discovered emotional feelings early that appeared to be necessary as reactions to parental and environmental demands, and that became less necessary later on when Self-confidence, patience and understanding had become developed within us. After discovering our spiritual natures, we may be concerned that certain normal, yet immature behavior patterns of childhood have tended to become habitual practices with us. Consequently, we may feel blame, shame and remorse as a result of their persistence in our adult lives long after we presume that we know better. As we become aware of this, our best actions lie in accepting that our lives are well lived by lifting up our expressions of love into Love, and in recognizing that this includes the physical ways which are involved with these actions.

Therefore, although we are crediting our interest in Love and Its spiritual emotional manner as our preferable activity of expression, physical emotions are very much involved with It. Life works best for us as we acknowledge that many of our very physical experiences have been necessary ones, at least for awhile. They were the vehicles that enabled us to take care of ourselves for a long time. They are contained within the spiritual reality, the Love presence within us; and It can use them for higher and higher ends to the extent that we let It know Itself in us. For instance, the physical experience of love is the basis for relationships, sexual activity, ordinary justice[1] and community care. The spiritual experience of Love includes these physical bases; however, beyond Its bringing us together into families and other affinities, into experiences that are sexually satisfying, protective and hospitable, *a capacity to limitlessly experience excellent communication, joy, trust, peace, other desired provisions and understanding is possible too;* and therefore individuals, families and wider communities can be helped immeasurably by Love.

Our best understanding of the physical and spiritual aspects of our lives comes to us as we cease comparing these two explanations of life as though there is an opposition between them. Although we all do our best when we practice Love in all our situations, we cannot achieve this until we practice love prior to our upliftment in Spirit, and come to the awareness that the physical activity of it (love) also belongs as much to Love. That is, we need to esteem physical activity as some part of Love's increasingly purified expressiveness through us.

We are spiritual beings; this *includes* that it is good for us to have experiences of physical bodies and things. However, until we find the interest to lift our physical activities into lofty pursuits, we mostly feel love and we largely experience our emotions only physically. When we soar with high ethical ideas representative of a benevolent idealism, we become aware of meeting with Love

---

[1] Ordinary justice is my term which refers to the kind of relationship most people try to experience with others. It means that they think they find as much satisfaction as they can have with others when other people give them equal consideration, opportunityy and returns of their own treatment to the others. Until Love is known, love is only underestood as fair play and equal treatment, as the best we think we can expect of life. There is a higher justice that is not ordinary and that never ceases to be. It is the true potentiality that awaits us in the experiences that are made possible when we are letting Love express us.

frequently, and we experience It spiritually in most of what we do. There are still physical aspects experienced in all of this, actually just as many as with love. And we are no better persons because of living more largely in Love. However, we are happier, healthier, more harmonious, more productive, finer citizens and more fulfilled.

Living in Love and in the richness of our spirituality is essential to our becoming expressed as we have been made to be. So long as we judge ourselves as wrong for experiencing any physical emotion, we entrap ourselves unnecessarily with an immature emotionalism that keeps us from presently mastering our behavior; it builds a mental field of guilt, self-rejection and anxiety around us which invites self-punishment and we can easily remain this way for a lifetime on earth. Additionally, our capacity to feel our spiritual emotions is thereby dulled.

It is not wrong that most of us have thought much about love and little about Love. However for many of us, our consciousness about life is rapidly evolving at present, and we are discovering that it helps us to think more about Love. *We are especially helped as we notice that Love and love are not two different natures, but that Love is our entire experience of life, and that love is simply a lesser awareness we have often had of It.* Love is sometimes seen from a high vantage point and other times from a low point of view. It is of greater advantage to us to now be open to the discovery of as many high vantage points for viewing Love and all of our emotions as we can.

Eventually, people in general will begin their lives knowing more about Love than love, but for now -- we must instill a higher viewpoint in our thinking. Otherwise, we will often mistakenly think that there is nothing more to Love than can be found in love.

THE UNITY OF LOVE WITH REASON AND EMOTION

Strangely enough, our misdirection in the near future will largely come from an attempt to explain that emotions have no existence except as the consequence of our thinking. Whereas most people have felt that their emotions have been a more basic cause for their behavior than have been their thoughts, a new regard for our capacity to use our thoughts constructively, is already tending to reshape enlightened thinking by giving rationality all the responsibility for our actions. We will come to know that Love is the combination of Supreme Intelligence and emotion, as well as being that of Friendship, resourcefulness, Self-givingness and far more (as I explained under the sub-title "Love And love" in chapter two). When this becomes understood, we will know that the combination of reason and emotion, along with conscious and unconscious thought is rooted in Love, and that neither reason nor emotion can account for the existence of the other. However, lower emotions tend to be expressed in association with less rational thought. Higher ideas are complemented by spiritual emotions. Again, security, Self-acceptance and the maturity of people are in further association with lifted Intelligence and with lifted emotionality.

As we greatly lift ourselves to a higher viewpoint in our livingness, both our logic about living in harmony and our feeling Love as It is, are included. We are wise to observe this and accept it as authentic, because otherwise our reasonings and our attempts to be loving cannot rise high enough to allow humankind to satisfactorily resolve its differences. And when we become convinced that Love is the common denominator of both our feelings and thoughts, we shall usher in all the experiences of life that have been missed by those who most truly care about our future.

This unity of thought, emotion and everything that is, cannot be denied or there will be an inability to discover life's essence temporarily. Because evolution is as real in our spirituality as is the idea of its existence in physical phenomena, everyone will eventually know all of life's nature; however, as our present attention focuses more upon how Love has already united everything, we can know and we can express life at its best in the here and now.

I mean then, that our ideas and emotions have always been, are now, and always will be of one essence, OF ONE CONSISTENCY. I further mean that our emotions do not originate from our ideas.

Nor are emotions merely momentary feelings that we have when we express thoughts. Again, emotions are not simply the way thoughts look when they are felt. Once more, emotions are felt in union with the content of our thoughts. And the emotions that we feel are indivisibly allied with the thoughts which we express.

Emotions are felt in union with the content of our thoughts

The indivisible unity of thoughts and emotions constitutes the nature of our consciousness. It is fortunate that we cannot break this oneness of what we think and feel. It is also Good that we can direct our feelings as a result of the thinking that we do, and that we cannot direct our thoughts from our feelings. It therefore seems that our thinking is in a position of dominance. LOVE PROVIDES OUR THINKING CAPACITY WITH THIS APPARENT SUPERIOR ROLE, BUT ONLY ENABLES US TO USE THIS FOR SELF-IMPROVEMENT TO THE DEGREE THAT WE ACKNOWLEDGE "WE ARE LOVE." Through such recognition we choose to live with Self-direction. Understandably, the extent of our acknowledgment is in direct proportion to the interest we take to increasingly benefit ourselves.

LOVE AS JUSTICE

When Love is not conceived as an unbreakable and eternal unity of both high reason and high emotion, It can only be seen, felt or experienced from a low viewpoint. It is not Love, but rather this low estimate we have tended to make of It, that has brought about all the lesser and somewhat disappointing experiences we have attributed to It. The experience of ordinary justice is the most outstanding example of this misunderstanding of Love's Way. Yet, we all tend to first meet Love in this manner of love's action. Afterwards, we discover Love as it truly is.

"Ordinary justice" is the customary experience we have usually had with life, in which equality (1) is either avoided through prejudiced actions (2) or is forced into our experiences because we suspect it cannot be otherwise achieved. An example of (1) is when a high percentage of a minority group is refused better employment by people who desire to keep the group an under-privileged minority. In the case of (2), attempts to bring equality to those who have been refused (in the instance just given) often result in procedures that contain a better experience of justice, but which disallow some more qualified people to gain the employment they deserve. Such coercion of justice ordinarily requires us to compromise ourselves so that a "fair" exchange of services, gifts or environments occurs. An instance of this is when a person feels compelled to "do a favor" for someone (perhaps something against his or her moral principles) in order to get a job. If we were not compelled by ordinary justice to live in a compromised behavior, competition and struggle could be rampant with most of us. Therefore ordinary justice serves us well. However as we discover Love, such justice is proven inadequate because a higher experience of coequality flows into our relationships.

Ordinary justice cannot show us Love; nevertheless we must begin with it, because that is where we are, with love. *Love will come through it somehow, and when It does we will experience the Universal Justice that spontaneously provides us all the trust, confidence, fidelity, serenity and continuous loving care that we need and desire.* Stepping into Love's spontaneous or flowing manner happens with us as we accept that where we are with love contains the higher experience, and that we can expect our lives to unfold It by using a plan of action that intends for our lives to be justly experienced.

To be successful then in discovering Love and Its attendant Universal Justice, we need to take two mental steps. The first is to become aware that ordinary justice shows us love, but not Love. When we understand and accept this, we can launch our discovery of Love with a clear sense of what we must do to individually instill in ourselves a great sense of Love's consciousness (See definition of "consciousness" under "The Consciousness of Love's Presence"). It includes that we thoroughly observe where we are with ordinary justice and love. Secondly, by anticipating that Love will come through our desiring a higher basis for living, we can let go of the conditions of love and experience the higher justice.

1. When we have only understood Love from a lower point of view, as though It is an emotion that has merely resulted from our more affectionate thoughts, or that It is a feeling that needs more intelligent direction than It can possibly have of Itself, It appears to be ordinary. It results in our believing that Love is merely a feeling of attraction with others who we hope will give us as many strokes as we give them. We may feel failed by it again and again. And yet, our "hope for love" may still remain an active pursuit with us. For does it not seem true that many people have found "their true love" somewhere? Yet, in relationship after relationship, most of us feel shortchanged. Perhaps we share affections, money, time or confidential information, only to discover that we give much of ourselves and seem to receive little in return. We expect to experience an equal sharing, but it does not happen. Eventually we conclude that to feel very much love is to become vulnerable, and we question whether such vulnerability is worth our while.

If any of these experiences of love become successful, our sharing with another makes us feel equals, and this seems just. *But, if we observe it realistically, we are looking for ordinary justice; we are calling it love. And so long as we continue to hope for love*

*rather than to let Love express us, the idea of ordinary justice may
well define it.* Because love has seemed like the best possible
experience that we might achieve, we may have gradually given
of ourselves even more than it seemed possible that we could ever
expect would be returned to us, but still with the hope that
equality would finally occur. We may have tempered our idea of
how an equal sharing should have been given us because of our
initial givingness, through our providing more and more affection,
money, time or through telling "our special other" more about our
private lives than seemed wise, wishing that it would eventually
be balanced in some way that would be acceptable to us. When
that did not occur, we may have felt let down by life itself,
because no one seemed to be "out there" who would truly share
with us.

There are many experiences of love that do seem to provide
equality. We could receive love if we simply wanted to take care
of someone or wanted someone to take care of us. Many people
feel one of these ways and attract another person who feels the
other way. One enjoys being a dependent and easily receives; the
other one enjoys taking care of the dependent and easily provides.
We could do the same, and many readers already do. Then, we
would have a "just" marriage or a nonmarital relationship that is
"just." (Again, we would have ordinary justice.) That is, some
people only approach love, for a long time, with the idea of
finding someone else who will meet their survival needs. In such
relationships, or with those mentioned earlier who want to share
equally, the same ring of justice is involved.

So long as we see love from such a viewpoint, love is experienced as a "reaction" to some form of kindness given us; or love
is felt and acted upon by us as a means to stir up in another
person feelings that cause a "reaction" around which we can feel
we are "in love." If we thus provide another person who similarly
gives back to us, or if we are provided with a relationship from
the other that is in accordance with our survival wants or needs,
we may feel it worth our while to return that kindness and to keep
returning further kindnesses, by giving that someone more and
more of what that one wants. Then love means to us that we

hope to find or may have found someone who gives to us according to our desires, and that our inclination is to give that person what he or she wants.

On this basis, let us understand that people generally expect to find love in a "just reaction." Many search for this, but do not find it. Yet others do! The satisfaction is easily found if only a dependency is desired, either in our being taken care of, or in our taking care of another. Many marriages that seem to succeed are such dependencies. However, these so-called successful marriages do not always last, and when they fall apart, it is because the needs change. Many people have concluded that as they grow and feel different needs, marriages may need to be sacrificed, and that we do well to let that happen. For instance, one marital partner may feel that the original attraction was for him or her to be drawn to another who demonstrated self-control or the feeling of affection, and that later the example was no longer needed. Nor was love any longer felt. But, when another relationship is formed, if love is still its basis, a similar experience with a different need again occurs.

"Just" love is often viewed as a fair exchange of gifts and services

2. When we review our sense of love, that is, when we think love can be better, it is possible to lift our vantage point and see Love, wherein sacrifice does not happen. When we see Love as a spiritual emotion, we need not keep changing love partners or be divorced and remarried over and over. *We can discover the larger sense of Love wherein justice as either equality or a fair exchange of services (ordinary justice) is replaced*

by Universal Justice, that is, by trust, confidence, fidelity, serenity and continuous loving care. The persons we then attract for our close relationships do not involve us with dependencies. This forms a higher basis for relationships. Because the Universal Justice embodies wholly honorable assistance, there is but One relationship involved with It; harmony, peace, joy and abundance are provided everyone.

The higher basis for becoming married or for being especially close to another includes our giving that which another wants, but not so as to serve what they superficially think they want or need. It comes about through (1) our sensitivity to their deeper desires, (2) our having the feeling of what they want that we too sincerely want, and (3) through knowing that as we give them that which we desire, we more truly have it also. The higher basis for Love comes as we cease feeling a need for ordinary justice to prevail, and accept that something better is feasible. Then we have a greater experience of justice; it happens with us when we give Love free reign. The higher basis is *TRULY JUST*; it is Universal Justice and Its availability always underlies experience; we can accurately name it "Love's Way." Ultimately we all have to turn to Love's Way to succeed.

THE FOREMOST SPIRITUAL EMOTION

Beyond our "just reactions," "ordinary justice" or our usual emotional actions lies Love's Way, a higher expression which I am calling a spiritual emotion. Our pathway into it begins when we choose to rise up and have our lives bettered. It commences from wherever we are with our emotions. This greater sense of love lies within everyone's immediate reach; as we dialogue within our own selves, expecting something more than ordinary justice, we discover a Friendship with Love. Thus we are implanted into the Universal Flow of Justice. I call the steps into this higher relationship with oneself, "the meetings" with the Lovefriend.

We can get in touch with Love via the Lovefriend while we are experiencing our lower emotions (as we shall learn through many references I will make to It such as that of my own personal experience in chapter three), and we can be lifted into our best actions -- without any reactions that resist this Good experience. But, if we then turn our backs on our lower emotions, as though they are in poor taste and have no further significance for us, we will have misunderstood their role in our spiritual development. This rejection can plunge us into emotional problems that will confuse, complicate and delay an otherwise natural, normal and beneficial rise of ourselves into a permanent state of great livingness. *We simply need to know that there are lower emotional experiences that we have to have on our way into an expanded discovery of Love.*

We simply need to know that there are lower emotional experiences that we have to have on our way into an expanded discovery of Love

It is our nature to express Love rather than love, but we are born on earth without knowing this in an outward way; Love must be discovered to be experienced. We do not need to suffer because of our lower emotional experiences; we only need to LET them be in our experience as we grow THROUGH love. Because we too often misunderstand this, it is wise to value all of our emotional experiences, even while learning the higher way to live through them.

Let us understand that various emotional actions containing some feelings of dependency and often attended with an excitement that will eventuate into some irrational actions, become our experiences whenever we both feel love and think about it. Such emotion is made up of physical and mental factors that usually excite us; it often has a dizzying effect and can easily blind us so that we act without wisdom. These feelings of love recur with us whenever we are crossing the bridge we naturally tend to build between our awarenesses of love and Love. It is through love that we are enabled to begin the discovery that our real identity is to be found in our spirituality. *Very much like the way we become deeply aware of anything that we especially enjoy, we have to begin with a small sense of what Love is. We begin to meet Love by feeling love.* As we give more and more attention to our awareness of love, and especially as we use our wisdom to discover love's deeper, kinder, finer values, such as its givingness, and as we open our feelings to experience love more completely, we gradually become aware of Love Itself.

We cannot experience love without feeling the lower emotional nature that is its basis. Such experiences of love began for us when we felt someone or something act friendly toward us and when we felt moved to give back a like action to the person, or to whatever thing that it was. If we did not easily feel this need to give back, we were told we should. As we felt love, we felt like reacting with kindness. We ordinarily continued acting with kindness so long as the other person or thing acted that way to us. *And so long as this remained reciprocal, we felt like we were "in love."*

As we grew up physically, our less conscious memories urged us to find new experiences of love, especially ones that were like those we felt in our childhood, whenever a parent or friend initiated a friendship with us that we liked. Also, many of us conceived the idea that we could act friendly toward someone else, and that we would be loved in return. Because of this idea, many people believe they are expert at loving. And perhaps it is true, but this is only a relative factor (relative to another's interest to reciprocally give and receive love). Many people are not happy that their "expert lovingness" leads them into dependencies, because they feel controlled or they tire of being a controller of someone else. Since love cannot otherwise be successful, people variously "fall in love" and "out of love." Until love becomes Love, love interferes with Self-fulfillment and happiness.

To accurately understand the feelings and actions of love, whether or not romance is involved, it should be noted that most people tend to try establishing either a just or "fair" relationship because of it. The experience of love provides the opportunity to attract someone or something that is desired, through the giving and receiving of some actions or things which are felt to be of equal value or equivalent satisfaction (achievement or failure of this is ordinary justice). When one or a few failures occur, some people in reflecting upon their feelings of unworthiness, impulsively rationalize the need to not accept further relationships. They conceive that life's nature caused this to be an inevitable necessity with them, and that life is therefore unfair. However, a great many people after considering the effect they feel from the failures of themselves or others, settle for a relationship with whomever they can get at almost any cost to them, because love as the lower emotion has generally seemed as the best experience of life that they could have.

Because love requires much personal sacrifice, other people sometimes go to great lengths to preserve the lower emotional feeling of love through trying not to give up that it will eventually help them find a relationship that is in every way just. However, if they fail after *many* more new attempts have been made, they cease searching. They conclude that life is exceedingly unfair! Still other people seem to never give up the search for a "right relationship" or "right relationships." But, let a person be disappointed by love a great many times, and the ability to feel it again lessens considerably (though it is never depleted entirely); that some people patiently try to love and gain justice again and again throughout their lives, and remain unsuccessful, seems even more unfair.

When the need for a just or fair experience ceases to carry importance, Love's announcement of Its presence and Its meetings is in some way heard. To hear Love and allow Its Self-givingness to express us is to experience the Universal Justice which is never unfair. Then, to experience Love, we act kindly whether there is any kindness displayed toward us or not. Our world will be wonderful for everyone when all of us regularly act with Love.

To experience Love, we act kindly whether any kindness is displayed toward us or not

And it is not only possible that this can happen, but in a small way--it already is happening with many of us. Sometimes Love simply slips into our actions because it is natural for It to do this, and because we are increasingly open to each other. And it happens even more, because Love has many meetings with everyone, everyday. ***But, in all instances, people who act with a sense of Love do so after having experienced love first. It happens then, in conjunction with people's becoming frustrated in their attempts to find lasting and true justice in love, and it is the result of their natural inclinations to look for something better.***

Since all love is within us, no one can keep looking for it without eventually discovering that in its same place, Love is also to be found. And it is possible for anyone to discover that Love is simply to be unfolded from love, as though love is a wrapping paper containing Love; or that love is a jacket which enshrouds each one's smaller conception of Love. The presence of Love is always with us; however, we have to be willing to extend kindness *beyond* that which seems extended to us, to express It. Consequently, our earliest awarenesses of Love can only bloom as improved attitudes that we form and in a growth in the manner of our personal behavior. *But once we clearly see Love in ourselves and nourish our experience of It, our recognition of Love grows, and we begin to see It in everything and everybody.*

Love is the presence of life that greatly moves the universal power of life to do Good. *Truly, Love provides us the Intelligence through which It causes our individual lives to have experiences that are as Good as we can believe.* Actions of Love are especially Good for us!

Some people may think that these statements about Love are too good to be true. And I agree that love as a lower emotion could never enable us so much! Yet, I acknowledge that it is sensible and practical to begin to understand Love by feeling the emotion of love. When we have felt love *deeply* enough, we will have discovered Love, and we will all find out that Love is a higher emotion. *The actions of Love are not common reactions; rather they are spiritual reactions, or responses of the highest caliber.* Love does not take our actions into consideration when It acts through us, even if those actions are unreasonable and very unkind ones. Love simply gives Itself without reservation through us, as us, and through all and as all.

It is natural to express Love as we mature, but we have generally kept ourselves from expressing It very much. Until we discover how to act with spirituality in our emotions, we make "our experience" of Love into love; that is, we keep It ordinary. And many of us do not even let very much love into our lives. The fear of love (and Love) is the largest fear that exists; most of us do not realize this. We generally think that love is not a fearsome aspect of life. Yet, our experiences of love have contained many disappointments; all fear develops out of our reactions to them. Who can doubt that there are millions of adults in the United States alone, who fear to become involved with love again? Many people involve themselves in casual sex and dating to be sure, but the fear of another broken relationship keeps them from marriages, serious companionships and intimacy; fear keeps them from sharing on the other levels where love could be most supportive.

Still, many of us are drawn to love, to feel it over and over. If we desire to discover love's deeper and truer nature, we can. Best of all, the Lovefriend awaits us! *If we simply dare to look deeply into love, we will find Love.* And Love's life will be everything we have ever dreamed it could be!

Whether we live in love or express Love, there is emotion. In love, it is always a low emotion although kindness and joy may be sprinkled in it. In Love, it is always a high emotion, because all *need* for ordinary justice or even "fair" play is emptied out of It. For all of us, Love is first discovered as love because the human environment strongly encourages us to experience it, but our natural inclinations are still toward Love. These instinctual or intuitive tendencies that would have us live in Love also incline us toward physical experiences, and therefore it is fortunate for us that love is physically felt. It is not the physical aspects of love that make it less desirable than Love. The reason that love is less desirable than Love is that love does not give us the satisfaction that we more greatly need and desire. The experience of love is to cling; that of Love is to express us; Self-expression enables us to be Self-fulfilled.

In experiencing love, we commonly experience reactions toward something we think is "out there," and we can quickly recognize that our feeling of them is coming from a low sense of emotion. The higher understanding is more gradually unfolded to us, through our developing awareness that Love never elicits our guilt because It never demands anything of us. For instance, some people feel guilt in their relationships because they only feel love. Others feel no guilt as a result of Love's being their expression. Love never reduces Itself to a common emotion, although It acts for us in lesser ways when we sense Love as love.

This is only gradually understood by us; in time it is definitely comprehended. *This is because we are really divine: we can have unlimited insight into our nature. And Love is our foremost emotion.*

We have all been experiencing love as a low emotion. We can grow through love and let Love be the high emotion that lifts us up in all we think, feel, say and do.

CHAPTER FIVE

A HUMAN METAMORPHOSIS

Can you discover the amazing kindness within you that enables you to Love yourself and everybody else regardless of what you and they have done? YES, YOU CAN! YES, YOU CAN! YES, YOU CAN!

Our physical appearance and our spiritual nature are interwoven, even as a caterpillar and potential glorious butterfly are both within the larval stage of a crawling, wormlike creature. In the beginning, the butterfly looks like a worm; often there is on it a suggestion of colorfulness; *however, it is really an exquisite creature that is made to glisten in the sun and enchant us with its fluttering about, setting its dazzling standards for beauty through flaunting colors and the unique markings in the pattern of its wings.* All humankind carries beneath the cloak of our doubts a similar magnificence of being spiritually resplendent.

You can fly; Let go of the cocoon

127

Edmund Sinnott,[1] the late world famous biology professor and author, explained it well. Briefly, his description of every moth and butterfly was that tiny islands of embryonic tissue exist within their larvae from their beginnings. The embryo substance is neither developed nor harmed, but simply kept afloat in various regions of the anatomy until a cocoon or chrysalis is built. While we generally presume that there is a quiescent state beneath that protective covering, in reality, an immediate, inward occupation of great activity is occurring. Although these covered insect larvae appear dormant, their many phagocytes (like white corpuscles) change their activity from a mere devouring of bacteria into nearly destroying everything of their physical bodies. However, they leave the embryonic tissue alone, whereupon these minute substances develop themselves into the moths or butterflies that soon emerge from what had appeared as inactive states of being. Sinnott likened the proceedings of emerging moths and butterflies to the developing spiritual quality of human lives, as the divine Spirit in each of us.

We have been born with evidences that Love is a spiritual emotion or a spiritual reactiveness inhabiting us, although at first, we have presumed Love to be but a common emotion and a common reaction. We have identified our sense of Love as love; we have usually believed that we can rarely experience Love, if at all. We have searched for love and generally have not even felt we had enough of it. At some point in our growth, Love becomes the whole action of all of us, because It is the foremost spiritual emotion. But, we must first come to the awareness, that our apparent lowly state is being replaced with Love's higher expressiveness. It does not happen in a lasting way until after we have *accepted* that our lesser capacity of living is initially all right as love, and that it is good for us to feel love in any of the usual ways that people feel it, which includes living by judgments and feeling guilty. After we have achieved that acceptance, love can next be felt as *a forgiveness.*

---

[1] Edmund W. Sinnott, "The Biology of the Spirit". Science of Mind Publications, Los Angeles, California. 1973.

For most people of today and for the majority of those to come far into the future, forgiveness is a link which connects our feeling love to our feeling Love. We do well to notice that until we choose to be forgiving, we cannot be giving of the most essential gifts. *ONCE A FORGIVING NATURE IS GENUINELY ESTABLISHED WITH US, THE TRANSITION FROM love INTO LOVE, OR FROM OUR USUAL MORE PHYSICAL EMOTIONAL REACTIONS TO OUR SELF-GIVING LOVINGNESS, HAPPENS. IT OCCURS AS WE INCREASINGLY VALUE LOVE AND SPIRIT'S HIGHER IDEAS OF HOW TO LIVE. ALTOGETHER IT IS A HUMAN METAMORPHOSIS, WHICH ALLOWS US TO STEP OUT OF THE COCOON (OR TEMPORARY CONDITION) OF LIVING IN THE GUILT OF HUMAN REACTIVENESS.*

Let us notice that our "usual more physical emotional reactions" are not any more physically expressed than our spiritually uplifted actions. In both kinds of expression, actions equally involve human bodies and things that we notice with our physical senses. As I said, under the subtitle "Love As Emotion" (in chapter four), physical emotional reactions are simply the result of our giving primary attention to our physical experiences rather than to the higher ideas that are developing within the Spirit of each of us. Love is expressed physically just as much as spiritually, although Its orientation is entirely from our spiritual natures. Our best action on earth then, is to shift our attention to these ideas of Spirit and thereby lift our thinking about Love and life, uplifting our manner of expressing love into Love. But to accomplish such upliftment when our usual physical emotional reactions drag us down, something must be discovered that will help us. The Lovefriend is that helper, although to conceive of It as merely a helper is to ignore or forget that It supplies us with *everything* we truly need and desire. The Lovefriend provides for us entirely by acting through us, or even more completely through Its acting as us.

The Lovefriend is the Self-givingness of the Spirit within us. This givingness of the Lovefriend is achieved through Spirit's ideas, which are communicated through us by the Lovefriend; they uplift us, and give us away. As we receive Spirit's ideas, we discover who we really are. It happens to the extent that we allow the Lovefriend to express Itself through us and as us.

We are wise to urge ourselves to be increasingly receptive of the Love- friend. This is achieved by concen- trating our attention through using the right combination of spiritual action prac- tices as explained (in chapter two) under the subtitle "Being With the Love- friend." Unless that method for concen- tration has become clear enough for us to meet the Love- friend with ease, we

The Lovefriend is the Self-givingness of the Spirit within us

are wise to review the method. It makes us receptive to the high ideas of the Lovefriend. These ideas always represent our deepest interests, which when well expressed provide a magnificent experience of harmony with people and with nature.

If in reviewing this procedure we observe that we have not yet become greatly uplifted, we need to supplement it with acts of forgiving, forgetting and acting anew. In this way the human metamorphosis most assuredly takes place.

A RISING THROUGH FORGIVENESS

The solution to living happily, effectively, peacefully, healthful- ly, prosperously and harmoniously with others, lies in our developing the interest to attend the meetings with an enthusiasm, and in contemplating ourselves as being very open with the

Lovefriend. We do well as we conceive of the Lovefriend as being everywhere present, which It is, and by declaring that we desire It to act as us from within particular physical and/or emotional experiences. When we do this before we could suffer something, we do not suffer it! These meetings with the Lovefriend become the most essential experiences of life that we will ever have. They produce results!

It is within our most physical emotional experiences that this all begins. For instance, within the feeling of love, we find we can cause ourselves to do better by telling our emotions to accept redirection from the "better ideas." This does not require any coercion. *Our emotions always follow our thoughts, and with a quickness when right thinking is used. Again, I remind the reader that I do not mean our emotions are merely the way our thoughts appear to us. Emotions and thoughts are of one consistency; they have always been unified, and will remain so. However, our emotions function entirely in accordance with the declarations of our thoughts.*

The "right" idea that will stir love into higher action includes the conception that there can be "a rising through forgiveness." The "lift" of forgiveness is contained within the even larger conception of "serving others." The lower emotion of love is enlisted into higher action as we *make* ourselves aware of a mental atmosphere around us that uses service as the highest expression of love that we can know. In service, we discover how to forgive and forget. We let go of our attachment to memories of what we used to do that we have wished we had not done, and with what other people have done that we have thought was hurtful to us. As we let go and let the Lovefriend act through us or as us, marvelous thoughts and feelings rise and become our better actions. As we notice this difference of thought, feeling and actions, our sense of divinity rises out of the somewhat dormant state of what appears to be a lower nature. The people, conditions and things of our lives, tend to act in concert with these higher thoughts, feelings and actions. It is in this way that we are introduced to Love's presence.

This greater expression of Good, of living with Love, can only occur when forgiveness is accompanied by a heightened sense of adequacy. Then, the spontaneity that was active in our childhood reemerges without our being pulled back into the old restrictions of a physical emotionalism.   We are thereafter no longer hampered by reacting to the differences among people, conditions and circumstances which surround us.

When we discover the value of service within love, and as we forgive and forget, the sense of Love that follows is the adequacy of the Lovefriend announcing Itself to us. The Lovefriend is our equivalent of the "isles of embryonic tissue" mentioned earlier. Our awareness of this larger presence of love lights our way into great living. As we open ourselves to Love's presence, we are born anew.

Forgiving is a necessary action before we can well express our Self-givingness. Forgetting is a necessary complement before we can achieve our desires. Forgiving is the catharsis, the cleansing out of resentful thoughts; it is the means of removing ideas of blame we have accumulated when we reacted to ourselves and others. Forgetting is the complementary catharsis to forgiveness; it enables us to receive Love's better ideas and their formative content. When we forget about the emotional awarenesses we have felt with love, we receive the divine awarenesses and experiences that Love desires us to have.

Our field of interest in this book is to discover how we can meet the Lovefriend, again and again, until we are aware of being at One with It everywhere we go and in all that we do. We will give attention to forgiveness and forgetfulness, but vastly more to the Lovefriend's presence, and Its adequacy, and to the renewal of life which It provides us. We will not examine very much of our lives as they were before our feelings of *FORGIVENESS, FORGETFULNESS AND ADEQUACY* developed, although we will examine them some. To feel forgiveness and forgetfulness is the early basis of our metamorphosis; it is the relative reason why we can be transformed. It is the stimulus that motivates us to let go and let "our embryonic isles of potentiality," or our adequacy, act as us. The sure foundation of, or the absolute reason for this potential, is the adequacy which I am naming as the LOVEFRIEND, along with Its ideas for better living. Or we can say, the adequacy is found in the attitude of Self-givingness.

BEING FORGIVING, FORGETFUL AND FORGETIVE

When "for" is placed in front of the word "give," it provides the meaning of how we can give forth. All giving means to contribute from ourselves. Such contribution is an expression of ourselves. The placement of "for" in front of the word "give" causes the givingness to be brought forth much as "for" does with the word "seen" or with the "word" itself. When something is foreseen, or when a writing is preceded by a foreword, a significant relationship exists between the subject and an understanding of it which tells us of something about it that is to be. Giving or bringing forth ourselves, is the essential subject of our greater livingness or of our reversing any difficulties we have in experiencing a fulfilled and happy life. To forgive, means to do something before we give that opens up the opportunity to express ourselves well.

Forgiveness is a change of attitude wherein we cease looking at our mistakes. Courageous actions follow forgiveness because it eliminates the entire basis for hesitancy.

Being forgetful ordinarily seems unnecessary or undesirable. Yet, forgetfulness is a great value to us when we use it to dismiss the effect upon us of past thoughts that have contained blame and shame. Those ideas have seemed to place us at a disadvantage and will appear to hurt us so long as we remember them. Subconsciously, they cannot and will not leave us in this lifetime. Yet, their seeming destruction of our confidence and well-being can be taken away when we move our attention from them to our potentiality for being able to think better about ourselves and others.

This disempowerment of the need to blame and shame ourselves and others happens all the more as we become "forgetive". The dictionary defines this as "Inventive, imaginative."[2] This inventive way of managing those destructive thoughts is the result of "the forgetting." By forgetting erroneous ideas, we are able to use the forgetive action that elevates our experiences into the realm of higher ideas, where our unrestricted imagination can express them fully. We cannot be forgetive, which means to greatly grow or achieve much by imagining distinctly creative ideas and placing them into action, until after we forgive and forget; and then we are empowered.

We become forgetive as we simply declare that we are changing our old thoughts from our past need to think in condemnatory ways, to the present interest of feeling unlimited in adequacy. Nothing enables us to achieve more personal or social progress; but we may think great effort is necessary. The ease comes about because there is an overlapping experience, from forgiveness to forgetting, from being forgetive to feeling adequacy. Our interests in each of these activities tend to attract us to participate in the meetings with the Lovefriend, who only knows an easiness.

The forgiveness of oneself is the acceptance that the Lovefriend is the truth of Self, and that the blamed and shamed idea of Self is the fictional belief that we are but selves. When our self is forgiven, the sense of being restricted, tormented, disabled or distressed falls away; the forgiven self is thereby exchanged for Self-resourcefulness.

We can all discover the Lovefriend who expresses us spontaneously and magnificently, so that joy, peace, happiness, success, abundance and happy relationships result. But, since all of this Good of life springs forth from within us through Love, and because It cannot happen until It is no longer locked up within us, the forgiving and forgetfulness are essential to our drawing upon the Self-resourcefulness.

The forgiveness, forgetfulness and forgetive actions are entirely

---

[2] Webster's Seventh New Collegiate Dictionary. G. & C. Merriam Company. 1972.

actions within ourselves. We may forgive other people, sometimes many other people, in the process of achieving self-forgiveness; nevertheless, it is the forgiveness of ourselves that we feel in our forgiving others that enables us to feel deserving of letting the Lovefriend express us. We have imprisoned our capacities to do well in life by restraining our thoughts, feelings, words and actions: only self-forgiveness releases us. However, once the forgiveness, forgetfulness and the action of being forgetive have occurred, discovering a sense of increasing adequacy and many other improved attitudes frees us more and more. Then we give ourselves away because the restraints to that action are largely stripped away. Our Self-givingness and receptivity become our greater livingness. And best of all, again and again in all of this we meet the Lovefriend, who carries us onward into further experiences that are unlimited in their value.

We are wise as we climb the steps of forgiveness,
forgetiveness and adequacy

Forgiveness, forgetfulness and being forgetive are the

beginning experiences that enable us to discover Love's presence and to be amazingly kind to ourselves and other people. They are essential and instrumental to our achieving great personal growth.

ADVICE

Advice is not of much value to us. Whenever it seems to be poor advice and we follow it, we might experience something that feels harmful. On the other hand, often when it appears to be helpful, we are erroneously thinking that someone else knows better than we do. *When we discover our individual capacities to think, feel and act, we find that no one else knows as well as we do what we should do about anything.* This greater knowledge is readily available to us when we trust ourselves completely and are forgiving and forgetive.

Still, before we feel love enough to sense the Love that is within us, most of us choose to value another person more than ourselves. We become dependents and live in discontent. We cannot find our "embryonic selves" until we divert ourselves from such preoccupation. It becomes necessary to place our sense of value on something that will challenge us to feel a cause for being alive; it must be something that is a natural interest to us, not one borrowed from someone we admire.

Generally, we do not notice that most of us live in dependencies. If we do observe our dependent ways, we often feel too little adequacy to desire to do better. Or, we hold so much against ourselves that to take the time to prove the difference forgiveness makes does not become a priority. *Again, many of us succeed in feeling forgiven, but we think there is nothing else that we can have. Nevertheless, we can live lives that are unlimited in doing that which we deeply desire to do. WE SIMPLY HAVE TO TURN AWAY FROM OTHER PEOPLE'S ADVICE; WE HAVE TO PRIZE SOMETHING THAT WE CHOOSE TO EXPERIENCE THAT IS FROM OUR OWN DEEP-FELT THINKING.*

VALUE

Let us observe that we first feel only a small sense of something's value before we are able to enjoy its greater deep-felt potential for us. At first, we notice that something is consistently beneficial to us and so we place the idea upon it that it is a value. If we are interested enough in a particular value, we explore it more. However, we cannot discover the value of anything beyond the degree to which we accept or embody it. In time, we naturally accept everything which we consistently value. However, time need not be much of a factor; feeling Love enables a swifter acceptance or embodiment of any value. This occurs because feeling Love and acting on the basis of It is the most positive action we can take. Love is only felt from a deep place within ourselves; Its action is fundamentally spiritual and unlimited in effectiveness.

We all naturally place considerable value on something. For some it is love; for others it is success or fame or money or things. No one values everything equally. Because we all tend to think we must have human considerations, we choose particulars that we value. Because some values never interest us very much, our sense of appreciation for them seldom increases with the passage of time. Some of us are like that with many things. There is much that we value a little, and little that we value very much. And if we do not open ourselves enough to the idea that there are for us some great values of life, we experience boredom, disappointments and pain. However, we can change our thinking and change our lives! We can begin by placing our attention on something we value, and then increase our interest with it until we enjoy it all the more.

Money is an example. The primary difference between people who are rich or poor is always that money is either greatly valued or not valued much at all. Those people who become rich, or who manage to maintain a wealthy status, are those who like money and who also continually grow in their appreciation of it. They cherish their ability to have money more than they value the things that it buys. Those people who are poor may think they like money or even that they love it, but they oppose their own belief that they can have money by valuing the things that it buys more than money itself.

To change from being poor, or to even upgrade one's economic position to a better one, there has to be a growth in the attitude of enjoying money itself. Opportunity frequently comes to all people who cultivate this attitude and desire to better themselves economically. The privilege of experiencing more money often comes to the attention of those who are open to it. But unless the opportunity is acted upon, it departs as quickly as it comes. To become rich monetarily, the primary ingredients are twofold: an attitude of enjoying money must grow in the thought, and the opportunities to have more money must be recognized. It is as simple as that.

Similarly, if we place great value on our experience of love, Love announces Itself to us through that experience. It happens through our developing an appreciation of love, which is our lesser awareness of Love. That is, through our becoming sincerely interested in experiencing love more richly, we place ourselves in consciousness where we value the idea that love can be better than it seemed at first. It is in this way, that (1) Love assists us to achieve a close Friendship with It, and that (2) we receive evidences of Its presence. Through all of this, we build conviction that we are having life's greatest experience. And we are! We can repeat this activity again and again, because it is the most basic format of our meetings with the Lovefriend.

I do not mean that the meetings with Love begin to occur when we make it our special interest to value love. *Love's meetings have always occurred with all of us. However, when our appreciation of love is great enough for us to acknowledge that Love is having meetings with us, and when we take an interest in the meetings, that is when we "really" attend them; then our relationship with Love takes on a higher dimension of meaning.* It is similar to the discovery that roses may have grown near where we live for as long as we have been there; yet, there is a particular point in time (the point of poise) when we stop what we are doing to smell them and observe their beauty. In the same manner, we have all experienced love; and we have had meetings with Love. However, we have not truly given attention to the meetings. It is in our not giving attention to Love's meetings, that we have not "really" attended them. But now, we are turning away from being preoccupied with love and trying to take care of our habitual conditions through it, and *we are noticing that Love has meetings with us; and we are discovering that our participation in these meetings is deeply fulfilling.* That is, the meetings with the Lovefriend are the most magnificent meetings anyone can have. And Love is the greatest Friendship we have ever conceived.

There has never been anyone who has not been deeply loved by the Lovefriend. The Lovefriend is always equally close to all persons. Therefore, anyone can grow through love into regular awarenesses of Love.

There has never been anyone who has not been deeply loved by the Lovefriend

In declaring that "Love assists us to achieve a close Friendship with It (1)," I do not mean that Love has ever been separable from any of us. Nor do I mean that Love Itself ever has to achieve anything. I mean that when we choose to especially value love--that we thereby place ourselves into a deeper relationship with Love (or with the Lovefriend), one that we have not before believed was possible. The achievement is actually ours because Love knew all along that it would happen, but we had to become ready or we had to accept the Friendship as something that we desired. Although I am saying that Love "knew all along that it would happen," the truth is that this only means that Love has never concerned Itself with when we would attend the meetings and if a deeper relationship with It would ever happen. For everything that could occur between ourselves and It, is already known by Love, and has always been done, so far as anything Love could do to bring it about. Our especial Friendship with Love is simply being unfolded from the eternal idea of Love's nature; and that unfoldment is gradually occurring within every person.

My purpose in writing this "as though Love always knew," is that we cannot understand how Love knows before we know, and at the same time still feel that we are freely choosing to be in Its Friendship, until we too know the Friendship is complete. And when we draw close to Love's presence, the Friendship is felt. Our deepest yearning and Love's greatest idea about us are then drawn together. In this way, we open ourselves to recognize that Love has always known of the Friendship we have with It. (Briefly, we can describe this as though Love has completed the Friendship by knowing this in the beginning and all along; however, *the completion for us does not appear to be there until we greatly recognize It.)*

Again, I do not mean that the Lovefriend could be closer to one than another. I really mean that we have been created to be unified with the Lovefriend, but that this has not been forced upon us. We have taken a great step forward toward feeling at One with Love, when we have come to the belief that there is much more to the substance of Love than there appeared to be when we presumed that love and its conditions were Love's entirety. When this happens with us, we tend to feel that Love has drawn close to our thoughts and feelings of It, which has always been true of It, but which we cannot have known until we have chosen to prize that experience for ourselves.

INNOCENCE

When we become markedly aware of the Lovefriend, the experiences of forgiveness and forgetiveness vanish from our lives. Our adequacy is reestablished upon innocence. *Innocence is the awareness that we have of ourselves when we feel at One with Love. Innocence is the experience of finding no fault with ourselves. Because of it, we no longer need to forgive ourselves. We probably still need to improve ourselves; however, it is not because "we have been bad or because there is something wrong with us," but rather because we have not acted in the elevated way that Love is now finding us more open to express. Now we know what we could have done before, that would have been good for us. That is, we have always acted as we thought we had to. Everyone has always acted in the best way each one thought was possible. This we cannot change. It means that we are all innocent of wrongdoing, inasmuch as we always do better when we know better.*

Forgiveness is no longer necessary when we cease being accusatory. We need to accept that all we have done or are doing now is the result of the place that we are in our growth into spiritual awareness. Throughout the evolving of our thinking until we know we are One with Love, we tend to think we are guilty because of our mistakes. When we let Love truly guide us, we let go of the need to feel guilt any longer. Before then, our spiritual growth necessitates forgiveness; after then, our spiritual evolution provides us the ability to feel innocent and more rapidly continue our growth.

Innocence relaxes us. The resulting serenity provides marvelous care. This happens increasingly with us as we attend Love's meetings with an enthusiasm. Attending the meetings and maintaining a high interest level in them is extraordinarily beneficial.

Because the awareness of innocence is the actual key to our being prepared for meeting the Lovefriend, it is the single largest experience of consciousness that we need to sense before entering the meetings. Innocence draws us close to Love. We are aware that innocence dwells within us to the extent that we convince ourselves that our feelings of inadequacy are not the result of being wrong or bad. We simply feel inadequate until we allow Love to be the foremost emotion and Intelligence of our lives.

If it seems that we can only be aware of innocence through experiencing long sessions with forgivenss, then we are wise to act on this understanding. However, *WHEN WE ARE READY, WE WILL EXPERIENCE LOVE MORE READILY AND REGULARLY AS WE SPEND MORE TIME IN DECLARING OURSELVES INNOCENT THAN FORGIVEN.* Forgiveness is necessary while we do not understand what "unconditional" Love really means. But once we realize how very unconditional Love and life are with us, we feel our innocence, and forgiveness is no longer necessary. To achieve this, we are helped the most as we identify ourselves as fundamentally divine or as spiritual beings.

THE MEETING

When we acknowledge Love's closeness, an outward manifestation of Love takes place. Then we feel Love's presence and that Its Friendship overshadows every other friendship we have ever experienced. Our sense of the seemingly increasing closeness is made possible by our having chosen this as our premium value, and the result is that Love has manifested with us what It has known of our relationship with It all along; Love has used our increasing desire to express It by manifesting through our feelings a more complete sense of Its unification with us than we have known before.

Love's announcement of Itself to us is not acknowledged by us without our feeling It as a deeply personal thing. And when we feel Love as such an abiding Friendship, something wonderful happens because of our consciousness. We instinctively attend a meeting with It. And we emerge from the meeting feeling happy, serene, resourceful, confident and whole. Something of these magnificent awarenesses of ourselves from each meeting is added to our permanent sense of Self-identity.

The Lovefriend cares for us so much that it seems our meetings with It are entirely of a personal nature. The truth is that our meetings with the Lovefriend are simply personalized with us. Actually, the Lovefriend is a Universal Presence and continuously Loves everyone. What we need to know is that the magnificent benefits of any and all meetings that we have with Love are universally available, but the particular personal experiences of the meetings are different for everyone. And the results of these meetings are experiences of our demonstrating more of that which we individually value in our lives.

The sense of value that we first find with love, escalates then for us as we prize it as though there is something greater about love than we first thought. This greater sense of love is something we must cultivate; this is because our valuing of love begins with us as a mere suspicion that those around us have not told us as much about the Good of life as they could have. Actually we were all born with a vigorous sense of Love, and before we *learned* to compare one thing to another and *thereby establish a value system,* we replaced our sense of Love with love by emulating the people immediately around us; then we learned to compare everything to them as though we *valued them the most.*

It was natural for us to imitate our guardians or someone close to us, at least in the beginning. It was also natural for us to make comparisons; it was a result of our having been individualized. It was just as necessary and natural for us to establish a valuing system. *HOWEVER, OUR PATTERNING OURSELVES AFTER OTHER PEOPLE AND OUR MAKING COMPARISONS NEED NOT CONTINUE AS A REPLACEMENT FOR OUR DEEPER LONGING TO FEEL LOVE AND TO EXPERIENCE THE LOVEFRIEND.* When we greatly adjust ourselves, so that the Lovefriend becomes our only model, future generations will still make comparisons and establish values, but Love's Way of being peaceful, harmonious, joyful, prosperous, successful and amazingly kind will, in time, be better known by them; and they will choose their values according to their individual interests. Along with this, forgiveness will rightfully be replaced by our accepting everyone's innocence.

Although there will come a time when many people will consider themselves and all others innocent, imprisonment, along with the enforcement of the law through courts and police actions, will continue to occur when actual crimes are committed. Then, people will not so much feel guilty as they will feel they are being reasonably corrected for their misdeeds. They will then understand that they are being shown how they could have acted in a better manner. Our society will have mastered the ability to provide protection and reform without being accusatory. Meetings with the Lovefriend will make this possible.

The meetings that we have with the Lovefriend are just as natural as anything else that exists. Although some people will tend to see a light or hear heavenly music in these meetings, most people will not. Therefore, most people are wise not to expect something that is strange or unusual, but rather to expect a heightened sense of the usual. Certainly the meetings with the Lovefriend are not of a common nature, yet ordinary experiences are involved. The difference between everyday occurrences as they have been, and as they will become in these meetings, is that our ordinary experiences will become *GREATLY* lived. Let us conceive how the most natural and normal experiences of life could be great by our really feeling Love in them; no better description of the meetings can be made.

As our metamorphosis takes place, the meetings with the Lovefriend occur nearly everyday. In them:

1. We place our imagination upon the idea that we are meeting with the Lovefriend. We may choose to go to a favorite spot where we can maximally relax, to make it easier to feel the presence.

2. When in our favorite place we tell ourselves that Love is always with us, but that we are right then using this experience to make ourselves sensitive to Love's presence.

3. We integrate the four practical actions from the chapter

"Meeting With Love," under the subtitle "Being With The Lovefriend." Their inclusion may have become spontaneous with us by now, but if they have not we take the time to study them and reach the awareness that they give us.

4. We explain to ourselves that our increasing sensitivity with the Lovefriend results in our ability to directly experience our deepest longings and innermost urges.

5. We speak to our deep yearnings, and we let them know that we desire to express ourselves well. We tell them that through our sensing them as evidence of the Lovefriend's presence, this meeting cannot be in vain. We assure ourselves that we are becoming One with their design of us, and that we are surely Self-giving.

6. Thereupon, we teach ourselves that our deepest and most genuine desires contain the Intelligence to express us with magnificence.

7. Upon leaving these meetings, we conceive of the Lovefriend as going forth through us in all we do.

The meeting will be explained more completely in the last chapters.

LOVE
PROJECTOR

As we forgive, and forget everything but Love, we experience Self-adequacy.

CHAPTER SIX

OUR NEW AWARENESSES

Can you cease reacting to everything and express Love without having to feel that someone else Loves you first? YES, YOU CAN! YES, YOU CAN! YES, YOU CAN!

Up until now, the world has not been very receptive to Love, but has rather been caught up in the belief that reacting to everything on the basis of what it brings up for us is the basic and necessary form of action. Our essential actions now, are:

1. to observe what we have done, what we are doing and what we can do to value love,
2. to discover a greater sense of love or to unfold from within love, the magnificent expression of life we are calling Love,
3. to notice how capably we can accept the idea that Love is very good for us by recognizing that our previously held ideas about love, and our corresponding reactions and emotions, have been largely erroneous for us (We are wise to refrain from equating error with the idea that we have been bad persons because of it. No one is evil, even though some of our actions have been mistakes and feel as though they have been bad for us.),
4. to choose to forgive and forget patterns of judgment and being reactive,
5. to contemplate the right combination of ideas,
6. to discover that our adequacy is the presence of the Lovefriend,
7. to take interest in the Lovefriend, so that It will lift us

into an expression of life that is noncritical of love reactions and physical emotions, and

8. at the same time, to actively and regularly express Love by acting entirely from an awareness of Its presence.

Of course, we cannot live by Love and be critical too! We cannot be critical of loving reactions and of physical emotions, while living by Love, because we would be reacting unlovingly to ourselves to do so. Neither can we cease feeling our erroneous customary reactions and living by our lowest emotions all at once, because we will continue to experience them to some degree while we are discovering how to live by Love. Moreover, we do not greatly live by Love by avoiding the expressions of our physical emotions. Love will move us to act in ways that are obviously very physical. Our growth **THROUGH** physical emotions is **NOT** to lift us out of them, but **TO LIFT US UP IN THEM**.

The difference between physical emotions and spiritual emotions is best understood then, by defining a physical emotion as the feeling and action that is entirely generated by reacting to the considerations of environment and heredity, without an awareness that a better or higher idea for behavior could exist; a spiritual emotion is the feeling and action that results from being true to oneself, which includes being kind, constructive and harmonious with others, and being very aware of, but usually not

Our growth through physical emotions is not to lift us out of them, but to lift us up in them

reactive to, an environment and one's heredity. Physical actions are always involved in expressing physical emotions. Physical emotions are always expressed by feeling physical appetites and physical instincts (and there is nothing wrong with this except that high ideas will help us to express emotions better), and by only considering environment and heredity in making a choice for an action (again, high ideas open up possibilities that often are not noticed this way). Spiritual emotions are always expressed by letting the inner presence, the Lovefriend, inspire us with higher ideas, ones that are gentle, beneficial, and that bring complete resolutions to our situations. The actions of spiritual emotion are carried out in ways that sometimes include reactions and always include physical movements. Sometimes the inspired actions are similar or identical to our physical desires and are already sensed by our ordinary instincts.

We proceed best by consciously observing what we are doing; this includes finding a way to lessen the extent to which we repress, depress and project ourselves. We accomplish this by observing ourselves in our customary reactions, including our criticisms of both ourselves and other people. In addition, we open ourselves to experiencing the presence of the Lovefriend. To the extent that we lift ourselves out of living judgmentally and become aware that the Lovefriend is present, we lift ourselves into Love and our lesser practices are diminished. Our best actions emerge in this way.

Some of us tend to feel that we cannot uplift ourselves. We think we must depend on a "savior," or someone who has never judged or wronged anyone, and there is a sound reason for this feeling. It begins naturally within our own thought. For example, if a person has been proven to be a thief, we would not ordinarily think it sensible to provide that one a job as the handler of large sums of money. However, we might rethink our ideas after his or her prison reform. Or, we might be more prone to build trust towards a proven thief if he or she chose to be reoriented towards society by emulating people who have always lived lawfully. We are able to think in these ways because something within us, deeper than our usual thoughts, is unblemished; it can assist us to live honest and wholesome lives; and we can discover it if we choose. Of course, an inner accusatory attitude can be of no benefit to us, but something deeper in our thoughts can help!

There is a savior within every person. I do not mean that the savior is really a different presence from one person to another, but I do mean that no one can put us in touch with the way that we truly are, and the way we truly are for each other, other than Love, or the Lovefriend. The word Lovefriend may be new; however, the conception of an inner unspoiled presence or the Spirit, which means the same, is as old as are the roots of every major religion of the world. Here we will not identify it with any religion; nor do we believe any religious dogma or doctrine is necessary in order to comprehend it. *ALL THAT WE ARE INTERESTED IN DOING IS ACKNOWLEDGING THE LOVE-FRIEND. IT IS THROUGH THIS AWARENESS THAT WE CAN FEEL ADEQUACY. WE CAN MOTIVATE OURSELVES BY CHOOSING LOVE'S WAY AS THE BASIS FOR OUR ACTIONS.*

The saviors of the major religions were all great people, who lived somewhat continuously with the quality of life that we are explaining here. They tended to choose their actions well. They largely lived "innocent" lives, but experienced forgiveness for themselves whenever necessary, were regularly forgiving and forgetive of others and greatly felt their adequacy. We have not succeeded well in explaining how they achieved this so completely and we may never understand; BUT THAT IS NOT IMPOR-TANT! The essential understanding we need about them is that they showed us how to live. The primary interest of these wayshowers was to tell us that we have a FRIEND LIKE THEM within ourselves. *WHEN WE BECOME AWARE OF THEIR MISSION, AND THE WISDOM THEY IMPARTED TO US, WE WILL FORGIVE OURSELVES, WORTHILY ADJUST OUR RELATIONSHIPS AND FIND ADEQUACY; WE WILL MEET THE LOVEFRIEND.*

NO MORE SUFFERING

None of this need be hard to achieve! If we *strive* to accomplish these ends, they elude us, at least until we give up the idea that we can be successful without feeling Love. Without attending meetings with the Lovefriend, we simply cannot discover Love's Way! The life that we most truly desire to live, that of maximally expressing Love, is the easiest way life can be lived. (It is true, of course that we can easily exist for a long time without discovering Love, but an irritation, conscious or unconscious, at not feeling well expressed or fulfilled makes such an existence a mere endurance; it is therefore a disappointment with what life could otherwise be.) For some of us, our only work in living Love's Way is to let go of our efforts to be like those particular models who have lived entirely in their reactions to other people, their environment and heredity. For others of us, our work is mostly to cease reacting to our own customary reactions.

It was this latter method that seemed important to my parents. However, they *tried too hard* to change themselves and so life became a struggle for them; and they suffered terribly because of it. I Love my parents (who passed on years ago) dearly, and I feel that some of my understanding has come from the modeling I did with them. However, to unlearn much of what they thought, felt, and practiced that life is a hardship we must suffer, has been a challenge. They suffered much and believed that they had to (though in his latter years, my father became expectant that someday people would suffer less). On the other hand, it was in their companionship that I discovered the inner loving presence. Where could I have found parents who could have thought differently about suffering and yet knew as much of the inner loving presence as mine? There have not been many. Yet there can be many now, and I desire to contribute to the manifestation of this possibility.

GROWING THROUGH OUR PHYSICAL EMOTIONS

Let us understand that all problems occur when we do not believe that our appearance contains more good for us than we perceive, even while we are being infinitely supplied with opportunities, growth and inner supportiveness. Just as frogs and toads appear to be tadpoles for awhile, so we appear to be limited. But, even as frogs and toads are not limited to life underwater, we are not limited to lives that are without the expressiveness that the Lovefriend gives to us. As they leap from water upon their discovery that they can, we express much greater life upon our discovery of the Love that is within us. We discover that we can

Tadpole to frog, love to Love

do anything we truly desire to do, because Love (the Lovefriend) wants us to be happy through our leaping out of our lower emotional turmoil.

Any limited experiences of life that we think we have result from thinking too little of ourselves. *We have thought we are only that which we appear to be; we have to feel Love to think better of ourselves.* And this happens with us as we attend the meetings.

The repetitious feelings of our lower emotions and the constancy of being in our consequent customary reactions keep us from uplifting our ideas of who we are. It is not that it is a mistake to feel our emotions. However, we delay our experience of discovering the Lovefriend if we place most of our attention upon feeling our lower emotions. On the other hand, we cannot grow through these emotions if we deny that they exist or avoid feeling them. Therefore, this is not a suggestion that we suppress our feelings. It is rather a presentation of how we can evolve into a larger expression of our true Selves by growing *through* our physical emotions.

When we have grown through our physical emotions, we will feel more of life than before; we will feel the Love which is present with us all the time. At a deep level within us we already feel the Lovefriend or Love all the time; we can outwardly discover this magnificent feeling of Love that we already have, and it is that which will greatly release us from our fears and ineptness. But, it cannot occur for us until we grow through our feelings of what we appear to be. Then it is that we leap forward.

THE WAY OF PHYSICAL EMOTION

When we live largely in our physical emotions, we believe that Love is but love; it seems it cannot be otherwise. Our lower emotional mannerisms result from believing that our world and life are full of problems, and that all the Love there is, is love. Instances are: if we think our world has not enough goods to provide for all the people of a swelling population, has not enough space for our wastes and is a breeding ground for disease, then we are unaware that a Universal Love exists.

The absence of Universal Love would mean that deprivation, crowded conditions and sickness would frequently occur or probably would be widespread all the time. Ample care might not ever become universally available, no matter what we would try to do. And such problems seem evident to many. It has seemed to most of us that a great lack exists of food, clothing, and desirable housing; there are many signs that our natural resources are being carelessly wasted; health problems appear to be on the increase; and the planet seems as if it is gradually being destroyed. All these conditions of hunger, poverty, waste, disease and carelessness, are looked upon by many as though they indicate that Universal Love is not present. However, the Truth is that Love is everywhere present, and is right now able to provide us with an unlimited resourcefulness; it is because Love is not generally recognized that poverty, squalor, widespread illness and irresponsibility are apparent at the same time that Love's solutions exist.

The question as to why people suffer if God is Love is superfluous, because the answer is easy. *LOVE IS EVER PRESENT; IT IS SIMPLY THAT IT IS BEING ONLY MEAGERLY RECOGNIZED. THIS IS THE CAUSE OF SUFFERING.* Of course, this does not feel reassuring to those who suffer. Nevertheless, their experiences of disease, poverty and squalor cannot continue longer than the time that they take to grow through their physical emotions. The solution is for us to learn from each other, not only how to grow up, but how to grow through our fears. If we feel we are our brothers' keepers, we need to grow through our lower emotions, both for them and for ourselves; for the only way we can help others is by being examples of a greater livingness that is founded upon the expressing of high emotions.

If Universal Love or the Lovefriend were not real, people would react to a shortage of supplies and overpopulation by trying to improve situations that actually could not be very much helped. Many of our lower emotional responses or customary reactions reflect a belief that such a critical condition exists. We often think we can make a difference with such presumed problems by fighting them and by struggling with them. But when we do this, underneath it all we feel considerable hopelessness! These are base reactions toward life. Other times, we act toward someone or something with anger, frustration, despair, lust, sorrow or other forms of lower emotion that we believe we must act out, so as to object to some other condition in life that we feel bothers us. In all these instances, *if we knew that nothing we legitimately need or truly desire would be kept from us when it was our Good to have it, our base reactions would cease to exist*. This means that we would not react fearfully any of the time because we would know we do not need to. *We can discover that Love can so assure us, and then commensurately act through us, as we participate in the meetings.*

THE LAW OF REACTION OR NEW ACTION

If we do not know Love, to experience our customary or even

base reactions is essential to our staying alive! To stay alive, or simply endure our experience of existence, there is that which I term Law that makes us react to circumstances as though they could hurt us or help us when we do not act spontaneously. The Law of the universe is that life is supported by continuous actions playing upon one another. One way to describe those actions is through explaining them as cause and effect. Wherever there are causes, effects follow. All causes begin in love (as fear, ignorance, jealousy, anxiety and guilt) or Love (as faith, knowledge, trust, confidence and innocence) and become mental actions; all effects are objectively manifested and can be reactions to circumstances that seem acceptable or unacceptable. However, when we know Love and we let Love guide us or act as us, the actions that follow are not necessarily the reactions of our liking or disliking circumstances. Often innovative new actions which combine fresh causes and better effects, based upon that which Love knows is best for a situation, replace what appears to be predictable effects.

Love knows what new actions to use independent of our customary idea of acting back to something on the basis of the previous actions we sensed from it. Sometimes the best action is a reaction to circumstances; often it is an entirely new action. In either case, it can be effortless, because Love knows what is best. Law intelligently complements Love's Intelligence. *Law always carries out our actions, and if Love is greatly recognized, the Law reacts according to Love's idea. If Love is not very greatly recognized, the Law reacts according to whatever intent we have.*

UNLESS THIS TEACHING ABOUT THE LAW OF REACTION IS UNDERSTOOD, THE NATURE AND PRESENCE OF LOVE CANNOT BE RECOGNIZED AS MUCH AS IS DESIRABLE FOR US. THE NATURE OF THE LAW OF REACTION IS THAT IT FORMS ALL OF OUR EXPERIENCES. WHEN LOVE IS NOT MUCH RECOGNIZED, THE LAW REACTS BY CREATING FORMS WHICH PROVIDE EVIDENCE OF THAT FACT. ON OUR WAY INTO LIFTING OUR SENSE OF love TO LOVE, THE LAW MAKES FORMS OR EXPERIENCES WHICH DEMONSTRATE THIS TRANSITIONAL STATE. BUT, BECAUSE LOVE AND LAW ARE COMPLEMENTS, LOVE ACTS AS US

(THROUGH THE LAW) TO THE EXTENT THAT WE RISE OUT OF love; AND LOVE THEN BECOMES FOR US OUR LAW OF ACTION. "LOVE IS THE FULFILLING OF THE LAW."[1]

The nature of the Law of reaction is that
it forms all of our experiences

AS WE GO ON, WE WILL REFER TO THE LAW PERIODI-CALLY. WE WILL MEAN THE LAW OF REACTION AS JUST DESCRIBED. WHEN WE REFER TO LOVE, WE WILL MEAN THAT THE ACTION OF LAW IS LIFTED FROM COMMON

---

[1] Romans 13:10 (RSV).

REACTIONS TO HIGHER REACTIONS, OR MORE OFTEN TO SPONTANEOUS AND INNOVATIVE ACTIONS THAT DO NOT ACCOUNT FOR WHAT HAS GONE ON BEFORE ITS EMER-GENCE; WE WILL FURTHER MEAN THAT LOVE HAS FULFILLED THE LAW.

TO LIVE IS TO ACT

To live means to act! "Act" means to use actions to acquire a desire or to fill a need. It is better to react to circumstances as though they could hurt us or help us than to not act at all. And for some of us, just the discovery that we are causing ourselves to live our lives in such reactions is what we next need to know about life. However, we will do better when we choose to let Love guide us so that we easily and regularly accept better actions. When Love is not felt, heard or greatly involved, we are still making choices, but rarely the ones that help us much.

Constructive action assures better living

Whether we know of Love or not, love enables us to act and to live. But, if love is our only guide, we are sometimes afraid to act as we feel we desire to, or feel we should. Unfortunately, when by conscience we keep ourselves from an action that we feel we need to do, we seem to injure ourselves. Fortunately, Love knows how to never experience hurt. As we go on, we are wise to remember this, because short lives as measured by earth time are often built upon the understanding that many preconceived actions should not be carried out. That does not make those short-lived people wrong who have not expressed themselves well; but, it does mean that they have felt wrongly (felt guilty) about their thoughts. They could have changed their thinking instead of shaming themselves, but they did not, because they had not discovered Love. This was not because anyone was to blame; rather, it was the result of people's somewhat generally knowing too little of Love. We are wise not to continue grieving over the past consequences of this, but to celebrate the wonderful difference people can achieve with this knowledge of Love in the present and future. Friends and family who have previously felt hurt through being too conscientious about this were not wrong to think and feel as they did; however, people cannot withhold reactions and stay alive for long. When reactions are not expressed, and when no actions take their place, the cells of the body or the health of the mind, or both, deteriorate.

Often we feel depressed when we question our right to react as we either think we want or think we should. Depressions cannot be replaced with happiness and effectual actions until depressed persons think and feel that they are all right to act as they see fit. If the actions could hurt them or others (and often that seems to be the nature of the situation), it is unwise, of course, that they carry them out. However, there is a marvelous solution for depressed people, and for repressed and projected people too. Rather than *withholding* harmful actions, they can *replace* them with better actions.

The whole idea behind feeling Love within us is that Love gives us the interest and understanding to replace an intended action, which could otherwise harm or disappoint, with a much better action that can help and greatly satisfy. So, we are happier and we function better when we do not react in a customary way with only ordinary justice in mind, and with elements of distrust, *provided* we are enough aware of Love to replace our intended reaction with a higher action. It is not hard to be that aware of Love. We have only to become interested in lifting up our actions and in doing that which is best for ourselves and others. In addition, we have to realize that we cannot know of Love's place in this unless we believe that Love is present with us.

GIVING LOVE

It becomes progressively easier to cease living within our previously customary reactions, which impede our greater livingness, to the extent that we have met the Lovefriend. *FOR THE MORE WE KNOW THAT LOVE IS, AND THAT LOVE IS OUR FRIEND, THEN THE LESS WE WILL REACT WITH DISTRUST AND OPPOSITION TO ANYTHING, AND THE MORE WE WILL BE SPONTANEOUSLY ACTIVE IN A BENEFICIAL WAY WITH EVERYTHING.* With a great sense of the reality of Love, we will act toward everybody and everything out of our awareness of Its Self-giving presence.

In contrast, the less we are certain that Love exists, the more we will reduce our idea of Love to love, to a reaction with negotiations and compromises; and then we will feel all the more, that love is but a physical emotion. And the more we feel love as only a physical emotion, the less of love will we feel. This is because it is not even easy to find love when we think we need to get it from someone else.

We think we need to get love from someone else

Who are those who will show us love when we are looking for it from other people? Admittedly **some** ministers, teachers, psychologists, nurses, psychiatrists and social workers will do this; however, their sympathy will be love, not Love. The degree of the givingness of their love will be slight, because they too will not be certain that Love exists, and they will also be seeking to convince themselves that at least love does. This does not make them inferior to more confident counselors, or unhelpful, because we may not be opening ourselves as fully to Love and to those who can more spontaneously give It; it is those to whom we are most willing to turn who help us to the extent that we can be helped. Giving love in that manner will make them feel good to a point; it will satisfy us to some degree. But, their love at best is "ordinary justice" in another of its appearances.

THERE ARE OTHER PUBLIC SERVANTS OF THEIR KIND WHO SOMETIMES SEE THAT WE ARE REALLY LOOKING FOR THE LOVE THAT IS WITHIN OUR OWN SELVES. THEY CAN SERVE US MORE BENEFICIALLY BY SHOWING US THE DIRECTION TO SELF-RELIANCE IN WHATEVER WAYS WE ARE OPEN TO IT. Yet, until we believe that there is much more to love than its being a physical emotion, we will prevent ourselves from receiving their help. Always, Love or love can only be discovered to the degree that we lift our idea of love from experiencing it with our customary reactions to one of a Self-givingness.

People generally give love only as a just reaction; that is, they return only the love that is first given them. Of those people who give love first, many feel starved for it, and they believe that by feeling sympathetic they are doing the best they can do to find love and feel it. On the other hand, there are others who give love to people, *who seem to have no need for it to be returned to them;* they are giving Love, because that is the major difference between love and Love. Once we understand this and we choose to Love others, whether or not they return love or even appreciation to us, we become less and less emotional in its most physical sense. This is because that which we give without thought of return is not given with physical emotion or attachment, but is given to express the Love (spiritual emotion) which has already fulfilled us. The gift of Love always comes back to us regardless of any particular recipient's reaction to it. The more we give, simply because we desire to give ourselves away, then the more we receive of that which we give. *We have all Love if we think to give Love, regardless of what any other person does.* When we have all Love, we are all Love. Then it is that we feel Love most completely, not so much as a customary physical emotion, but as a deep, inner, permanent joy.

*The gift of Love always comes back to us;
the more we give, the more we receive*

But right here, we are wise to check ourselves. If we think we are beyond distrustful, emotional reactions when we are not, we are not giving Love; we are in a repressed or suppressed state of thought. We may be giving love for love and even love for Love. Because we may be avoiding the responsibility of facing our distrustful reactions, we have not attended meetings with the Lovefriend. However, as we become willing to admit the extent of our concern for ordinary justice and as we establish an interest in replacing it with Universal Justice, Love shows Itself to us, and those lesser physical emotions become less necessary to us as our basis for action. Then, Love's meetings interest and attract us.

When we act with less physical emotion, we might think we feel less. Certainly, when we feel less emotional because we suppress ourselves, we do feel less. However, when we grow through our physical emotion by letting Love act as us, we feel vastly more than any other way enables us to feel. The idea that the mastery of emotions means that we have less feeling of ourselves and of our lives is a misunderstanding of our nature. When we have the awareness of Love, we become outgoing and we feel ourselves and our lives as they are. And these feelings provide us with a continuous joy, peace, success and well-being.

When we act with less physical emotion, we might think that we will not feed the hungry of the world, attend the sick and destitute or assist them in their needs. But, the reverse is true! We care greatly for both our friends and enemies as we allow love to be transformed into Love in our lives. Through converting our physical emotional expression into a spiritual emotional expression, love is manifested with us as the Love that It more truly is. It becomes our increased interest to bind the wounds, heal the sick, clothe the poor, feed the hungry and take good care of our planet. Moreover, we become convinced that everything we do is helpful. Therefore, we accompany our charitable physical acts with teaching actions that are thoughtful. At the same time, we do not relate to others in ways that result in dependencies. *PEOPLE WHO TRULY LOVE ARE SEEN AS EXAMPLES AND NOT AS INDISPENSABLE CARETAKERS.*

THE NATURE OF ADEQUACY

We would all give Love without thought of what we would receive, and we would just as naturally and easily attract the givingness from the Love of many others, except for our sense of inadequacy. Until now, most of us have tended to feel inadequate to express Love; because of our inadequacy, we have tended to feel love or we have only hoped to feel love.

Whenever we allow emotional actions to form a bridge from love to Love, we are feeling our inadequacies, and this makes us emotional (in physical ways); nevertheless, this builds the bridge over which we can travel from our small sense of Love (which is love) to a great sense of Love. A key question for us is how can we feel enough adequacy to give of ourselves, rather than to try to receive from others without expressing Self-givingness? Until we can give of Love, we can fall off the bridge and feel hurt. Yet there comes a time for all of us when we will never again fall off the bridge or become hurt. Moreover, before we reach that time in our livingness when adequacy places us in touch with such a great sense of Love that we are extraordinarily safe and strong, we still need not fall or be hurt again.

The feeling of adequacy builds in us as we meet the Love-friend. This lifts us up from mere physical emotion, up from love as it has seemed to be, and out of customary reactions. In the beginning, the meetings are very brief, but they are remembered and prized as is nothing else we have ever experienced. Even as the bridge seems to be lengthened, and the challenges feel as though they are increased, adequacy is building within us while we cross the bridge and until we reach the land of Love. That land is a place where everything is flowing, even the soil in which its Good ideas grow. Anyone can walk there in the flow; it is because Love supports anyone who is greatly aware of It.

The land of Love is not far away. It is right where all of us are. Yet, our awareness of it and our sense of flowing and growing cannot be known by us until we meet the Lovefriend. And we cannot regularly dwell in Love's land until we meet the Lovefriend again and again. We are always welcome! But we remain on the bridge until we fully acknowledge that we are welcome. Our entrance into the land of Love, unless we truly feel our innocence, awaits our willingness to forgive and forget, and our expectation that life is meant to be better for us.

UPLIFTED EMOTION

There is a consciousness of Good action that can become realized through Love's encouragement. Such consciousness is developed within us as we discover Love there. The potential Good action needs no development and is what many people label the Higher Self. When we tire of living only by ordinary just reactions, and we think something better can spring forth from within us, something else does. If we desire to encourage this experience to happen in our lives, we succeed by observing our distrusting reactions and by desiring that we discover better actions. We obtain especially desirable results by taking time nearly everyday to quiet ourselves and to talk with our inner selves as though Love is there, with the idea that Love hears us and that we are in a meeting with It.

We do best not to ***abruptly*** stop any of our reactions based on ordinary justice unless we are being harmful. Our best opportunity to successfully replace them comes by positioning ourselves into a meditative exercise. There, we may do well by meditating in the manner of our individual choice of teachers or books that explain meditation.[2] Then our "just reactions" are favorably transformed by our bringing forth an idea and an action from somewhere within the meditation, something that each one feels is his or her best.

As much as "the quiet" may seem to some people to be an experience of subduing the conscious use of Mind, I do not see it that way. Meditation helps us the most when we are consciously aware of our thoughts. *"The quiet" is simply a state in our thinking in which the struggle that we have believed we must have with life ceases. Rather than slipping out of our conscious state, we do best "in the quiet" to "see through" our continuing false thoughts or ideas about conflict.* We are greatly helped when we remove fear or any major aspect of it, such as anxiety or guilt, from our conscious thoughts, particularly as we remain conscious and in

---

[2] Or see my book on meditation, "Second Reflections" 1991.

touch with our deeper sense of self. Then we clearly hear Love speak with us as a Friend.

The whole idea is to feel assured that Love is with us in all we do and to experience the points of poise. When we get that sense from our inner quiet space, we can act with Love and rise above customary reactions that otherwise are only an "acting back" to what someone or something appears to be doing to us.

When Love's answers come through us, they are never reactions to our reactions. Love's answers are ideas of actions that can instantly place us into a desirable relationship

When we remove any aspect of fear from any conscious thoughts, then we clearly hear Love speak with us as a friend

with our environment; they are the best ideas of how to act that we would have conceived if we had known all the facts involved and were not falsely dissuaded by any of them. After we listen and prepare ourselves to let Love act as us, we do best to bring our meditative time to completion and then to rise and take action.

When we step out of "the quiet," ready to act with Love toward everyone, we have uplifted our sense of emotion and our past negative manner of experiencing emotional effects. At first, "the upliftment" may only last a few seconds or a few minutes at a time. We will succeed in achieving longer periods of these spiritually and emotionally uplifted experiences when we do not object too strongly to the return of the lesser physical emotions that sometimes occur with them. We need to stay aware that there is nothing wrong with feeling emotions. We are wise to accept all the feelings of emotion that we have, knowing that our upliftment into Spirit-filled emotion will mature our experience. An ease will come as we follow this procedure day after day, and as we develop trust. When the Lovefriend is truly known by us, we will be continuously uplifted by the higher emotion of Love. We will then feel especially vitalized. We will be more active than when our lower emotions dominated our sense of life; the new animation will be the activity of the Lovefriend within us, being us. Our actions will all be spontaneous, and they will be the right ones for us. They will be right because they will have been prepared in the "meetings."

Love is the presence of life that has a wonderful Friendship to express through us and as us.

CHAPTER SEVEN

THE GREATEST CARE

Can you give and receive as great care as has ever been experienced by anyone? YES, YOU CAN! YES, YOU CAN! YES, YOU CAN!

There is an evolution of care in our lives. Every form of care that we experience, whether it is a total protection, a healing, the presence of concern, an aggravation, or even an abuse, is altogether our experience of trust or distrust in life. Right now, some of us are being benefited by believing that our universe is Love and that it is giving us Love's perfect care. Others of us appear to be tormented by suffering burdensome experiences that come from our more negative ideas about care.

Fortunately, there is an orderliness in this. That is, when our belief about Love becomes keen enough to let Love have a considerable measure of Its way with us, we have matured enough to not suffer a return to the poorer care we had before. Again, once we know enough of Love, our sense of love will not lead us to feel regretful and to think we deserve neglect, as it sometimes has done to us before. But such heights of Love are not discovered until we feel innocent and cease thinking that our mistakes, or those of other people, need punishment.

Care can be positive or negative. On the positive side, we can rise above anxiety, fear and feeling harmed as a result of believing that we are receiving loving care while we simply are using our common sense to handle crises. On the negative side, we can be distressed, afraid and mistreated because of thinking that we are without friends and in bondage to bad care unless some strong and friendly person rescues us from our disappointments; we can add to our sense of torment by believing that every displeasure is a punishment.

Until we understand that Love never hurts us or lets us down, our sense of It must slowly evolve us. This is because *Love's care helps or love's care hinders us according to the extent that we expect Love to help us. This expectancy directly reflects the degree to which we recognize Love as Love or love. This is a principle of life within Love. That is, Love never hinders us, but Its care becomes for us the experience that we expect from Love or love.*

Love's care becomes for us the experience
that we expect from Love or love

Care is always present; we are being cared for every moment. Care is wonderful if we appreciate it; care is not the way we would like it to be if we believe we are receiving poor care. This is true because there is a tendency for everyone to feel strongly about care, and to give their idea of care considerable attention; and because "the Law reacts according to whatever intent we have" with our thoughts (chapter six, under subtitle "The Law Of

Reaction Or New Action").

That which we place at our attention rapidly becomes the idea of our intention, even if we think it is not. Our intentions tend to take place even if we wish they would not. When life feels threatening, observe what it is to which we have been giving our attention! It is what we have cared about! We have cared when someone has experienced the symptoms of heart trouble. We have cared if someone cheated us. We have cared if our country has become involved in negotiating with other countries that were having civil wars. We have cared about the destruction of our environment. If a woman friend has been raped and has felt much distress, we have cared about her experience. We have cared when we have had things stolen from us. It may have seemed that we should have cared about these circumstances, but such thinking was all negative. When we let Love do our caring, we discover that none of these conditions continue. However, when we conceive of love as our means of care, we give too much attention to negative things, and the Law of reaction makes them *increase* in our experiences!

When life feels threatening, observe what
it is to which we have been giving our attention

Before we are secure enough to trust that Love is providing us with everything we need, we settle in our thoughts some lesser levels of trust that we dare to have. Each bit of our evolvement on earth begins afresh from each new level of trust that we have reached. Our gradually rising level of trust is the mark of our individual personal growth. It remains intertwined with our sense of care. *We can only truly mature in accordance with the ways in which we let Love care for us.* Whether we are being cared for by another person or by ourselves, the success of that care always matches the trust we place in the idea that Love is within us, and the extent to which we are letting Love arrange our entire experience of care.

EARLY CARE

At first, we appeared to have been born into a conditon of helplessness....with an urgent need to receive care. Certainly, we were all provided care, but not with an equal pleasantness. A few of us were treated royally, but a larger number were tended with considerable abuse. Most of us experienced something in between. It would seem that there could have been something better for many of us and that our universe was too often unfair in providing us our particular experiences. But, it could not have been better than it was, though it can become better now. The cause of unhappy events is always in the ways we misunderstand the Love affair that we have with life. We can discover these misunderstandings of Love, and then resolve to let Love be to us the way It truly is. The resolution of disappointing experiences lies in opening ourselves to trust life and to choose to feel its Love of us; Love then acts out, through us, the same experiences in a new and very brilliant, high way of happiness and success.

We may feel that it is hard to establish the resolution to court the presence of Love. Such difficulty stems from our having kept ourselves unconscious of our real experience of Love. Life always knows it is in Love with us, and ever acts accordingly. Many of us have not believed that we could receive much Love from life and so we have tried to find It in other ways. Our earliest felt needs and desires for Love could have experienced Love's assistance had we let this happen. Some of us did. We have all felt Love; only some of us knew of our feeling of It then. Love continues to care for us every moment; there is nothing so close to us as the presence of Love. We are forever feeling Love's presence, but we keep making ourselves unaware of It.

Our original providers tended to ignore their own Love affair with life; they tended to distrust it and to resist it. Most of them thought superstitiously, and believed they personally had the mission of saving us from problems. When we were preborn and then again when we were infants, we were needing and desiring a sense of how to live on earth. There was in us a complete openness to learn and to feel everything of life. Our guardians represented to us what it meant to be alive; we felt dependent on them; as such, it was natural to let them influence us. Because we were exceedingly receptive and impressionable, we absorbed their ideas like sponges. As we grew from infancy into childhood, we reasoned out from a child's viewpoint, what those ideas could mean for us right then. That magnified the errors of such thoughts. Then we put those ideas into larger use. It is no wonder that we have often found ourselves fighting stress.

It is good that it is human nature to be open to the ideas and practices of our earliest protectors, because when the time comes that people are more generally trusting of life, their children will quickly feel the same way. Then little ones, from an early age, will absorb an understanding of how to experience and express lives of great happiness and sufficiency. But for now, even though it may appear that we originally received poor care, we do best to begin again by reconstructing the way it would have been, if we had been more open to the idea that Love was being our protector.

The first helpful reconstruction of our relationship to life is to understand that our guardians were agents for Love, and that Love is our greatest Friend. The care that we were given was possible because Love silently commissioned people to be providers of our care. In this connection, it is essential that we understand something within us knew of this provision, and so we have always felt Love and we always will. But, most of us erroneously thought the human providers were our source of Love, and that they were making themselves love us or that they were not making themselves love us. Actually, they were acting on behalf of Love, and some of them knew this; however, others had only a slight sense of It and most of them hardly knew It at all. If we had not made ourselves unaware of Love, by thinking Its agents were the source of It, we would right now be aware of Love as very helpful, everywhere present and much greater than Its agents, all of which It is.

We are right now feeling much Love. We are receiving Its care every moment. If we think we are not feeling very much Love, we are preventing ourselves from being aware of what we are really feeling. *WE ARE REALLY FEELING LOVE, WHICH MEANS THAT OUR MOST AUTHENTIC AWARENESS OF REALITY IS THAT OF LOVE, AND WE ARE FEELING IT DEEPLY WITHIN OURSELVES*. Buried beneath the lesser ideas about care that we have collected and placed in our subconscious use of mind, is the continuous loving assurance that all of our needs are being generously met.

We are becoming aware of our needs and desires to receive Love. Until we have enough awareness of this, our sense of inadequacy is interfering with our well-being. Where is our inadequacy coming from? *WE HAVE LEARNED TO REACT TO THE LIFE WITHIN US BY FEELING THAT WE LACK SOME-THING OR THAT THERE IS SOMETHING WRONG WITH US.* We have learned that from the people who have cared for us. Though they were agents of Love, most of them did not understand they were in that role or they would have taught us differently. We can change that for the future, and we will!

The evolution of care moves us to feel a need or desire to be freed of the care of our first protectors. When we disinvolve ourselves, we feel we need care from someone else, or many others; but somewhere in all of this, we allow an all consuming desire to be independent to form itself with us.

Independence means we get to take care of ourselves. Sooner or later, we must become desirous of this, for otherwise our self-esteem cannot establish itself.

SELF-ESTEEM

Everything described in this chapter so far takes some time to develop in our lives; it takes a very few years for some of us, a great many years for others. Our self-esteem does not become very well developed until after all of this has happened.

After we have developed enough self-esteem to feel our independence and to enable ourselves to achieve as much as the average of the human race, or more, there comes another new experience of care. *WE COME TO THE REALIZATION THAT WE ARE CARING SO MUCH FOR OURSELVES THAT WE ARE GETTING IN OUR OWN WAY.* When this becomes clear to us,

We realize that we are caring so much for
ourselves that we are getting in our own way

we examine our egotistical attitudes and find that they are disappointing us. We start to look for something in ourselves that we can bring forth which will make us better persons. We gradually find that this requires of us not to care about what others are doing. We judge them less and less, and we judge ourselves less too. We come to see that there are many ways of experiencing care in our lives, and that growth in our relationship with care improves us in expressing life. Many excellent books have been written about self-esteem and how we can care enough about ourselves to experience it -- but its lowest and highest stages have not been given as much explanation. Here we are presenting, though briefly, the entire range of our experiences of self-esteem.

Discovering how to let go of our control of care, after we acquire some self-esteem, is essential if we are to achieve the growth that leads to great self-esteem. Yet, when we release all control of care, an even greater sense of care is soon felt by us. It is THEN, that life becomes for us the magnificent experience it has always been meant to be.

Back and forth, like a pendulum, we swing with our idea of what care means. As we go through this, Self-reliance emerges. The continual succession of anxious feelings, because of the alternating experiences of feeling danger and safety as though they are intended by life as a game of see-saw, are eventually replaced by an EASE. As we let this poised sense of life assist us, we find that it is an early expression of our potential Selfhood; it proves itself to be infinitely resourceful and it is completely secure. More and more we come to know that Love's unlimited givingness is acting as us through our increasing esteem of Its care.

FEELING LOVE

Love knows best how to care, and can be conceived as the teacher of how we can care for ourselves and become independent; nevertheless, Its greater nature is to provide us care by giving Itself through us and as us. ***WHEN WE OPEN OURSELVES ENOUGH TO DEEPLY RECEIVE IT, WE "REALLY FEEL LOVE";***

OUR INTEREST TURNS TO UNIFY WITH IT, FOREVERMORE.
This does not make us Its dependent, at least not in any ordinary
sense; It causes us to be interdependent with everyone and everything.

The Oneness we find with Love, when we have become
matured as just explained, heals our thoughts and feelings; it
follows that everything in our lives is made whole and complete.
This is because the human race has generally been thinking that
the outward and inward sense of our lives are separated from
each other. We have misunderstood this aspect of our growth.
This is why God has been assumed as being a reality that is away
from the place of the rest of our reality. Again, Love has not
been consciously felt except in a vague way, and generally not as
something that we feel is plentiful enough for everyone to have
a full sense of It. It is of great benefit to us to correct our
misunderstanding about this, because until we do, we cannot
interpret the place, value and meaning of Love. Of even more
significance, this misunderstanding keeps us from "really feeling
Love" as It is. Unless we feel the true nature of Love our
existence must contain disappointment, because knowing the truth
about Love alone is what enables us to experience and express
life in its greater possibilities.

Let us not misunderstand the phrase, "Really Feeling Love."
It refers to an especially strong awareness that Love is present in
our lives. Actually, all people feel much Love every minute
because It maintains our very existence, but we are most generally
insensitive to It and thus unaware of our deeper feelings of It.

LOVE'S ACTION

Whenever any growth is felt that particularly involves caring
in any of its stages, then there is an awareness of feeling Love,
but It is usually felt as care. When care is felt, it is the discovery
of the action of whatever degree of Love we have accepted.

Love Itself is best understood here as always being a noun and
always as the actor. Though we should be able to feel the
presence of the actor directly, we ordinarily have not -- unless we

have truly made ourselves into believers that Love is the actor. In this writing, we are conceptualizing Love as the actor within us -- which we are also calling "the Lovefriend." The phrase "Really Feeling Love" means the sense of Love that we get when the actor is deeply felt and greatly appreciated. When this happens, the power of life is productive of wonderful benefits for us and those especially close to us.

Love does not result from something we think, feel or say. Rather, It is the all-healing Creative Presence of the universe that acts in the ways It knows are best for us through our thoughts, feelings and deeds, to the extent that we receive It as It is. Love is not becoming something; It is, has always been and always will be, a Self-givingness. Love and Its Intelligence is another name for Universal Spirit. Care is best defined as the behavior of Love. Whatever recognition we have of Love's giving Itself through and as us, we feel as care.

Love is the actor within us—which we are also calling "the Lovefriend"

DEFINING LOVE AND CARE

Love can never be defined as easily as care can be; *Love is the nature of the greatest truth there is; care is Its expression;* we can only abstractly explain the essence of the greatest truth; we can concretely explain the way It acts -- by telling what It does. Of course, there is Love's great activity of care and there is also a lesser care, a pseudo care; that is, there are people who feel Love almost entirely in a negative way. They recognize that it would be better for them to care; but, they do not know how to cooperate with Love to give and receive that care. Love, to people who think negatively is always love; it is something they think they must make happen. Care is somewhat easily confused too. Love cannot be changed! Love is never qualified; It is never restricted; but our *experience* of care is modified, reduced and distorted when Love's agents misinterpret Love. Although Love and Its care cannot be misused, there is a substitution of care that occurs when we feel that there is an effort in caring; of itself it is an action of questioning the reality of Love. And Love is misplaced when we go searching for that Good which we forget that we already have.

Love is the nature of the greatest truth there is;
care is Its expression

Love comes into our lives from deep within ourselves and we can feel It. When we observe that we feel Its care, we have already moved our awareness of It to the way It is being effective. When we do not feel Its care very much, It is only being effective in our lives to that extent. Of course, Love cannot act ineffectually, but if we have only a small sense of Love, we are only aware of that much effectiveness of It. We too easily think that any kind of care is the best provision that Love can give us. We easily confuse the pretense of caring activities that are not of Love's care with Love Itself.

Think of Love's care this way. An old friend comes to your city and visits for a day or so, but you happen to be away. Someone in your family entertains the friend. Soon after, you return home. You feel that your friend has been there. You discover a gift was left for you. You notice how the pillows on your divan are propped up the way your friend always used to arrange them. You feel that you have a sense of your friend's visit, but not the direct feeling you sometimes had before. Love is the friend you did not see; the evidence of care in the visit supports that Love indeed visited you.

On the other hand, a visitor who pretends to care could come to your home and convince your family that you need to have a new divan, or roof, or something else that you do not need or want. An agreement could be signed, and false care could be arranged. This would not be a visit of Love; such a visit could only happen if Love is not yet a certainty with you.

But, let us understand that Love never ceases caring for us. If we mistake a visitor or a false form of care for Love, we are not receiving the high care Love can give; nevertheless, we are still being cared for by Love. Always, we are receiving Love's care; however, some of the time we are receiving a pseudo care; often love is that way. We can learn to distinguish the difference, and it is desirable that we do. Then we can invite Love to continuously express through us Its own bighearted idea of care.

Care is remarkable; in all of its activity, it always leaves an effect. The kind of care that is given is the evidence that Love is effectively channeled or displaced by love. Feeling care is helpful; it can give an assurance that Love is near, that Love is directly expressing Itself, or that love is all of the Love that we are accepting. If Love is misinterpreted or not really felt, false ideas of care will appear to represent It. A false idea of care is the experience of apprehension that is acted out as though there is something to be feared. Even when people assume that they must take full responsibility for us, if it is because they disbelieve or forget that Love is within us in an innate way, Love's care is being displaced by love. Whenever we believe these false ideas of care deserve that we embrace them, we cannot experience Love in Its richness. But, when we believe enough in Love, we feel an awareness of Its high care. We then feel relaxed because we are convinced there is nothing to fear, and there never is. Still Love is something more than care; care simply *comes from* Love.

There is no evolution of Love because It is absolute, unconditional and always in full flower. There is an evolution in our experiences of care; those incidents are our most frequent experience of Love's action: care, but not Love, is different at different times to us, depending on the extent of our own spiritual evolvement. That is, when we are fully open to it, Love's care is expressed with amazing kindness, such as Love always gives. When we are anxious about what Love can be to us, we become aware of love's lesser care. Care, at first, represents something that Love or love does to us through someone else; as we build the idea of Love, we greatly appreciate care and we rapidly give ourselves greater care. To the extent that we build the idea of love, care often feels negative, we think about it with some or much suspicion. Then care is variously a hindrance or of some help, but not as great as it could be. When care feels negative, it is because we appear to abuse ourselves with the idea that life must contain abuse. Someone or several persons carry out the actions. The apparent abusers may have been those very people from whom we received the idea that life has to contain abuse. We could help ourselves and deny them such actions with us, but we must first believe no one and nothing can hurt us. Unfortunately, until we discover the Lovefriend, we tend to believe only what we are told. We can change this for ourselves, our children, and all people in the future, as we all become aware of Love and the Lovefriend. We can make that choice; gradually we will! Love does not provide us this false kind of care; but love sometimes does.

AN EVOLUTION IN THE WAY WE CARE

The first step in the evolution of greater care is to move experiences into Love's care from love's lesser care. Some of us evolve without the negative experience of love's care being abusive; others of us feel much abuse. *As we grow,* the better feeling of care comes to us from our *consciously* experiencing the Love of ourselves. Taking care of ourselves, or of someone or something else, is different for each of us, depending on the circumstances involved. But Love's nature is always the same; if Love has seemed different from one time to another, we have not been truly aware of our deeper feeling of It, although we have recognized some form of Its care. This does not mean that we cannot frequently feel Love, for we do so all the time, and can always feel Its magnificence fully and directly. However, we have tended to be more aware of care; we have seldom been as aware of Love. We are ordinarily quite insensitive to Love. We can change that! We can really (consciously) feel Love, if we so desire. That awareness becomes the great acceptance in our lives. It takes an evolution in the way we care--for that to happen!

Subconsciously (at a very deep level of our subconscious thought), we feel Love all the time, but we are ordinarily not consciously in tune with It. Whatever conscious sense we have of Love, from time to time, is frequently interrupted by our lack of receptivity to It. Why? It is because we have chosen to live in a relative understanding of reality; we have thought we must be conditioned and controlled, which means that we are not yet "flowered out." Therefore, we act one way, and then the other, sometimes allowing Love to have Its way with us; then in an unconscious opposition, we turn to the doubts of others and give them so much attention that they displace our ability to sense Love's presence. But this is not bad; our actions resemble the ebb and flow of ocean waves, the breaths we give and take, and the zigzag activity of changing weather. Our greater wisdom is to discover that we act with this behavior because we are choosing to feel Love alternately one way, and then the other. This is the early sense of the "natural method" through which we reveal Love to ourselves -- *until* we come to know how to spontaneously express nature even more.

SUPER CARE

The natural method is the only way we have discovered to this point that we can truly experience Love, because our natures have so far proven to be the basis for how we experience everything. Our natures at first feel a need to search, but eventually find in themselves all that we seek. When the search is over a sense of calm reigns with us. Therefore we do best to simply let this means of discovery be what it is. As we allow ourselves to experience this method, our anxiety diminishes over the way that Love seems to sometimes be absent.

After pursuing the natural method for awhile, we find that we need not experience any strain or stress in our living. We simply need to let Love express us. We come to trust that Love is taking care of all our situations. This gradually forms in us the feeling that we do not need to care for anything in our lives or in the lives of others. And we need not care about anything negative that occurs. The less we care, the more we feel relaxed, protected and enabled. It might seem that our disinterest in taking care could be unloving, and as it develops with us, at times we wonder if it is so. However, it turns us into persons who at last greatly care, for the very reason that we abandon the act of caring for ourselves and we "take care from deep within ourselves." Too much anxiety kept us from this before. Taking care from deep within ourselves means that our outward sense, at last, is feeling at One with Love. This does not happen.... until we cease reacting negatively to other persons and other experiences of reality. The cessation comes as we give to them that which we would most deeply desire if we were they, and as we act in manners commensurate with the needs of all our situations.

The achievement of being at One with Love is healing to everything in our lives. It occurs as we trust that Love enables everything, and as we become receptive to Its Self-givingness. Then the ebb and flow are no longer separate actions; they are

One. It is as if there is only air to breathe, and we are that air, and we need not search out how to breathe in and out, because we are the whole of breath. As we let ourselves be at One with Love, care becomes evolved in us on a large scale. Care is then given us in greater measure than we can use. We discover that we then distribute care everywhere we go, not only through our giving to charities, although they are some part of it, but more largely in our entering into the feeling and activity of assisting everyone and everything in their discovering how they can express their potentialities with unlimited joy and completeness.

It has been proven that Love heals! But, often we have thought that we had applied Love, and nothing was healed by our effort. Now we know that we have feared to let Love act without our providing care for It. It is as we let Love provide all our care that we let Love be, and in this way, Love rises up and uses us to triumphantly care for us and all that we touch.

THE AGENTS OF LOVE

We cannot understand Love until we notice that It is the primary actor of the universe, and that care is the active expression of It. Its care is acted out through many agents. When we feel Its activity without an agent involved, we are feeling Love directly. For us individually, this is always happening within our own selves. However, though we can feel It there, we are almost always indifferent to It. Many people on earth have never been aware of feeling Love. Still, this is changing -- we will all become aware of the feeling of Love. It is worth our cultivation; *our feeling of Love is the greatest experience of our lives.*

The agents of Love are all the people that It uses to provide us care. Some of the agents accept that they are channels for Love to use, to do Its caring, and so their care is more in alignment with the truth of Love. But, even when this is not understood, Love still trusts them to provide care.

Sometimes the care others give us, or even the care we give ourselves, is abusive or otherwise harmful. The evidence of that poor care is often obvious. Admittedly, it is a pseudo care, and not what Love knows we should have. However, when this happens Love still provides an inner care, so that if we trust that our development has not been hindered because of poor care, and we turn to Love by declaring our confidence in It, an inner resourcefulness marvelously reestablishes our outer conditions.

Always Love is caring for us and there is never a moment that we do not inwardly know that. Outwardly, we often question it, and this keeps us from being aware of how wonderful Love is with us. But, if Love were to prevent people from caring for us outwardly, because of their irresponsibility, we would cease to live on earth; we cannot live here without receiving some attention from others for our physical needs. When we believe that we can have better treatment and attract better agents, and as we desire to better express our roles in providing care to others, we gain better care outwardly. When we come to the understanding of how the implementation of better beliefs and greater desires enable us to have reasonable care, we do not feel disappointed about the manner in which Love uses people as Its agents. It means some people are provided better care than others, but we can upgrade the lesser care simply by observing how and why it happens and through generally educating people until there is a common awareness of how to give good care: and we can develop our own interest in taking good care of ourselves and others. We can also appreciate Love and care by recognizing that if the universe functioned in any other way, it would tend to be either anarchic or deterministic.

If the universe were anarchic, carelessness would be its only rule. If it were deterministic, it would mean that we could do nothing to improve our experience of care or well-being. As it is, Love is taking care of us so completely, that inwardly we can feel It and thereby be healed of anything outwardly. Also, we can be so aware of Love that *It will show us* how to greatly increase the good care we take of ourselves and of other people. To the degree that our intent is genuine, we are expertly *guided in this* at any time that this is our desire. Even better, we can discover *how to let Love act out* Its care superbly *as* us.

We are wise to keep reminding ourselves that Love is the actor and knows best how to give care. Our *attempts* to care for others or to *make* Love be what we think is best are mistakes, unless we use those ways as a practice to feel that we are needed as caring agents of Love. As we use them to discover that we can improve our care, the attempts are then replaced by higher care. The mistakes are all right for us, when necessary, for they are something we tend to do preceding our awareness that Love can and will better direct us in the care that we provide. *However, when we are unified enough with Love's presence, so that we do not conceive of ourselves as anything but Love, all our care is Love's care. Then we no longer try to care for others, nor do we try to make Love. We know then that we are Love, and we let Love express us in Its unconditional manner.*

ATTEMPTS TO MAKE LOVE BE

There were earlier times in our lives when it was natural for us to try to care for ourselves. Self-esteem came to us as we cared. Becoming independent also required us to try to take care. This was essential for awhile, but eventually, as we have come to understand that we are persons of worth, we have had to let go of further attempts to care for ourselves, so that Love can evolve us more. Now, we are being prepared for something of especial splendor. Love can lift us into a reality where effort is unknown. It is now time to cease trying and to let Love have its total way with us.

The greatest benefits we can know of Love are achieved as we enthusiastically express It; this is the only way we can know Love in depth. Our greater interest in Love will therefore mean for us that we will do all we can to lavishly expend It. But to do this, we must become authorities on Love, and know when we are giving It and when we are only expressing love. *As we will discover, we express Love best as we let Love give us away, and as we give Love away. But Love is not well expressed by our giving away our sense of It.*

We give Love away and Love gives us away as we become especially kind. Certainly, all kind actions give evidence that the reality of Love exists, except when they become manipulative. It is when our actions are motivated by high self-regard that they naturally become kind. We shall discover here that Love prompts us to esteem ourselves and then to act as kindly to others as we do to ourselves. When we take an interest to feel Love and feel loving, there is a healing result that shows us that we are functioning out of a benign nature that provides for us an attractive behavior: when this happens, we become amazingly kind. Always, an empowerment --" to move mountains" is provided in It.

When we take an interest to feel Love and feel loving, we become amazingly kind

Love does not provide us with Its best expression while we

imitate other people, even if those people are remarkably kind. In so doing we restrict Love by trying to make It look like something It cannot and need not be, in us. The test of our ability to express Love as It would show Itself in our lives, is to receive It into our imaginations with trust and confidence. Love best moves through our thoughts from an origination that It has provided us from deep within our thoughts. Love, for us, always comes from there.

Beyond this explanation, that Love comes into our outer expressiveness "from deep within our thoughts," we can say no more, except to speak of deity. "Man is a stream whose source is hidden. Always our being is descending into us from we know not whence."[1] Emerson wrote on, explaining It as the "Over-soul....that common heart of which all sincere conversation is the worship....when It flows through his affection, It is Love."[2]

Love is never truly found by our trying to be understanding, cooperative or appreciative of others. We emphasize that any time the action of *trying* captures our imagination, it is not Love; it is exertion or the attempt to be loving and results from the feeling that we are not loving.

Emerson bade us, "Trust your emotion."[3] This means, trust Love, the king or queen of emotions. By trusting Love, I do not merely mean that Love is safe to express and that love is not as sure. More than that, when we trust Love as It comes from deep within us, we discover an unlimited helpfulness that can be instantly and forever used exactly as It is. And better yet, we can always trust any use It makes of us. It need never first be tried.

WHEN NATURE AND LOVE ARE TRUSTED

We have all tried to be loving, but then admired more the easy way that Love flows through certain other people, those who are

---

[1] The Over-Soul. Ralph Waldo Emerson.

[2] Ibid.

[3] Self-Reliance. Ralph Waldo Emerson.

truly open to Its presence. Here, we are establishing that kind of receptivity with the flow of Love. We are thinking of Love as the presence of the Supreme Intelligence of life. When Love seems elusive, it is not because It is not everywhere present. It is always right where we are. Our capacity to know this requires us to trust that life's nature is able to be expressed limitlessly through us and around us because it is both loving and intelligent.

Love is behind, within and around all thoughts and all experiences. We find Love in our thoughts to the degree that we trust life. Life could not have otherwise evolved, and no greater experience of happiness can now emerge among us, except as we trust that life has more of Love's givingness within it.

If we try to trust only what we think we want of life, and let Love be in our experiences only to the extent of those choices, we can never discover Love's depths of expression. This is because our ability to accept further values of life is then hampered by too little sense of Love, too little awareness of Its being unlimited in Its givingness. Some people may have a considerable trust of some aspects of life, and their experience may be that they are provided with all the wealth that they think they want or need, but at the same time, they may be assuming that life must contain experiences for them of diseases or problems in their relationships. All people tend to find such voids in their experiences of life until they trust all of life and its natural manner, and until they Love enough. Life proffers the opportunity to feel successful, healthy, wealthy, resourceful and to be happy in relationships, all at once, and on a continuous basis. No break should ever occur in any of these privileges. Love knows how this can be; Love does not even know that any deviation from such Good could ever be, because it is life's nature to intelligently and boundlessly express Love. It is our interest here to fully open ourselves to Love, to know that we are very intelligent, to let It give us away and to let life reflect that Love back to us.

We will discover that Love and nature are in union. We cannot really trust and feel Love in any deep and lasting way without trusting and feeling nature's way too. *Our greater trust of life emerges as we trust its nature and Love. So, although we are opening ourselves to especially feel Love, we are wise to include a deepening of our appreciation for nature, and for the nature of ourselves.*

LETTING LOVE CARE FOR US

If care could not be abusive, we would not be at liberty to choose the ways we act. We are wise to be grateful for this obvious freedom, but then deepen our sense of life's enrichment by discovering the Lovefriend and upgrading our experiences of care. Nature is on our side and we find that its support is always healing everything as rapidly as we find the way to cooperate with it. Nature does everything for us that we ever need and desire as we align ourselves with it. Most of us understand this to a fair degree, but we can increase this understanding and greatly enlarge our reception of nature's care. However, the presence of Love in nature is not as generally known. And Love is our greatest resource. We do best to simply let Love care for us.

*Love is our greatest resource. We do
best to simply let Love care for us*

How can we believe more in Love? We must first forgive and

forget as much as possible, or discover innocency; secondly, we must feel our adequacy as much as we can. Then, we do well to let people and circumstances be however they appear to us, letting nonresistance dissipate any further negative reactions we otherwise could yet form toward them. Everyone and everything will then manifest its eesence; at center, all will be disclosed as fine expressions of Love. For Love will greatly exhibit Itself as us and everything when we feel no need to react negatively to anyone, and as we choose to still be actively involved with others. *Love is our adequacy and the greatest of care when we let go and let Love express us. For then we are One with Love.*

*As we trust Love enough, Love's great care
becomes all our care.*

CHAPTER EIGHT

DISCOVERING LOVE

*Can you believe that you deserve to feel Love? YES, YOU CAN!
YES, YOU CAN! YES, YOU CAN!*

We were often told by our parents or original guardians that we must do something to earn their love. Some of us actually heard a mother or father tell us that she or he would not love us unless we would be more pleasing. And when we did not hear that idea expressed in those actual words, it was still subtly conveyed to most of us. For instance, it was taught through rewards and punishments that were used to show us when we were considered good or bad. It would not seem that the placement of those incentives upon us could have affected us so severely, because on some level deep within us we knew that Love could not be held back from us. However, all infants are exceedingly sensitive to the thoughts, feelings and voices of people around them. Therefore, we all tended to believe it was necessary to listen to everything we were told, and to act in accord with it or be hurt. The innocence of infancy generally made it possible for guardians to influence the outer sense of ourselves in any way that they chose to do. Their success paved the way for us to later ignore the naturalness, goodness and rightness of innocence.

We were not the only ones who were influenced by erroneous thoughts. Our guardians were similarly entrapped when they were young. We could have been fulfilled through Self-reliance, but most of us do not find this out until after we have taught the lie to our own children, and many of us do not discover it in this lifetime.

Some people will not punish a child in a manner which is

considered to be abusive. But they often fail to notice that when they give benefits to children or deprive them (when they use rewards or punishments), they are teaching the idea that love (or Love) is not to be found within the child, and this is the greatest abuse that can be felt! It is the inevitable result of thinking that children have to be taught by guardians as to how they can be good. Furthermore, in some form or another, most people have believed this to be the only possible way to take good care of children.

AN APPROPRIATE BEHAVIOR FOR EVERY SITUATION CAN BE UNFOLDED AND ENACTED FROM WITHIN CHILDREN, PROVIDED THAT WE BELIEVE ENOUGH IN THEM. BUT, UNTIL PEOPLE QUITE GENERALLY EMBODY THE CONCEPTION THAT LOVE IS TO BE FOUND WITHIN THEIR OWN INDIVIDUAL SELVES, THE FALSE IDEA THAT LOVE IS TO BE FOUND IN ANOTHER IS LEARNED, AND THAT MISLEADS CHILDREN SO THAT THEY ASSUME THEY MUST SEARCH FOR LOVE'S PLACE OUTSIDE THEMSELVES. ALL PEOPLE HAVE HOPED THAT THEY WOULD FIND LOVE IN A PARENTAL FIGURE. AT FIRST THE MOTHER WAS BELIEVED TO BE THE SOURCE; ALWAYS, DISAPPOINTMENTS FOLLOWED OR NEARLY UNALTERABLE DEPENDENCIES WERE FORMED. SOME CHILDREN TRIED TO FIND HAPPINESS BY REDEFINING LOVE AS love, BUT love EVEN IN ITS SMALLEST CONCEIVABLE FORM STILL SEEMED TO BE MISSING FOR THEM.

The most essential aspect of experiencing life has seemed to be our search for Love. Many people have felt frustrated in this search for a long time, and a great number for a lifetime. Many others have given up the search. They have concluded that it is unrealistic to expect that Love, or even love, can ever be found. However, Love is the most basic reality there is, and is Itself undisturbed by the wanderings of our belief.

WHEN THE EXPERIENCE OF FINDING LOVE IS REALIZED, OUR LIVES ARE FILLED WITH ONLY ONE DESIRE, TO GIVE OURSELVES AWAY. WHEN THIS OCCURS, OUR DESIRE TO GIVE BECOMES A PASSION FOR EXPRESSING SIMPLE LOVING ACTIONS WHICH REGULATE OUR LIVES.

*When we find Love, our desire to give is
simply a choice that quietly regulates our lives*

BEFORE OUR CONSCIOUS DISCOVERY OF LOVE

It can accurately be said that infants and little children are more aware of Love than the rest of us. However, they do not exercise that awareness in the manner of helping themselves as they could, because at first they express Love by cooperating with their parents or the people of their environment. This leads them away from sensing Love as much as they naturally could; they rapidly learn how to displace It with love and its attendant anxieties and insecurities. All this happens before birth or very soon after. However, infants and children are always able to return to Love. The return must be, for them and us, a more conscious discovery of ourselves than we at first seemed able to achieve. Since we have largely evolved ourselves in this way, we all carry individual memories, some less conscious than others, of a search for Love or love, which cannot be satisfied until the conscious awareness of truth becomes developed. The awareness that Love's presence lies immediately beneath the seeming evidence of Its absence is available to everyone.

LOWLANDS OF LOVE

After we begin our search, and before we discover much Love within ourselves, we hope that love is at work in the world around us. We do not greatly feel love from others in this very early stage of our growth, but we tend to feel that love exists with some of them or that Love may be the essence of reality and that we can in time experience It.

Before discovering how wonderful we are and how splendid are the other people we meet, and even before we notice love at work around us or believe that we will eventually find Love, some time is spent in our being ignorant of Love and these personal values. At first we judge everyone, and this includes ourselves. Even though our most severe judgments moderate in time, generally the critical comparisons remain and disturb us until our sense of self-esteem is established. Additionally, there seem to be too many ways for us to feel hurt for us to believe that Love and personal endowment could in some way provide a resolution of the difficulties experienced by ourselves and others.

When we live in judgments and feelings of having been hurt, our ideas of love lead us to seek out people who feel comfortable to us, and to criticize and avoid being involved with people whose actions are not as comfortable to us. If we do something which is socially unacceptable, and we react to being severely criticized, love then seems to us to be only an action of sympathy.

Perhaps love at its best is largely sympathy, but Love cannot be explained only as sympathy because It does not know how to merely help us, only to fully heal us. (Even then, Love does not think as we do that It is healing us, because Love never conceives of us as diseased. Love simply expresses Its givingness continuously, which heals.) Of course, we ordinarily think that Love, or even love, often helps us; from this perspective, we often feel helped by Love. My references to Love's helping us are many, and until we feel completely One with Love, Love will continue to appear helpful. Yet this difference between pure Love and pure sympathy will always exist. We often hope that sympathy will feel helpful although most sympathy until now has cried over our disappointment; love acts similarly, but when Love is most truly engaged, It does not merely help us, but entirely resolves any hurt.

We have often thought that our typical sympathetic care of others is our best expression of love. But people need better care than our usual sympathies can provide. When we recognize this, we discover that our sympathy can be successfully joined with the other aspects of Love's nature.

We have sometimes believed that sacrifice and martyrdom are Love, but they are not, except in a small way. Turning away from our own interests, so that we can make others more comfortable, restricts their awakening to the Love that is immediately within them. When we try to be loving, something forceful within us takes the place of Love, and we drive away the sense of It that would otherwise be felt.

An early sense of really feeling Love comes as we think that all people have been created with great capacities. Love is especially felt as we also think that these capacities can be used to benefit ourselves and other people, and even our planet. This results in Love's springing forth from within us; we become examples of the kind of life both others and ourselves most truly desire to experience. Then again, the activity of Love comes our way from others. We acknowledge their giving by receiving their gifts with joy, rather than by ignoring them or merely storing them away.

These early senses of feeling Love do not come to us as automatically as does the growth of our bodies. They occur as we think that our sympathies need refurbishing, because our past sympathies have been built upon sacrifice, suffering and struggle, and have kept us from lifting our sense of love to Love. These early awarenesses of what Love really is happen with us as we build an authentic self-esteem, especially that Self-reliance which brings into expression our inward reserves.

MIDLANDS OF LOVE

We show Love to other people after we have discovered It within ourselves. We cannot Love others until we know that we ourselves are noble. As we gain this sense of personal magnificence, an elevated endowment is then evident to us in nearly everyone we meet. We finally notice that no person lacks admirable qualities. Our world is enriched because Love then uses us to help draw out of others their unique identities. When these awarenesses have come to us, we have risen from the lowlands of Love. It is not that Love is ever low or lifted, but it is that we have let Love lift us to a greater sense of It.

Love enriches our world because Love helps us to draw out of others their unique identities

Love is not something we can directly give to the people of our affection. On our part, our Love for them is best expressed as we show the willingness and interest to believe that the way they are unfolding themselves is already through Love, and is not dependent upon our friendship. This requires of us that we require nothing of them. We serve them best by letting them be where they are in their need, and by respecting their methods of personal growth, which brings magnificence out of them according to their belief.

When our friends and family believe that we no longer judge their behavior, they are released from thinking they have to do what we desire. Until then, all our friends who have low self-esteem are burdened by our thoughts about them. Their ideas about love revolve around our helping them or their having to please us. Afterwards, however, they are able to conceive that there is value in what they choose to express; love begins to be recognized as Love in this manner. Love reveals Itself through them as they simply feel free to face whatever they presume they must.

Those close to us may express Love greatly through finding ways to lessen our importance to them, or by seeing themselves as persons of value. They may wish to believe they have many needs which interfere with their being able to express life better. However, when they feel they own their needs, and that we are not needing to control them, they act with responsibility. When they are convinced that we have no right to control them and that we have given up advising or judging them, a desire to do better for themselves brings Love forth from within them to help (or heal) them. To some extent, they may continue to believe that we are not receptive to their decisions, or sensitive to their feelings, or aware of their needs. We Love them as we let that be. Their freedom to think of us as they please is more important to that phase of their growth than our trying to show them that we care. As we become aware of their growing ability to maintain a sense of purposeful direction, we gradually appreciate that they are meeting challenges, and that Love is evolving them.

This awareness, of how to Love people by letting them be, comes to us as we desire to understand and as we become sensitive to their experiential needs. As we relate to people in this way, an openness to the sense that Love is an inner, wise Friend is felt by us, and we are uplifted in constructiveness and creativity. When we think this way enough, the goodness of Love provides experiences that are incredibly beneficial. It is an unseen form of care; it is as though we think we are there for others, but that Love has made us appear invisible.

We dare not feel Love too much unless we are willing to be used by It, for even when we do not seem to understand how to be Love's agent, It teaches us. That is, we cannot truly Love another without thinking, feeling and acting in ways that lead to

changes in ourselves.   Love takes the coldness out of our
dispositions.   As we feel It, we are like icebergs relocated in the
waters of a tropic sea, for our inflexibilities and judgmental
attitudes are quickly thawed.

Then, we no longer give people what we think they want. We
let them discover what Love can do for them and will do through
them. No other person should be substituted for an awareness
of the Self-resourcefulness that Love has already given them. This
results in our giving them what we would want if we were to
become the persons that they becoming. However, we err if we
give what other people do not want or what they are not ready
to receive, especially if we sacrifice ourselves for them.

HIGHLANDS OF LOVE

We have reached the beautiful highlands of Love as we let
Love pour Itself through us according to the highest idea of It
that we can think for ourselves; in this we let Love make of us
an avenue of expression that radiates joy. Once this has happened
in our consciousness, something remarkable occurs. We become
persons who are able to express Love in a sublime way. We
transcend dependency, martyrdom or mere indulgences. There
is no possibility of doing this unless we first give away what we
most desire to receive. Then it happens: as we give what we most
want to gain, we realize that it is the same as what some other
people in our lives most desire to receive. It means that we find
out for ourselves that no sacrifice exists; not really! We discover
that we are the givers of something of which there is no end of
abundance in ourselves.

When Love moves through our lives unhampered and acts in
unlimited generosity, the forcefulness of desires leaves us.
Although we try to make our desires and needs a significant part
of our behavior for a long time, the urgency disappears altogether
when we become open enough to Love's presence.

But, unless we first Love ourselves deeply, we will feel we have
simply sacrificed ourselves, and Love will be less believed by us
than before! Our basis for Self-givingness must be that we are

letting Love act as us, never that we are trying to prove the reality of Love by acting.   Of course, we are wise to act out our convictions so as to experience them; but we are foolish to act out something which seems to make us suffer, especially if we do not really believe that it can be.   When to act and when not to act; that is the great question.   The answer is within us.   Are we convinced that Love is in our acts or not?

Love in the highlands is also our *right* attraction.   Our right attraction is an experience of being pulled into deeply loving relationships; this happens when there is a maturation of Love in our personalities.   Love matches us with others who are like us even in our most inspired growth.

If all that could be said of us were at any time gathered and explained, what we did with Love would be of the most interest. By the time we reached Love's heights within us, the scenario might go something like this: We began by seeking Love....Love that would be beautiful and stabilizing.   The search was long. When Love seemed so elusive that we felt too tired and frustrated to continue, we let go of any idea that we could possess It. It was then that we were drawn to Love. We gave of ourselves. We were made beautiful by It. We found ourselves matured and secured. The deepest desires of ourselves and the other people in our lives were found to be the same. And we became so open to Love's expression that the forcefulness of our desires vanished entirely, and Love flowed through us as a river that knew no restriction and needed no help.

It is natural and normal to feel Love.

CHAPTER NINE

OUR DESIROUS NATURE

Can you express Love well and, at the same time, have what you most desire? YES, YOU CAN! YES, YOU CAN! YES, YOU CAN!
We are living in a friendly universe. If some or many of us are not certain about this, let us consider what is least friendly to us. It is not the nature of our environment nor our particular physical heredity; it is the nature of our most frequently thought ideas. It has "seemed comfortable" to us to make a personal collection of the thoughts of various other people. We have thought that if we could but imitate their ideas they would become good friends. But, as we have made their ideas our own, we have not felt their presence, our environment or our heredity to be anywhere nearly so friendly to us as we have desired. This is because our philosophies of life, constructed from their ideas, contain a doubt that any "great Friendship" could be present anywhere in life; with most of us that doubt has been a trying question. Can any genuine Friendship really exist for us?

We can change our ideas about the absence of Friendship. As we assure ourselves that a marvelous Friend is present, we are assisted from inside ourselves to discover the resourcefulness of the Friend who has always been with us and who will never leave us. Moreover, we will gradually experience meetings with this Friend: we will walk with It, talk with It, think, feel, speak and do everything in our lives with a sense of It; and some of us are already doing this!

We have never been without this Friend; and right now, we can expect to never feel friendless again. *We will become certain of this when we come to know that we are accompanied everywhere*

198

we go by the person we are becoming.

We have lived long enough not knowing who we are. It is time to cease thinking that our physical heredity, environment, and the people in our lives have produced us. They have been and remain the stimuli which we use to motivate our self-expression. But, they have only caused our experiences to be as they are in a secondary way. They have caused us to *temporarily* have our past and present experiences, because *we have given them this empowerment.*

We are accompanied everywhere we go
by the person we are becoming

But, it is the combination of thinking that Love is love, and the steadfast willingness of Love Itself to let us discover It at our own chosen pace, that has given our physical environment, heredity and so-called friends the formative influence to make us appear as we do. However, our deepening sense of the Love that is within us, and our letting It more fully express us, will yet lift us into vastly better experiences of life.

Let us now expect to experience a sense of unity between who we appear to be and who we can know we are. Such a growing experience of unity is the greatest Friendship we will ever have. For instance, the Lovefriend is not ever interested in our being less than who we are; It is desirous of our being more than who we have appeared to be.

THE CAUSE OF OUR EXPERIENCES

The human race, as a whole, is evolving toward the understanding that all of our experiences are caused by the thinking we do. This is an essential and inevitable realization that is gradually enabling us to live more effectively than before. Yet, there is an even greater cause that has its way with us! It is Love!

The tried and untrue belief is that everything is caused by our physical environment and heredity. That concept fails to recognize that thought controls us. Our physical environment and heredity affect us only to the extent that we think they do. In a similar way, our thought is interfering with our capacity to realize that Love is our Supreme Cause.

Sorting out the empowerments of Love, thought, heredity and environment, we discover a hierarchy of influences. Love is the underlying cause of everything that happens; Love causes perfect actions and love causes actions which appear imperfect, but fortunately these latter manifestations exist only temporarily. As Plato indicated, there is that which is perfect: it lies behind or within the imperfect actions and things, and they are made from it. His mentor Socrates, had taught that an intelligible order is the essence of everything; Plato named that orderliness "the forms," which meant universal ideas. Here we are identifying the "order," "forms" or "ideas" as the Lovefriend. In accord with platonic explanations, this teaching is that reality is infinitely intelligent and thinks ideas which are copied in the experiences and things which we see. I am adding that Love is this Intelligence and Its ideas, and that Love is not in any way separate from us, but rather is also us or that we are One with It; however, our awareness of this is dim. The copies of the ideas appear imperfect to us and will continue to, until we deeply recognize that we are Love. As we do, the imperfect will be adjusted so that its imperfections are less; as the recognitions become more frequent and truer, the perfection of the Lovefriend will reveal itself incrementally.[1] In the meanwhile, Love is continuously with

---

[1] For students of philosophy, the only real argument that Aristotle had with Plato is resolved with this explanation: Love is "behind or within" the apparent imperfections of life; however, there is no separation.

us in all that we do.

Love provides thought with high motivation and love temporarily gives it low motivation. High motivation is unconditional and low motivation is conditional. Thought directs all actions whether unconditional or conditional in nature. While at first, our heredities and environments appear to cause all experiences to be what they are, gradually we discover that love and low motivation have subjected us to the belief that our lives are being controlled by people, places, things and our genes. We tend to think we are victims, but we are not; we actually regulate our experiences by the extent of Love that we sense. As we let Love express us more (and love express us less), Love's high motivation establishes within us the awareness that we can function as we really desire. Then, unconditional thought allows Love the liberty to perfectly shape our circumstances according to that which is best for us. On a practical basis, this happens to the degree that we conceive and accept Love's better ideas for us in the meetings we have with It.

Conditional thought temporarily gives direction to the forming of circumstances according to prior conditions that existed in our heredities and environments, many of which we find disappointing. Our experiences then, are especially happy and constructive when we meet frequently with Love and Its unconditional manner of thinking. However, when our meetings are infrequent, our lives are variably happy and unhappy, constructive and nonconstructive according to the level of love that we accept. When we meet but

---

Oneness cannot be known as readily as Aristotelian philosophers would usually have it (as though the appearance of something is its whole). A deep inner recognition of being at One with Love (or "order," "forms," "ideas") must occur, in order to embody both Platonism and Aristotelianism simultaneously. Although this may seem unnecessary, both of those grand teachers taught "pieces" which when placed together enable us to discover the Lovefriend. However, this awareness does not dawn on us through trying to piece their philosophies together. Rather, it is when we sense the Lovefriend's presence that we can come to know that Plato and Aristotle were in aggregate correct.

little with Love, we cause our heredities and environments to largely control us. Nevertheless, even without being at One with Love, we can think in ways that enable us to gain what we think we desire to some extent. We can use the Law to advantage if we believe that we can; however, the lesser degree in our sense of Love will disallow us to experience much that we truly desire. At best, we will think that we want many things and experiences which when gained, will either disappoint us or arouse in us a sense of our feeling dissatisfied with our results.

The truth of Love's supremacy is known by everyone, but for most of us It is not known in a very conscious manner. Because there has been little awareness that thought guides us toward our experiences, the increasingly popular conception of our day that our authority resides in our thinking, is a tremendous step forward for many of us. Once we discover what thought is doing in our lives, it might seem that there is nothing more we need to know. Yet our greater wisdom lies in the discovery that Love is our basic source of productive living. *Thought is creative, but Love is the essential inspiration for its becoming both more constructive and productive.* And Love provides these gifts without limit when thought releases the belief that the conditions of our present circumstances are necessary to our human experiences. This is the higher way of life's empowerment, Love's Way.

Why have we not all confidently and consciously declared that we can do whatever we think we can? We have delayed this greater self-expression because we have not been interested enough before now to more completely experience Love as the very essence of this confidence. Many of us have thought that it is only through the controlling of our worldly experiences that we can do that which we desire. And others of us have believed that to be controllers of our world is to invite disasters to occur because of our egocentricity; and so, not a few of us have distrusted our thoughts too much to bring about control. We will cease thinking these ways when we open our awareness to the work that Love is doing in our lives. One aspect of this work is that *Love is letting us do as we choose with our thoughts; It knows that our thoughts will eventually turn to Its ideas; because Love is letting us be, It will ultimately lead us to Itself.*

There are some among us who think and act somewhat freely, but do not know the presence and power of Love; those of us who are this way get much of what we want by controlling everything we can. The Law of reaction (which complements Love's Intelligence) acts as us, according to our thought, but we are not always happy with what we do. *We want complete ease and cannot have it, unless we let Love have Its higher way with us. In time it will happen, and we will be humbled by it, not because Love wishes us to feel inferior, but because we cannot feel true to ourselves without turning more to Love's presence. Being controllers is hard on us! As we yield our attempts to control to Love, It then acts as us in Its better way without hesitation and It brings us ease. Our humbleness thereafter turns in rapid succession to modesty, to strength and then to nobility without pretense.*

We will all eventually let Love guide us and gradually act as us, by lifting ourselves up through love in all we think and do. It cannot be otherwise, for it is human nature to be truly interested in experiencing that which is maximally Good for us. Love knows It will rise through our human nature and bring us into a full expression of Good.

Love knows that our nature is inherently Good. Love knows we are happy, whole, honest and unlimited in resourcefulness. Love knows we will come to know this, too.

A bad human nature does not truly exist; a misunderstanding of the goodness and innocency of our nature generally occurs with us for a time. This will not happen as much with people in the future, but until most people feel Love more than love, the tendency will be for them to not be aware of their Good nature.

Our understandings and misunderstandings about our nature result in our feeling life in two different ways, as though there are two levels upon which we can experience our living. We can give the greater part of our attention to only one of these levels at a time. Yet there is also a tendency of human thought to think about the alternate level, and we are always in some way aware that we could shift to it. Our attention at any given time is given to the level we most believe is real for us right then. When we are observing our nature as Good, we are really feeling Love, and we are attending the level that Love knows is best for us, the one in which our emotions are uplifted. Until we think of ourselves as inherently Good, we largely or entirely experience the lower level. The lower level is made up of the lesser understandings, in which our emotions are for the most part felt only physically; when we place the larger part of our attention on that level, we feel inadequacies. It is never wrong for us to think of love on a physical level, but too much attention there depletes our sense of resourcefulness. This is misunderstood if it means to us that we are unwise to involve ourselves with physical experiences of Love; they are good for us, but our greatest experiences of life, whether physical or nonphysical, come to us as they are felt through high ideas.

THE WAY LOVE IS SUPPORTIVE

Our thinking deprives us of the gift of Love until we recognize that the gift has already been given. The feeling of Love is always there; but, we cannot accept the feeling except as we acknowledge it. If a friendly relative visits us, but we think this person is neither a friend or a relative, we cannot enjoy the visit or the deepening of an already very present friendship. Since Love is not a visitor, but always attends us, we can make the recognition anytime and the Good feeling will then be discovered. But until we do, we will not know that our Lovefriend and Its magnificent supportiveness even exist.

So long as we do not sense the Good feelings that are natural to us, we make ourselves vulnerable to bad feelings. Because the Law of reaction (described in chapter six under the subtitle "The Law Of Reaction Or New Action") supports us in our choices, and since the thoughts we have are those choices whether we know this or not, It intensifies our bad feelings and they dismay us. Why does the Law do this? It is because it is the nature of the Law to give us what we choose. Of course, our choice to feel badly is not because we like to feel that we are bad; it is the combined result of our assenting to the belief that we hear from other people around us that any person could be bad, and that unless we live by the judgments of others we probably are bad.

Why does the Law not consider that we have been unsuitably influenced by others when it creates our experiences out of the idea that we are bad? It is not because It intends us harm. It is because the Law accepts us as being the sole and rightful judges of our lives. *THE LAW DOES NOT KNOW THE DIFFERENCE BETWEEN GOOD AND BAD. NOR DOES THE LAW EVER INTEND ANYTHING; IT ALWAYS ACCEPTS EVERYTHING. IT HAS NO CONCEPTION ABOUT WHAT WE SHOULD EXPERIENCE EXCEPT THAT WE SHOULD HAVE THE RIGHT TO CHOOSE THE IDEAS ABOUT OURSELVES THAT WE DESIRE TO IMPLEMENT. CONSEQUENTLY, IT INCREASES THOSE FEELINGS AND EXPERIENCES TO WHICH WE DIRECT OUR*

The Law acts upon the ideas and fears to which we give attention, and expands them into our experiences

ATTENTION. THIS NEED NOT BE PROBLEMATIC. BECAUSE LOVE IS ALWAYS WITH US, AND BECAUSE WE CAN CHANGE

OUR THINKING, WE ONLY NEED TO AFFIRM LOVE AND THAT OUR LIVES ARE GOOD, AND THE LAW WILL EXPRESS LOVE'S IDEA OF GOOD IN AND AS OUR LIFE EXPERIENCE.
Those who choose to think with Love feel wonderful about themselves. *Gradually* the entire human race is using more Love in its thought. Perhaps we think our rise into a greater sense of Love is too gradual. If we do, we can change that for ourselves; others will follow suit. However quickly or slowly it may seem to be, we are all moving toward the thinking that enables us to choose ideas that are especially worthy of the Law's multiplication. We are preparing ourselves to feel our inherent goodness more and more and to "really feel Love" within us.

LOVE AND LAW

Love is the cause of everything; without Love nothing would exist. But, have we not said that the Law is the maker of everything? We have; the Law creates all that is. *Love is the cause; Law is the creator. And the Law only makes what Love desires. However, the Law responds to Love's desires as they are communicated through thought. This includes the thoughts of every human being. Every thought communicates something of Love. If Love's idea is not felt strongly enough, Love's idea is reduced by love's concern, and the Law makes results that mirror "concern." Because a concern is an anxiety, the Law makes disappointments of our concerns. This cannot be avoided, because to live is to experience Love. And when our sense of Love is only love, our lives can only be expressed at the lower level of being. When we recognize Love greatly, Love's action through us is Good. But, when we think love is all there is of Love, love's action through us is not always as good as we would like to experience.*

We are alive because Love has thought of us, and caused us to be. Law, reacting to Love's idea of us, has created us in Love's image, and has provided us with Love's capacity to be constructive and positive. However, we cannot use this elevated capacity beyond our recognition of Love's presence. To the degree that we achieve recognition, we creatively express lives that are abundantly blessed. Yet, even when we do not recognize Love, Law enables us to creatively express everything that we think, and that we do not deny.

It appears unfortunate that there are some things that the Law makes for us that hardly seem becoming of Love! Moreover, we often feel guilty about our thoughts that are creative of such experiences. We need to know that guilt is but another action of love; we do best to open ourselves to Love and expect It to reform our reactions along with the guilt that attends them. Love does not count us as unworthy of Its presence because of our having had these lesser thoughts of It. Rather, when we turn enough to Love, the Law acts creatively to transform all of them into an attitude that is restorative.

Whatever sense of Love we have, even if it be love, still Love is there in it, to let us think as we will. No one is alive except that some degree of Love or love is felt by that person. No one who feels Love or love is ever denied the Law's creating the ideas that one thinks. *HOWEVER, THE PERSONS WHO HAVE THE GREATEST SENSE OF LOVE ARE THOSE WHO ARE MOST EMPOWERED!*

Love is flowing through all people. It is like a deep lake high in the mountains that endlessly supplies many streams of water throughout the hills and valleys below. The movement of Love is streaming through us, and to the extent that we recognize It, It is flowing through our thoughts and actions.

The results of Love's activity within us are not always satisfying. But, this is not because there is any lack of kindness, creativity or empowerment in Love; it is because we often do not recognize Love as we need to. Then the Law of reaction gives us likenesses of our fearful and undesirable thoughts. Our lives, because of our reactions, are sometimes vehicles of disease, poverty and strife. This is not because Love would ever have it that way. However, Love cannot give us Its Good beyond the extent that we think and feel It. Sometimes we feel bitter or sad about our experiences. In those times, Love seems absent; nevertheless, these experiences happen because we simply do not acknowledge Love's presence and let It act through us with Its better ideas. It is not that any person entirely fails to recognize Love, but that many only acknowledge It as love, and some with a very small sense of love.

We all think we desire health and peace. However, many of us become preoccupied with love's understanding which includes the fear of our experiencing diseases and of aging. We may then try to change our focus by placing attention on disease prevention and anti-aging. But, we then become diseased and aged. It is the result of trying to avoid conflict by hoping that we will not have disease and that death will not disintegrate our bodies. Attempts to resist these conditions is a fear of deterioration that love conceives. This causes the Law of reaction to create the state of being that we have wished to avoid.

The Law of reaction makes certain that we have deteriorating health and conflict as long as we expect such conditions in our lives. We may think we do not really expect them, but we generally do. *Our expectancy is rarely what we hope could be. It is whatever we think about with regularity. Expectation builds in our thought from the ideas we hold in our attention. Unfortunately, we are unconscious of many of these thoughts, and our placing attention upon the Love that is within them and that could help us, is too infrequent.*

We are meant to have serenity, success, prosperity, Good health and very happy relationships. Law is able to provide all the Good experiences of life that we can conceive. What we get can be what we truly desire, but if we think that this is unlikely to happen, we will tend to receive lesser desires. We may have the experience of receiving many lesser desires because we may think that we are undeserving of anything better.

Again, that to which we give our attention becomes our expectancy; it is ordinarily what we think we want. What we think we want and what we hope to have are different. We generally hope for something that we deem is better than what we think we want. We do this because *we think we cannot have what we most truly want.* We dwell, somewhat unconsciously, on the thought that there is too little good in the world to provide for the interests of everyone. Therefore, we think we must be lucky in order to realize our true desires. We do not feel we can be very lucky, therefore we choose to settle for less, or for what we think we want under the circumstances that prevail.

We tend to think we do not live in a world where Love is supreme, but rather in one where circumstances must rule Love. We are mistaken, but the Law works for us at the level of our understanding and recognition. Therefore, we temporarily repeat our disappointing experiences, again and again, until we understand and recognize Love as supreme, and that It only acts constructively for us to the extent that we identify ourselves with It.

The bottom line is that we get to experience life as good or as bad according to our expectancy. WE GET WHAT WE THINK WE WANT, BUT WE COULD GET WHAT WE REALLY WANT. As we lift up our understanding, we become aware that Love truly longs to do this for us. Better yet, when we turn from our deliberated desires and let Love give us what Love knows is best, we are given a life of happiness and resourcefulness beyond our old thoughts of what could be.

We get what we think we want but we could get what we really want

When we think something happens to us that we have not expected, we are thinking erroneously; we are using our hope fancifully, covering up our awareness of what we have actually expected. But in the very end of this lifetime, we will individually become unmistakably aware that what we experienced is what we actually expected. Then we will see that our life experiences matched the beliefs that we had been holding subconsciously. If our experiences are then shown to be different than what we consciously thought they should have been, the cause will show itself to be the result of our having used the subconscious mind to store many fears about what desirable experiences could have occurred. Those fears will be seen as a mixture of hopes and doubts; they will not have been very much admitted into our conscious recollection, after our having originally thought of them, because of our having conceived of their manifestations as being especially painful, and of our having pulled back from our awareness the memories of our having feared such unpleasantness.

The Law's action is always assisting us to discover the void we place between expectancies that are based on the thoughts that are likely to be formed into realities, and those which we pretend, but do not really expect that we will experience. Its assistance is the constant provision for each of us of experiences that are mathematical copies of all our thoughts and the ways we have assembled them. When we feel ready to discover this, we come to the awareness that every experience aids us, because we can determine from it the results that we can expect to have from similar thinking that we do in preparing ourselves for our next experiences. We can then discover the value and process of focusing our thinking more and more on the Good, Love would have for us. It is through this that Love acting with Law replaces the experiences we have had with new ones that better represent our deeper interests. And it is never too late to find out how this happens; our lives and experiences will continue beyond the few years we spend on earth; and they will become happy, successful and satisfying immediately upon this discovery; and our implementation of these gains will happen upon our focusing thought more upon Love.

DISTINGUISHING THE INDISTINGUISHABLE

We have believed that there is too little Love and too few lovers. Love has seemed concealed, sometimes nonexistent, yet It is everywhere. Love is in us. Why do we not see It? We will never physically "see" Love, any more than we will physically "see"

Its Intelligence, yet most of us would not think of denying or doubting the existence and presence of Intelligence. We cannot ever physically "see" life itself, but we cannot intelligently deny our livingness, our consciousness of being.

If we could actually "see" life exactly as it is, Love would not be distinguishable from it as a separate thing. Life and Love are inseparable. There is no life without Love, for life is Love; Love is life. But we are blinded by our misunderstanding and ignorance about the nature of Love. Because of blindness, though we believe ourselves to be alive, we do not see the "nature" of being alive. Being able to fathom the indistinguishable is for us now a grand and important step.

When we *begin* to see *into* ourselves as we are, Love is discovered as very distinguishable; in this way, the nature of life is comprehended by us. We come to the point of feeling that life is special when we distinguish Love; yet neither life nor Love is more a reality than the other, because our entire basis for existence lies in their continuous inseparability from each other and from who we are.

Our present experience of life is enhanced as we distinguish the presence of Love in it. It is the greatest discovery we can presently achieve, for it opens for us the ability to see ourselves as we really are. Next, we can distinguish Love as being everywhere around us.

Whenever Love is identified by us, we feel life as a beautiful and happy state of being. At first there seems to be more beauty, happiness and Love in some places and on some days. Eventually, the degrees of Love, beauty and happiness are not as apparent, because they are noticed as being present as much in one place or time as in another. The earliest awareness of this discrimination, despite its lesser sensitivity to the manifesting of even better experiences that will follow it, is a most splendid benefit. It enables us to open ourselves to the realization that Love gives us all Good in life. It happens through our interest to increase our awareness of Love: in this, we become increasingly receptive to deeper and more wonderful desires, and then to the even greater experiences of the manifestation of them that will surely follow.

TWO KINDS OF DESIRES

The nature of everyone is to desire that life be happier, more comfortable and more in accord with one's interests than it seems to be. It is generally presumed that such desire must forever be denied; and that the desirous nature is faulty or even bad. We need to know that our desirous nature is not only good, but the generator for all action. Except for desiring something better, nothing would grow; life would terminate itself.

Many presume that their legitimate desires are bad

There are two kinds of desires, those that we feel pull us toward our Self-fulfillment and those that seem more immediately reachable, that draw us away from supporting our being fulfilled. As long as we do not embrace our desirous nature as an essential characteristic of the living process, we must torment ourselves with desires that make us feel guilty, anxious and competitive. Accepting that our great desires are realizable, enables us to rise above stressful living, but it often has not seemed that way.

However, failure is simply the result of trying to achieve our sincere objectives without letting Love help us. Love knows how to express us well, how to manifest our real interests; and we can experience Love's helpfulness in every situation we face, simply by meeting regularly with the Lovefriend, removing the conditions in our thought and letting Love guide us through our activities.

When we try to live without being aware of Love, we have to have disappointments; it is because of them that we become mired in addictive behavior. Dysfunctional lives are seldom the result of our having excessive desires that harmfully involve us with bad habits which seem unshakable. Addictions are largely the result of not actively pursuing deeper, more sincere desires, and of disbelieving that Love is our friend.

POTENTIALITY AND OUR DESIROUS NATURE

We can embody all that we truly need and desire so as to be wonderfully happy. We do not usually hear about this from other people. We discover it for ourselves as we open up to the Love that is within us. We do that best as we think highly of ourselves.

Until we "really feel Love," we tend to think very little about the Good that is within us. We feel far less secure than we truly are. This results from our attempts to *try* to feel good. When we try to feel something, it is because we think we need or desire it; and rather than feeling Good, we feel bad--we feel unloved. This is a fearful state and it is critical, mostly because we tend to use it to accuse ourselves. Nevertheless, Love attends us. Because of a temporary ignorance, the realization of greater needs and deeper desires is not more than potentially possible during these experiences. However, they will be expressed in time; every person is filled with a unique talent which is most Self-fulfilling and which will someday in the here or hereafter, be well expressed; nothing can interfere with that or take it away.

Distinguishing the presence of Love in life makes it necessary that we turn from fears and criticisms of ourselves. Our desirous nature proves to be the means. We may not be presently able to express our deepest desires, but we can begin to, by letting Love do more of the things through us that give us great satisfaction. Our desire for Love requires us to care more for ourselves. (All people Love themselves some; none are completely care-less.) We do this by telling ourselves that we love who we are. We think of some things that we really desire to have happen. Then we watch, and Love does them as us, as we begin to simply declare them as done. Speaking of our desires develops our ability to feel more; as we actively feel desires, we feel Love in action.

Anyone can feel the desire to experience life in a better way. The Law always carries out the actions we most think about. The potentiality of getting even better results resides within every person. Love desires it even before we do, and the Law will act upon Love's higher ideas as quickly as we desire It enough to let Love help us.

We may think we would like Love to be seen in ways other than the activities we experience in needs, desires, tendencies and potentialities. But that is impossible, for *Love only expresses "through" the focus of attention, and we tend to focus on needs or desires. At first, we do not use attention to really represent ourselves; we think too much about lesser needs and lower desires. Eventually, we place a stronger focus on the potentiality of gaining greater needs and deeper desires. That change comes as we take enough interest in discovering how to best feel the needs and desires that really represent us, and to "really feel Love," which makes all of this natural.*

Love is always present in the thoughts of all of us. This does not at first seem true, but certainly, if it is the case, we want to find it out. We make that discovery by becoming aware that Love is rising up through our nature as just described. Love unfolds Itself through us step by step.

We find that our desires and desirous natures contain impulses of Love, but not because our desirous nature is a force of itself. The contrary is the case! Desires are misunderstood when they are conceived as a force which makes something happen. In the ordinary references that we make to desire, and in the usual definitions of desire, a strong action is presumed. *But, the strength of desires lies totally in the naming of a choice that is then turned over to the power that resides behind or within the thought of the desire. (I believe this well explains what the momentous discovery of the Great Buddha[2]could better mean for us: it is not that we should not have desires, but that we do well to not TRY to manifest them.) That power belongs to Law, because all power is Law. However, when Love's action has no unnecessary reaction mixed into it, the desire that sets it into motion appears to be the power. It seems that way because, Love's own impulsiveness acts WITH all power to manifest our desires. Consequently, to the extent that we "really feel Love," It cannot fail to manifest our deepest and most splendid desires. Again, "Love fulfills the Law"!*

Let us understand that desires are essential to well-being; they are the longings that name our interests, and can be manifested effortlessly. If we put effort into our desires, the impulsion of Love recedes. *When we turn any desire into a passion, unless it is an all consuming enthusiasm to express Love, we divert from it some sense of Love. When we empty desires of all passion, everything we would Love to do is empowered to happen.* As we grasp this, we seek to choose higher ideas as our desires.

Our desires will be best expressed by Law without the slightest effort on our part

---

[2] Briefly, Buddha's discovery was that suffering can be eradicated from people's lives by their cutting off the roots of their desires, or by their ceasing to give any further attention to being desirous.

We recognize that Love is at work in us because we succeed. We continually upgrade our choices and cause our world to be a better place.

THIS DOES NOT MEAN THAT WE DO NOT NEED TO EXPERIENCE PASSION. PASSION IS ESSENTIAL IF WE ARE TO SUCCEED WITH ANYTHING. BUT THE DESIRES AND OUR DESIROUS NATURE DO NOT EXPRESS US WELL IF THEY ARE MADE INTO PASSIONS! OUR DESIROUS NATURE MUST BE SURRENDERED TO LOVE IF WE ARE TO BE TRUE TO OURSELVES!

There is the possibility of doing almost anything we desire, because there exists in everything and everyone the potentiality of being used to serve humankind in greater ways. Engineers, for instance, are hired to design ever greater and safer dams. Their ever unfolding scientific understanding enables them to achieve their goals. That understanding is largely knowledge regarding the nature of water flow and of the composition of the surrounding soils. Where did that nature come from? It simply is given in the kind of world we have. Because of the nature of water and soil, a potentiality exists of building great dams, bridges, and many other marvelous forms.

We live in a world that is potentially all that we choose to make it. This is because Love is in everything. The nature of Love is that It desires to be used by everything. Love gives results as marvelous as can be conceived as we discover how best to recognize It, and to practice Its way.

LOVE IS BEST USED BY US AS WE LET IT BE THE USER OF US. This is because Love's Way is the sum of Supreme Intelligence, Self-givingness, sympathy and emotion, each in the right degree. When we truly let Love express us in this perfect synthesis of Its capacity, it is because this has become our passion, while we are simultaneously experiencing a quietness and trust. This combination of action enables us to act with magnificence.

Our own lives can be expressed as wonderfully as those of any individuals who have ever lived. Our lives can be even greater! As we simply believe this, Love does the rest. However, to express life this magnificently, there must be a "feeling" that this is true. We succeed as we feel the impulsiveness of Love.

It may be questioned whether the people who are successful as scientists and psychologists, and who have been able leaders in their field, really feel Love. It is likely that many of them, if asked, would say they do not know what it is that we are talking about. However, the feeling of Love comes in different ways to different people. And I am indicating that such resourceful leaders generally experience it, even if it might be that it happens in a very different way with them. Though I am encouraging us here to be open to an imaginative sense of the Lovefriend, the imagination of Love's presence and a real feeling of Love can come in many other ways. All people who have high self-esteem, no matter who they are, feel a presence of Love within themselves: they may call it a secure feeling, a self-reliance or a strong confidence. That is exactly what I mean by Love. But, to have security, reliance and confidence, *and* to feel a companionship of the Lovefriend too, is especially dynamic. It requires meetings!

Realizing the potentiality that is natural is accomplished through keeping our attention on deeper desires. It will lead us to the success of being a fulfilled person; we will then masterfully express ourselves. Remember, Love is interested to express us as we naturally desire. Love supports us to be successful as we seek to be an office worker or manager, a factory worker or foreman, a student or school teacher, an electronic engineer or biochemist, a farmer or doctor, lawyer or construction worker, housewife or house husband, mother or father, or through any other function that we conceive. This is especially true if we attend Love's meetings regularly.

Love is showing us that our deepest desires are those which most interest and best represent us; these desires can all be manifested.

CHAPTER TEN

LOVE AND SACRIFICE

Can you express Love well to other people, some who are near and dear to you, others who but casually touch upon your life, without making sacrifices of yourself and of your interests? YES, YOU CAN! YES, YOU CAN! YES, YOU CAN!

Many feel that Love is found more in the chains of sacrifice than in the free expression of their natural desires

Many of us tend to think Love is found more often in the making of sacrifices than in the expression of desires. It is common to think that our desires should be somewhat suppressed in reverence to those who have suppressed their desires almost entirely. That idea is a peculiar twist of self-denial. It means to honor, most of all, those people who have denied themselves the expression of their greater interests. We tend to use that idea to think that some or many natural desires could be bad, that we should not even feel them. Therefore, we feel that we must not do much of that which we desire to do. We bind ourselves with prohibitions. We severely restrain our ambitions. We feel those restraints as mental chains.

218

We cause ourselves to fear what we might do if we broke through our self-confinement. Often that bondage is erroneously taught as the nature of Love.

There is a better way to experience self-denial and it is achieved when Love is felt with it. It is the opposite of the traditional understanding of self-denial. The better self-denial is an activity that brings forth Love from within us. It is in denying ourselves the paltry compensations we feel are necessary when we think we should not reach out to be, do and have our deep felt longings. We do best to deny ourselves indulgence in debilitating habits that we have erroneously hoped are less harmful than the expressing of our individualities. We are wise to exchange those habits for the expression of our greater desires. Rather than being sacrificial, such action gives up nothing of ourselves and is wholly enjoyable. If we stop thinking that circumstances must upset our lives and those of friends, and realize that we do not need to continue to act sacrificially, our natural and normal urges enable us to pleasantly express authentic supportiveness, serenity and well-being.

It is not a sacrifice to give up something of little value, such as "the self-punishing habitual depressants," to achieve happiness or a high ethic. Neither is it sacrificial to live in a thrifty way to build capital, or to deny the self any lesser thing in exchange for something better. However, these gains occur only as we let Love's action replace our preoccupation with low desires. And this makes necessary the dismissal of all thoughts that we are bad persons because we have been experiencing legitimate emotions and legitimate desires. It requires us to not deny ourselves moderate and reasonable experiences of the "ten normal habitual action" needs. However, it also includes a willingness to let these legitimate desires be *lifted* in their expressions.

We will not cultivate the willingness to lift our desires nor discover their points of poised expressiveness, until we let ourselves become greatly aware of the presence of Love. Sacrifice is a different action! Sacrifice is the forfeiture of a natural behavior, or it is a disciplined action that crushes it. Unlike Love's action, if through sacrifice or discipline alone a better experience seems to be formed, a new negative experience emerges and similarly encumbers a person in the way the previous circumstances did.

Love has often been equated with being sacrificial. Love need not be caught up in sacrifice, suffering or struggling, because we do not create Love by something we do. We let Love flow through us by intending to act constructively. Love, naturally and spontaneously, arises from within our desires to express our high intentions. Through sacrifice, we keep ourselves from really feeling Love; *we cannot truly feel Love when we are attempting to be Love.*

Love never acts sacrificially of Itself, because It is unlimited in Its capacity to express Its ideas well. Therefore, Love dwells less in the person's life in which there is commitment to sacrifice. For sacrifice is our chief method of displaying a false report of Love. We cannot look upon ourselves as really loving while we sacrifice. Sacrifice is unnecessary when Love is free to be. Yet, occasionally some emerge who successfully mix sacrifice into an uplifted expression of Love; such persons are rare, and their examples are best followed by our subtracting the impact they make upon us with their sacrificial manners, from their other more authentic loving actions.

Sacrifice has three modes of being: we use sacrifice to hide from Love, to hide our sense of Love from ourselves or to project Love. That is, psychological repression, depression, and projection are the tools of sacrifice. When we practice any of them, we are sacrificing ourselves.

Repression, depression, projection
are the tools of sacrifice

When we think of famous historical religious figures and other heroes, we are reminded of sacrifice. Yet sacrifice has never been a requirement of Love. Many have seemingly suffered and died for great causes and on behalf of other people. It appeared necessary that they experience sacrificial lives because they were resisted by other people. But it was not necessary! True, they faced challenges that even great people have thought insurmountable. But, if they had thought of nonsacrificial ways to achieve their goals, Love would have supported them just as completely. It is not wrong that they gave their lives, because Love used their gifts of Self to reach others. We are wise to appreciate the greater livingness we have come to know because of their heartfelt choices. But our appreciation of them should not be an endorsement of sacrifice as though it is a requirement of Love, because it is never that.

LOVE AND JESUS

In the case of Jesus, we will never truly understand him if we believe that he sacrificed himself. He allowed himself to be crucified. He premeditated its likelihood. ***BUT IT WAS NOT SACRIFICE IN THE ORDINARY SENSE!** Rather it was a demonstration of faith that nothing could really hurt him, not even the experience called death.* Most of us could not see a crucifixion in our future without thinking of it as bad. We would do all we could to prevent it, unless perhaps we felt that it would serve other people and ourselves if we were to be sacrificed. Thus, the difference between Jesus and ourselves. Jesus did not see crucifixion as bad, because he was convinced that no one could really be killed. He believed he could prove it through his being crucified; he thought people who believed as he did would discover afterwards that he was still alive, ***thus proving that life goes on.*** He was earnest to express this; it was a deep desire for him.

Jesus wanted us to understand that God is wholly Good, is our Friend forever and will support us just as much on the other side of this life as here. The crucifixion became his most opportune experience to prove this. Though Jesus appeared to die, his closest friends were later overjoyed when they realized that he had not really died. Eventually, the whole world was given a new confidence and a new direction!

It may be difficult to comprehend just how much Jesus understood the benevolent nature of the universe. However, we can fathom it as we observe that there were no doubts in his thinking about God's being with him every moment. We have forgotten to take into account his faith, and have been swayed more by religious leaders who speak about Jesus as though his resurrection must have been a miracle. Actually, he had faith that the eternality of life was certain, not just for him, but for everyone.

If we take it for granted that Jesus was sacrificed, how can we explain it? Why would God have allowed it? Some say that God was hurt by it and suffered a sense of disappointment. If this were true, God would have been shown as insufficient to cause all to be as Love desires it. This viewpoint has been shared by many. The concept of "a hurting god" is widely taught; it is a thoughtful resolution of why there seemed to be a sacrifice. Still, it leaves too much unresolved. First of all, it would have to mean that God is not unlimited in power and is therefore less of an inspiration to us than the mightiness of creation demonstrates. Secondly, if we believe in "a hurting god," we cannot really feel how very triumphant Jesus proved himself to be. His ministry never showed an insufficiency. A frustrated or suffering God would be too weak a power to enable Jesus to have found such great strength as he showed that he had in his many other successes. Love always shows itself victorious; there is nothing to indicate Love was any less that way on the occasion of the crucifixion, since Jesus proved himself to continue to be very much alive.

But did not Jesus himself say that he was sacrificing himself? No; never did he say this! All the teachings, rites and beliefs about Jesus' sacrificing himself have been misconceived and taught with misunderstandings. All the times that are scripturally recorded of Jesus' using the word sacrifice, including all of its derivatives, are in Matthew and Mark. Two times in Matthew, he simply said,

"Go and learn what this means, 'I desire mercy, and not sacrifice'."[1]

The only possible Old Testament references that he could have had in mind in saying this are these two:

> "For I desire *steadfast love* and not sacrifice, *the knowledge of God, rather* than burnt offerings."[2]

> "Behold, *to obey* is *better* than sacrifice."[3]

In Mark, in the only time there that Jesus used the word (sacrifice) so that it has been generally accepted as authentic by most Biblical scholars, he said, to love God and one's neighbor *"is much more* than all whole burnt offerings and sacrifices."[4]

It is clear that so far as biblical information is concerned, Jesus saw sacrifice as a considerably lesser practice than Love. As we shall soon notice (under the subtitle "Self-givingness"), he *chose* to be crucified, so we cannot correctly presume that he was sacrificed.

The reason he made the seemingly preposterous choice to be crucified, was because it was his obvious opportunity to ably teach about life's everlastingness, and to challenge the beliefs of his people. From very early in his ministry, he foresaw it as his necessary action. And were it not for his deep conviction that life is certain to be ongoing, it could have appeared like a sacrifice to him even as it may seem to us.

It was in the belief that God's greatest blessing with the people of Israel was in His releasing them from their bondage as slaves, that Jesus' idea of being crucified was conceived. The authority

---

[1] Matthew 9:13 and 12:7 (RSV).

[2] Hosea 6:6 (RSV).

[3] 1 Samuel 15:22 (RSV).

[4] Mark 12:33 (RSV).

of the Passover,[5] that eventuated in their being "the exodus," revolved around the sacrificing of choice lambs (symbolized in the Passover lamb or paschal lamb). Many have considered that Jesus' life has been analogous to the paschal lamb; and it was, but not for us to admire sacrifice, but to build faith in immortality.

The original Passover occurred about 1400 years earlier, and was explained as though an angel of death passed over the homes of ancient Israelites who had the blood of the paschal lamb smeared over the doors of their dwellings. Now then, is it not true that Jesus' choice of "accepting" his time for crucifixion during Passover, was suggestive of being the symbol of a paschal lamb for the purpose of liberating his followers from their fear of death? There are scriptures that show this could have been the case such as the one Paul wrote, "For Christ, our paschal lamb, has been sacrificed."[6] But, why then did Jesus' references to *sacrifice* explain *it* as not desirable? It is because his motive for crucifixion was to prove that life naturally goes on for us, but his greatest opportunity for its expression involved him with the inevitable connection with the sacrificial lamb; his being misinterpreted ever since has placed an emphasis on sacrifice that has been misleading. He simply wanted people to know that we are not wise to fear death!

The truth then about Jesus was that he felt Love very deeply and desired to express It in the way that would most help people. If he could help them to discover that they have everlasting life they would feel maximally secure. Because he knew there was no void of Good in Love or life, he trusted the impending crucifixion as being his way to accomplish this.

It may seem to some that Jesus was sacrificed because there were certain violent reactions set up to control him, and because it *seemed* he could not stop them, and that he then *appeared* to be destroyed by them. If we reason this way, it means that we believe his action was less powerful than one of resistance. But,

---

[5] Exodus 12.
[6] 1 Corinthians 5:7 (RSV).

had he not shown himself able to resolve everything else? Rather than there being a weak spot in his otherwise powerful ministry, it is obvious that Jesus chose the experience which we call death to prove that life is eternal. But let us look at the way this idea of a weakness has been used by us, to falsely believe that limitations rule our world and that Love is only supreme through sacrifice. And let us observe how Jesus believed that death's appearance was *not* a weakness in life, but something *he could use* to prove that life is forever strong.

SENSING LOVE AS GOOD AND STRONG

We have tended to interpret everything as having a beginning and an ending. The beginning has never been satisfactorily explained by those of us who think this way; the ending has always been seen as decay or a more sudden action of harm. Birth then, is ordinarily understood as a sweet mystery, something that we welcome, while death is thought of as a more or less inevitable disappointment, one that we seek to delay as long as possible. Death is generally explained as necessary, but something which we may at least sometimes, put off for awhile. The length of any form of life, or the durability of any material object, is considered from this point of view as being limited.

A tension appears to exist in everything. It is a fact, that so far as the physical sciences have been able to test material things, they have not been able to stretch the substance or usefulness of any of them beyond a certain point. This seems to imply that everything is limited. Consequently, it has been common to measure the resistance to durability and life. But resistance implies the existence of an opposition, for otherwise there would be nothing that would resist. Is there something that has the power to cause decay or death? Certainly not! It is only Love that has given life; Love is nonresistance, and by Its nature, cannot take away life. However, Love regularly reconceives new expressions for everything, and in each instance the forms of prior expressions disintegrate or die. Death is not a termination of anything other than forms that seem to be shell-like coverings or appearances. It is simply the name we give to that which occurs when a *particular form* of something ceases to be.

Death is a concept then which represents a change of forms. That which animates any given form is its Spirit; Spirit goes on forever; forms decay. When death occurs, the power (Law) that expresses Spirit creates a new form; the old form disintegrates, but its atomic composition is newly assembled to house the capacity to achieve another expression.

People, animals and things keep changing forms. We know this, and some of us fear these changes. We can face our fear and lift our feeling of it to a confidence that all is well. A very sensible basis for this confidence can be established. It is done by making ourselves aware that death is only feared by material-ists! Things and people are ordinarily explained by them as having a certain endurance factor because they believe that each physical appearance is all there is of it, and therefore its entire construction is best measured by particular physical factors. I do not see that it is wrong to think this way. But life is more com-pletely disclosed to us as we also discover that a spiritual essence exists within each thing or person. Everything has a spiritual identity, and that is its actual basis for being; and Spirit has no tension, no limitation, no endurance factor.

Endurance limits or breaking points of the things in which we observe deterioration, are generally the result of what was believed about them when they were first conceived. When Love is adequately felt, It can cause anything to be as permanent for us as we desire it to be. It is the Law of reaction that does this work for Love and that makes something be or breaks something down. The Law can pull anything apart or put anything together; the Law does this in our experiences as we "think" the idea of what we desire or what we do not desire. The idea that some-thing can be lost is the way we have generally used the Law to form experiences that frighten us. As we evolve in our under-standing, we will use Love and Law to establish our experiences of life with more security, reliability and durability.

Some people think the difference between the spiritual and material natures of life is that some things are spiritual and other things are material. They say Love, joy, honesty and serenity are spiritual states of being. The material world is explained by them as the visible things: the trees, grass, buildings, physical bodies, water and earth. It is understandable that some people think this way. However, Jesus had a higher understanding, and all really great spiritual leaders have known better. We can know better, too.

The spiritual nature of life is everywhere, is in everything, and is everything. We can understand this as we no longer judge things as good and evil. We can reach this understanding as we conceive of everything as being made because of Love. We may notice many people, places and things that seem devoid of Love, and we may often see ourselves in that way. But Love is in all places, in every-thing, and in everyone. If we desire to see something Good expressed in unexpected places or things, or from ourselves, we must join our loving attention with that desire, and then Love will cause the Good to show Itself with a splendor. It is never too late for anything to re-emerge or `make a come back, no matter how old or decayed. There is an eter-

The spiritual nature of life is everywhere, is in everything, and is everything

nal source of life givingness within the Spirit of everything that can return its splendor with anything. We have only to maintain an attitude of expectancy and acceptance through opening ourselves enough to Love, to discover this as true.

Nothing need decay because of time. Everything can last as long as we can believe that it will. This may seem far-fetched to many readers and that is very understandable. Yet most of us can believe in the durability of something. It might be the belief that people who are rich tend to maintain their wealth, and that those who are poor tend to remain poor. We might think that the oceans are durable. We might think that most people will always have to work to earn a living. If we can but believe that there is much that is potentially more lasting than we have formerly allowed ourselves to think, we will have begun to detect the spiritual nature of life. If some of us are convinced that at least some aspects of life can go on and on and on, we benefit by that. If we can believe that everything made by God could last forever, we will find its evidences, and this will be even more helpful. Finally, there are those of us who believe that nothing is made except that God is involved, or that Love causes it. As we believe that God or Love is eternal, Its resulting creations may be thought of as something which will never decay or die.

Let us suppose that the invisible aspects of life, such as Love and faith, are as lasting as life itself. If life is forever, then these high qualities of life will also always be. If we are not certain about eternity, then perhaps we can believe that Love and faith will be sustained at least as long as the stars will shine. We could go even further with that idea of durability, and think of Love and faith as being the kinds of starlights that never will burn out.

Let us be aware that some might choose to stop here and argue that it is not believable to think of anything as everlasting. They may think that the statements of the last several pages are not adequately based on fact. I do not disagree. I only point out that reasonings which are based on acquired facts entirely reflect assumptions that are based on materialism. The facts of materialism can only remain important to us for as long as the tests of reality are made with materialists' instruments. My purpose right here is to indicate that the greatest of spiritual leaders believed in a permanent reality and that their beliefs have been proven to last in the thoughts of the masses. We do well to see what those leaders saw.

Nothing here is intended as an argument; it is not necessary that it appear conclusive! That is, everything here can be proven, bit by bit, but it could take thousands of years to see the whole of it. Therefore, we will not really meet the Lovefriend, feel Love, nor distinguish It from sacrifice in this lifetime, unless we let go that this is a debate.

What then is our overall purpose in pursuing the ongoingness of life? It is to meet the Lovefriend and to really feel Love. How can we do this? We can meet the Lovefriend, and feel Love, as we believe It is the most basic reality. We can meet the Lovefriend and be at One with It in everything of life as we believe that what is worthy is lasting. If the only way we can do this is to think that it may be true, but that it does not have to be -- that is sufficient. This view will open us to the awareness that Love and faith can last as long as we can conceive anything as being lasting. And if we find any basis for Love and faith to continue that long, could not such continuance be as true of other invisible things? And is it not possible that our lives will be greatly benefited by conceiving that Love, faith and the beneficial ways of life could go on forever?

The invisible things of life will come to be known by us as everlasting. Joy, happiness, success, integrity and Good character cannot die, because they are permanent Goods of this universe. For example, a Good creator would not endow human beings with the gift of Good character only to have it wasted. We do not have to prove this to believe it. But if we can believe it, it will tend to prove itself.

Is there really a difference between the visible and invisible? There are many stars, solar systems and galaxies that have lasted twenty billion years or much longer. Talk about durability! We cannot unassumingly conceive of that length of time. The visible things will ultimately be shown to be as strong as Love and faith, whenever our sense of Love and faith intends that of them, because there is a spiritual nature in everything. Love is the sufficiency of all things, and can cause anything to be seen with a continuous reemergence of life's vigor through making the death of its young forms succeed each other in new but similar images.

Like an overflowing fountain, Love,
faith and life flow on forever

Behind or within every visible object is the cause of its being, the idea that enables it to be. Most of us do not see the cause except in the idea of it that we imagine. The physical part of it is outwardly seen, but is usually poorly represented in the perception we have of it. Our true observation of any cause usually begins as we think of an image of what it might be, and "as we conceive of a finer conception" than the appearance seems to allow. When anyone thinks of someone else this way, the possibility is provided that the image can bring forth a better presentation of itself. This is because all creation is formed through the expansion of an image; the idea of a good image encourages the expansion. When Love is felt, one always sees a good image. When we feel Love in this way, the creative effect is a lasting one.

As a person regularly "sees" this way, the value to the overall community of people on earth is great. That person feels connected with the overall mission of Love. We can easily believe that if anything could be immortal, first of all, it would be the person who could do this. By feeling the Love connection, the belief in everlasting life is assured. Now suppose that one of us has succeeded in this. If any one has, then everyone has this potentiality. And, if we all have the capacity, then we are all immortal, and only need to be shown that we are immortal by the one who first achieves the goal. The one who knows it--shows it. The rest of us will likewise show it -- as we come to know it.

People are immortal; Love has made it so! One there was, who has convinced much of the world that he was loved enough by the very HEART of reality. But Love cannot be partial and still be true to Itself. It is bringing all people to the knowledge of Its care for them.

The most wonderful truth that we can know, is that nothing ever decays, except as we "think" that it can or does. There is a way in which some things appear to decay, but they are actually the old forms of the real things which decay; new forms build around that which inhabited the old ones. This happens continuously; everything is constantly being "transformed." For instance, Jesus was confronted with threats, yet kept his sense of Love lifted high; the threats dissolved; the idea of decay was forgotten. When a personal stand was taken on the stability of Love, everything reversed itself; Jesus was supported by Love and his death was demonstrated as his greater experience of life.

Unless Love abides forever, we have nothing upon which to establish any real confidence. Unless faith can be maintained in something that cannot be extinguished, all other life is without meaning. If we believe that Love and faith are forever, we have an understanding that there need not be any weakness in our universe.

Since there was no resistance at all by Jesus we are wise to recognize that he knew he could not die to his essence. Materialism met its Waterloo long ago, at Jerusalem! Sacrifice was not involved, but rather courage! It was used to prove that Love would make all things right!

A suffering God would be too helpless and too weak a power to explain why Jesus could have been motivated to be crucified. There was no sacrifice, no error and nothing wronged! The crucifixion was the courageous way for one of us to show that nothing could damage the heart of Love, nothing could harm the nature of Good, and nothing could prevent people from coming to know that we are all immortal. The fact that Jesus' disciples did not mourn for long in the aftermath, but understood that Love had won, tells us that Love was unhurt through it all.

Some teach that God did not create people with the ability to live with enough goodness to be worth eternal life. They believe that Jesus sacrificed himself to appease God's intent to destroy us. And again, many people actually think God sacrificed Jesus to appease a second power, such as a devil.

All these speculations as to why there could have been a sacrifice have a morbid ring to them. Sacrifice has been conceived by those people who were not sure that Love, and a tendency toward goodness, is the heart of the universe. And others have not believed that the universal heart is necessarily stronger than that of a violent power which might be struggling with it. *But suppose Jesus really did believe that God is Love, that Love is our infinite resource for living, that It is forever and It makes Its home in us. Suppose he was right? AND HE WAS! Then there would not be, AND THERE IS NOT, a need to think morbidly or TO MAKE A sacrifice.*

No one needs to sacrifice to enable Love to do Its work. Love protects Itself simply by being what It is. If It needed any other protection, It could not be relied upon with certainty as our protector. Love must be forever, or nothing else could be eternal. If anything could last without Love or could outlast Love, it would not be worth our keeping it. But, we cannot know that sacrifice is not needed until we *sense* that Love is Good and strong.

Fortunately, there was no reservation about that goodness and strength in the ideas and feelings of Jesus. And what he knew we can know too, if we but open our minds and hearts to Love.

SELF-GIVINGNESS

Love is never sacrificial. Rather, Love supports all interests to express life better. It is time that we see Love for what It is, and let It do Its perfect work within us.

If we choose to sacrifice ourselves, the Law will assist us to experience as much value from sacrifice as we believe should be there. Also, love will do this, but not Love!

There is a Self-givingness inherent to us, not toward death but toward life ... abundant life. The feelings of sacrifice and Self-givingness are not the same. When we feel sacrificial, we can lift ourselves to Self-givingness by letting Love express us more. This is possible because *sacrifice is naturally an early understanding*

The feelings of Self-givingness and sacrifice are not the same

of Self-givingness in which the divine idea of Self-expressiveness is not yet greatly unfolded. Therefore, it is understandable that sacrifice has seemed necessary. People have not made mistakes by performing sacrifices. Yet, *as we evolve, sacrifices will only be remembered as either primitive actions or insufficient understandings of Self-givingness.*

Many primitive religions began by using sacrifice to gain favor from the gods. They understood some things and misunderstood others. Their understanding was that life became better when people gave away what they most valued. Their misunderstanding was the idea that they needed to sacrifice firstborn boys, children and young women whom they prized. This primitive rite contained within it the rudiments of an activity for personal growth that is clarified as people prize their individual lives, especially the unique capacities given them by the creator. When we identify our abilities to make things with our hands and then use those abilities to be productive, we give something of ourselves away. Then we become increasingly productive. It is not because of sacrifice; it is because of Self-givingness. When we give money to beneficial organizations or when we volunteer our help, we give something of ourselves away. If we feel sacrificial, it is because we have not chosen to give of ourselves from the heart; if we wanted to give, it would not be a sacrifice. When we give because we want to, it is Self-givingness. This is Love!

Jesus did not die, if we conceive of death as the end of him. He did not have the option to live or die as such; no one ever does! All people are immortal, and all people have no alternative but to live forever. Jesus did have the choice of whether or not to allow his crucifixion. Moreover, he could have made the crucifixion into a sacrifice. He could have (by choice) allowed other people to take from him the experience of vitality that he felt on earth. Or he could do what he did....simply appear to die....and he did so, because his mission was to teach that life cannot really be extinguished!

Jesus chose to allow the crucifixion, but no one took his life from him. He said he chose to do what he did:

"I lay down my life, *that I may take it again.* No one takes it from me, but I lay it down of my own accord. I have power to lay it down, and I have power to take it again; this charge I have received from my Father."[7]

This was Self-givingness with no sacrifice involved. If we cannot see how that was true, it is because we feel we cannot live nobly except by sacrifice. This concept hurts anyone who thinks this way. It is not necessary for us to feel hurt. But we must discover how to be lifted in our idea of Love or a hurt will tear at our hearts -- as it is already doing for most people whether it is acknowledged or not.

THE CROSS

The usual attention placed upon the historical cross of Christianity's beginnings tries to make of it a tragedy, and presumes it was the result of a sacrifice. On the other hand, my view agrees with another ancient explanation that explains the cross as the inevitable intersection that appears temporarily with life when its indefatigability is not accepted. The vertical beam of the cross represents the onward, upward, immortal example of what is possible for humanity, and the crosspiece represents the doubt that life could be so good. Jesus let doubters do all they could to prove their doubts about life's being everlasting unless sacrifices could buy it; and they correspondingly acted to curtail his ability to express life except through sacrifice. When we conceive his Self-givingness as sacrificial along with them, we misunderstand his mission, his teaching and his achievement.

It is true that Jesus spoke of experiencing trials and that he had his disciples prepare themselves to witness his death. But, I reiterate that the confidence that life was not being taken from him (Jesus chose the experience to teach us that Self-givingness leads to life, "not to death") and that he would be alive afterwards is the significant underlying factor. If we focus on his being hurt,

---

[7] John 10:17-18 (RSV).

it is because we fear life for us must mean our being hurt, and that is the way we then tend to conceive of its being for someone else. If we really desire to experience life without harm for ourselves and others, we have to find a way to conceive that someone else has achieved it; this is his example, whether we can easily see it or must first view it conversely for a long time.

When we really observe that life never hurts us, we are readied to give of ourselves. Then, our "daily crosses" become not suffering states, but are rather the awarenesses of joy we have as we let Love pour through them. We are never hurt except by the Love we withhold from others.

When we really observe that life never hurts us, we are readied to express Love and joy

A frequently quoted verse of the Bible would nevertheless seem to make Jesus a victim of God as though he was sacrificed for us,

"For God so loved the world that he gave his only begotten Son that whosoever believeth in him should not perish, but have everlasting life."[8]

But, when we realize that everyone has an inner relationship with God, that the "only begotten Son" is the Christ within all of us (the crystal clear sense at the center of our beings that knows we can live by Love), then we express a consciousness of the Christ, and the inner Son goes out into our world through us. Then too, we readily see that Jesus was simply an example of one who understood this, and that he accepted his Christ Self as all of us will do when we turn to Love's presence. Because we all live forever, as Jesus was showing us, Love places no pressure upon us to enable Itself to express us. However, when we become aware of Love's value and let It express us well, "the only begotten Son" is discovered as another name for Love or for the Love-friend.

It may seem that when Jesus declared,
"....even as the Son of man came not to be served but to serve, and to give his life as a ransom for many.,"[9]

the evidence of sacrifice was present. But, the ransom was not something given up to life, God or the Jews, but the price he paid for being willing to experience whatever was necessary to prove his belief that the crucifixion would not cost him his life. The ransom was paid so as to draw out of the rest of us an understanding that we also have, but that we have hidden from our conscious awareness, that we too are made to live forever despite contrary appearances. As we examine the achievement of Jesus, we can discover our agreement with him. He succeeded in showing many people that he would remain alive after the crucifixion; therefore, he did not sacrifice himself nor was he

---

[8] John 3:16 (KJV).
[9] Matthew 20:28 (RSV).

sacrificed. Although his friends had considered it too great a risk for him, they later believed as he had, that life was forever.

Unfortunately, the believable evidence of immortality that resulted was soon relegated to a lesser teaching, because many people felt unworthy of immortality and felt that some kind of sacrifice must be paid, so as to establish worthiness. So although we have the proof that life is forever, we are still saddled with the idea that we must do something good to earn immortality or to receive forgiveness in order to establish worth and ample virtue. We have ignored the fact that love only needs to be lifted to Love within us to alleviate our guilts, anxieties and other thoughts of inadequacy. When we become Self-giving, love is lifted to Love; it is then that we understand all of this. And although we have made it clear that we cannot know Love unless we "forgive and forget," or discover our innocence, Self-givingness results when we do.

THE CHALLENGE

Of course, there were those moments, sometimes minutes or even hours, when Jesus was not certain that he really wanted to be crucified, when it seemed to him terribly like a sacrifice. At such times he said,

> "My Father, if it be possible, let this cup pass from me; nevertheless, not as I will, but as thou wilt."[10]

and

> "My God, my God, why hast thou forsaken me?,"[11]

but those brief intervals amidst the persuasion that he wanted to do what he did and that he was sure of what he was doing, were

---

[10] Matthew 26:39 (RSV).
[11] Matthew 27:46 (RSV).

not true deterrents to his basic decision or he would not have recovered his composure from each incident so quickly and so surely. It is sensible to understand all of them this way. His mission in life was especially daring and was at certain times questioned even by himself as being somewhat risky. Yet beneath all of those hesitating moments, he *knew* he was right, and so there was little wavering when compared to the steadiness he had as he set "his face to go to Jerusalem"[12] and all he understood that to mean.

We will better understand how Jesus faced the crucifixion if we quietly reflect on how we have wondered at times whether a decision of our own to do some heroic thing was right or mistaken. Such hesitation was *sometimes* short-lived, because our deeper feelings embraced the decision. Some of us know our life's intention from early on, such as achieving the goal of a lofty profession. Many who succeed in this may never have thought of the necessary preparation as a sacrifice. But, if we think we are making a sacrifice by taking many years to carefully prepare or train ourselves and to deny ourselves material things, we become afraid of the preparations to some degree. As a result, (1.) we do not achieve our goal, or (2.) we mishandle the experience after presuming too early that we had succeeded, which happens because we were not willing to sacrifice as much as we thought we must, to meet the grueling requirements we believed must be some part of it or (3.) we are never happy with our profession afterwards because of the demands that we feel it placed upon us. Those of us who are doing well with our greatest lifetime goal, and who feel happy in every way that we stayed with it, do so because we feel we have not actually sacrificed for it! It has not been a sacrifice for us because we did not fear that we could not succeed, nor did we feel the need for many distractions, nor did we regret the time or cost it required of us. There have been some waverings of thought, but they are hardly conspicuous when we count our satisfactions.

---

[12] Luke 9:51 (RSV).

Of course, many of us do not yet know how to conceive of living a life of worthy service without feeling it as sacrificial. And many of us who agree that sacrifice is not necessary, and who think that it is not existent in our lives, still live sacrificially and simply are not aware that we think, feel and act this way. Nevertheless, there has not been only one person, but many, who have given themselves to others and to whatever expression of life that they naturally felt represented them from a deep place within their thoughts, and who were Self-reliant, happy, successful and peaceful despite tremendous challenges. And there are many people alive today who are this way!

Although we may have questions at times about how well we can handle everything, and we may wonder whether we are on the right trail because other people question our rights or ability, we can all build self-esteem through meeting regularly with the Lovefriend. As we do, we question ourselves only in a small way, and can quite immediately reaffirm our idea of success. When we do this often, with sincerity and desire, the doubt we feel becomes small and is generally overruled by our confidence that some particular interest is what we most want to do; the sense of sacrifice then becomes too minute to be dramatically conceptualized and may not actually be felt anymore. When our Love for our daring interests is great enough, all cost is seen as no cost, because expressing our Self-givingness is that which we most want to do. *PARTICULARLY, WHEN WE KNOW WE WILL ACHIEVE OUR GOAL--THERE IS NO SACRIFICE. THIS HAPPENS BECAUSE LOVE HAS LIFTED US INTO THE CERTAINTY THAT FAILURE IS IMPOSSIBLE.* Even so, some small part of us may still wonder momentarily, and why not? We are on the mission of fulfilling our sincere and particular individual desire, one that no one else dares do. We simply know we are better trained or readied for it than are others; we were born for its undertaking; it is our Self-fulfillment and our Good.

Our reason for being hesitant is not because we did not really make a particular choice to begin with, but because we are free every moment to reconsider and to make a new choice. Jesus chose not once, but more than a thousand times a million times, not to be sacrificed, but rather to be crucified, so as to live more completely than he would have otherwise. If we weigh his billion moments of feeling certain against those in which he questioned the cost of giving himself to prove that life is all there is, we see that the latter were like one in a million, and we can recognize that he was not sacrificial; his actions represented his chief desire and his overall choice, but it took many meetings with Love to achieve this. (If we calculate each moment as being a second or less, which is reasonable, and if Jesus from a young age rather continuously reaffirmed his belief that he could be crucified without really losing his life, a number such as a billion is realistic.)

Jesus succeeded in proving that life is everlasting for all people. It was not accomplished because he was different from us, for that would have proved something for him, but not necessarily anything for the rest of us. He succeeded because he had a nature exactly like our own; how else could his experience have been made convincing for us? He also knew the nature of Love and he let It express his heartfelt desire.

For all of his success, Jesus' achievement only benefits us because of his likeness to us. If Jesus had never hesitat-

Jesus succeeded in proving that life is everlasting for all people

ed about accepting the crucifixion, if he had not at times felt that "the Spirit is strong but the flesh is weak," and if he had had no lower inclinations, he could not have been an example for us of how to live, nor could his resurrection have meant that we too live forever. Because he had his times of challenge, but was largely a successful person, we can find in him something to follow; that something is Love as he knew It; he simply was conscious that *Love can inspire us to "no end."*

We like Jesus, and every other person who has ever given deeply of Self, can only succeed as we know *that of ourselves* we do not have the ability to be Self-giving. Therefore, we have to discover that *whatever we do for the greater good of ourselves and others will tend toward sacrificial action unless we allow Love to inspire it and express it through us.*

LOVERS, FIGHTERS, MARTYRS

The Law of reaction supports any behavior we choose. On the other hand, Love's greater support comes to us only to the degree that we choose to feel Love or believe in Love's reality. Our thinking discloses the sense of support we are able to generate. We generally think low, and the Law enables us to experience our sense of lowliness. Love will change that, but not unless we feel It or in some way *MEET* with It. Love always has the highest conceivable idea for us. We make many poor choices, but through Love we can upgrade all of them.

If we mix sacrifice or some other form of suffering with a lifted idea of Love, we have to experience Love intertwined with suffering. *WE SET THAT UP.* It is not Love's way; it is the way of sacrifice or of suffering mixed with Love. It is possible to experience such a mixture, but many will never have experiences that are so jumbled. This is because we ordinarily reduce our idea of Love to love if we conceive of suffering as being with It. Only a *few* people have been able to mix an authentic idea of Love with suffering and sacrifice, without severely reducing their sense of Its essence. And this is the difficulty that we have had in getting a clear awareness of Jesus' practice of Love; we have thought that he was one of those people; *HE WAS NOT!* Nevertheless, a very few of his followers have been; they have successfully conceived of Love, suffering and sacrifice as compatible. They have *greatly loved* while making sacrifices; still, they have not loved as greatly as Jesus did, although they could have had they understood this. The difference is that people do not *TEND TO* express any great sense of Love to others if they appear to hurt themselves. When someone achieves the mixing of Love and sacrifice, the sense of Love is not as complete as It could be; persons helped by them still feel hurt, but in a new way; that is, they learn to sense Love more completely than before, while still appearing to hurt themselves. But now they think they hurt for others, by emulating sacrifice in the development of their own Self-givingness.

I reiterate, only a few succeed in greatly experiencing Love while being sacrificial; and those who learn from them generally change the form of their seeming personal hurts from thinking they are victims of other people to thinking sacrifice is the only way they can help other people. THIS MEANS THAT THE FOLLOWERS OF THE FEW WHO ARE MOST NEARLY SACRIFICIAL IN AN AUTHENTIC WAY CONTINUE TO FEEL THEMSELVES AS VICTIMS, BUT NOW AS VICTIMS OF THE NEED TO SACRIFICE THEMSELVES FOR OTHERS, AND SUCH ACTS OF PRESUMED HELPFULNESS ARE NOT WHAT THEY REALLY NEED TO EXPERIENCE. NEITHER IS IT WHAT STILL OTHERS NEED, WHO RECEIVE FROM THEM THE IDEA OF NEEDING TO PROLONGATE A CONTINUED CHAIN OF SACRIFICIAL ACTIONS.

Great lovers include then, a few people who could both Love others and sacrifice themselves too. Wherever these few people have also become martyrs, in the sense of their appearing to die for a great cause, they were "authentic martyrs." Some martyrs carried lesser degrees of authenticity in that they had less awareness of the nature of Love, but if they loved themselves and others enough to die to help a legitimate cause, rather than to prove themselves as being all right, they were Self-giving and martyrs worth mentioning. But, most people who have appeared to die for a great cause were not among them; the majority of humans who have voluntarily sacrificed their lives did so because they were made to feel that it was their responsibility to die for a cause. They thought that they could not feel good about themselves unless they did do what others expected of them. Unfortunately, no one can really feel Good by forming their activities out of what others tell them they should do. However, many people think they can feel especially good about themselves if they can show that they are suffering. It is not wrong for people to give their lives that way. Yet the wars that claimed our loved ones for such a reason were the unnecessary result of the mass ignorance of better solutions that could have been achieved. A void of more conciliatory thought, and actions, which could have been carried out long before any governmental leadership could have developed hostile strengths, has occurred within the reasoning of the entire human race. We have generally thought we could not communicate with each other when national loyalties demanded that we fear people who have a different history.

It still remains good for us that we praise our soldiers who have died in action, or who have dared and then succeeded in protecting people whose lives and freedom appeared threatened. Such support is sensible because all of them have always naturally acted as each one believed was necessary. However, either fighting to protect others or refusing to fight to safeguard the ideals of Love and nonresistance, have both been the result of convictions that were sincere. While giving genuine and praiseworthy attention to the actions of each of these persons who felt challenged to react through resistance or nonresistance to wars between nations, and who sincerely acted as each one felt was necessary under the circumstances, we do well as we also evolve our concept of love to Love.

Gradually but surely, we will see that authentic martyrdom does not lie in a fervent patriotism, no matter how sincere it is. Neither does it lie in religious crusades, in battling over religious doctrines or in any differences that could be settled over a conference table. It may be, that for the time being, numerous individuals must continue to be imprisoned to protect the public from their misbehavior; however, it is rare that governments and social groups do not contain persons who can skillfully conciliate group differences. Our first interest with government should always be to establish a representative body which will "keep the peace" between its interests and those of other people who think somewhat differently. Such procedure will *gradually* remove all forms of criminality; soon there will no longer be any ample reason for people to suffer or die so that others may live. But of course, people will continue to die for others until we support ourselves and each other enough with Love.

When someone appreciates an authentic martyr or any greatly loving person enough to emulate that person, he or she often thinks that dying for others still has its place. It seems that the example of that individual's sacrificial activity must be followed. However, "the authenticity" is not well established in this way. It appears easier to observe sacrifice than to observe Love's presence, and so most people miss seeing what is truly exemplary about the leaders who truly care and who have mixed sacrifice with their caring.

There were martyrs worth referring to in the real or mythic battles of ancient Hinduism, martyrs of Christendom worth mentioning in the earliest of Its years; since then, here and there an authentic martyr between them, and even some in the dark and middle ages; also, there was "Mr. Authenticity" himself, Socrates, the "model man," who was martyred by his being forced to drink hemlock. More recently, there have been "some" presidents and kings worth mentioning. The "authentic martyrs" of modern times have included Martin Luther King and Mahatma Gandhi. Surely, there are many more worth mentioning who were sacrificed or who gave themselves as a sacrifice for a cause, because they thought they had too. All of them did right! But the greatly loving persons who will also give themselves away in the years to come, will know that it is not sacrifice that will make them deeply loving, but something taller than any "essence of suffering" can impart. Certain past heroes (who died in their suffering for others), are to be prized because they loved so much; but, in the future, sacrifice will not be as much mixed with Love.

When Love becomes known for what It is, sacrifice will be

replaced with nonviolent solutions to every problem. In this regard, we can be encouraged that most people in political and social leadership today are more open than were their predecessors, to the idea that peaceful solutions can be found to settle all differences. And yet, the language of both world and local leaders often includes that nonviolent solutions will be followed only *if* they can be found, and that otherwise violence may yet be necessary. When solutions are discovered, they are often compromised ones. So, it is essential for our well-being that we meet often with the Lovefriend, because It knows that perfect solutions without compromise exist in every situation that troubles us. And when we discover the meetings, attend them, and let Love carry on with us, sacrifices will recede into the past and Love will motivate us in all that we do.

This does not make a person better who dismisses sacrifice and who only Loves. The purpose for dismissing sacrifice as an authentic need is simply because it is time that we let go of an imperfect idea. We are to become aware that Love makes all martyrdom and all feelings of hurtfulness unnecessary. One man knew this long ago; but, among those who have loved him most have been many who thought they had to give up life in his name even though *he never gave up his life, but rather, expressed it well.* He died, or appeared to, that we would in time understand the infinite heights and depths of Love, Its boundless lengths and breadths, and so that no one would need pay the price again that seems like death in expressing life and Love. Even as the early discoveries of electricity, motorized transportation and wireless communication had temporary limitations, so we thought Love had Its limits, but now we can know better. *Disease, suffering, hostilities, confusion and lack can all be forgotten, because Love can heal them all without price, and always could.*

Many interpreters have established theologies and rites that have reflected their particular ideas that all the Love that Jesus expressed was in his activities of sacrificing himself. And this has led to numerous acts of martyrdom for the single purpose of promoting sacrifice. In these instances, people died not to show that one never dies (which was already achieved and has therefore been evident for a long time), but to try to prove that their deaths were activities of Love, which they were not! Many other people gave several decades of their lives to help less fortunate people while they repressed their own worthy interests, not at all because they wanted to, but because they believed that God and Jesus suffered and that they could not feel good about themselves unless they did too. Myriad numbers of people have sacrificed themselves for others in their everyday experiences, in the name of Jesus, erroneously thinking of him as a martyr and not realizing that their activities had no similarity to his particular activity. Such everyday sacrifices have included: "nice" mothers denying themselves their own needs so that their young children could have more food, clothes and pleasures than they, and "nice" fathers and mothers sacrificing the legitimate desires of their "middle years" as their children mature, so that they could provide college educations or automobiles while the children barely expended themselves for those needs. Similarly, sacrifices have involved "nice" marital partners prohibiting themselves from expressing their true feelings while not ever conversing about their different ideas of how they could live happily together, because suffering their differences seemed more important than being communicative about the presumed reasons for not resolving the challenges they had. None of these practices have anything to do with Love; but, so far as love goes, these practices all belong to it. While Love is never sacrificial of Itself, love is!

THE CORE OF LIFE

How can we think of Love as untainted with the suffering that is traditionally associated with It? There is a way. It lies in meeting the Lovefriend, and because of the upliftment of that meeting, to then feel Love without thinking It is something other than It is. We achieve this as we separate from our idea of Love the belief that It is the result of something we have done or should do. Love is not what we do! However, Love comes through our willingness to do the beneficial things of life; Love does this to the extent that we recognize It is not made by us, but

Love is an everlasting Friendship at the center of ourselves

is given through our interests to receive It. Love is in our lives because It is the central core of who we are. Again, Love is not a product of something we do, but an everlasting Friendship at the center of ourselves.

Love cannot die, if we mean ordinary death. Because Love's Friendship is the core of all life, Jesus did not sacrifice himself nor was he sacrificed! He did not actually die! *His body was severed from his spirit and soul, and that might seem to have been his death, but it was not--because his body was simply a temporary vehicle which was no longer needed when people came to believe that he was alive without being in it.*

Jesus did not actually die; his body was surely destroyed, but simultaneously his expression of Love expanded his presence. Neither he nor Love were his body. He was Love, as we all are, but he knew himself to be Love, which most of us have not yet learned.

When he appeared to many people after the crucifixion, his body seemed to be representing him. And at times he demonstrated that he could be as much a human form as he was before. Nevertheless, it was Love that enabled him to appear in form in those moments and to seem formless in some others.

Neither will we die! Neither can we! But we can continue to mix sacrifice with Love and life, and thereby go on as before, experiencing Love as love. And all people who think this way about us and themselves must continue to believe that we are only alive because we have bodies.

The truth is that life is Love, and Love is never sacrificial, but always Self-giving. We have quite generally misunderstood this! It is worth our while to rethink the nature of Love.

Self-givingness is the high way of life that we discover when we cease walking the low way of sacrifice as though it is Love.

CHAPTER ELEVEN

LOVE AND BEING NICE

Can you frequently be with people who are addicted to the negative activities of life, and not merely act as though you feel sorry for them, but Love them in the deepest sense of your Self-givingness? YES, YOU CAN! YES, YOU CAN! YES, YOU CAN!

Most of us have "acted" nicely to people who are in trouble. We have not realized that the nice things we said and the ways we acted were not especially loving. When someone has an addiction and also experiences with it a lack of money, of employment, of friends, of self-esteem or all of these, such a person often believes that anyone who takes an interest in or feels sorry for him or her is a friend. It is not necessarily so! Sometimes someone provides care, but expects payment in a demanding, personal manner and only "acts" nicely to the extent that such demands are met. With some others, the only thing that appears "nice" is the provision of barely acceptable shelter or non-nourishing foods, given while even greater demands are made. Still others act with niceness and make no demands at all. Although it might seem that the latter arrangement is desirable, it is not necessarily true that any of these actions really help the problems of needy people.

Nowadays, we are often encouraged to break the bonds of dependency when a relationship has nothing beneficial within it other than the maintenance of the other's negative habit patterns. But most people who successfully let go of a negative relationship immediately attach themselves to another one....That which makes for a truly nice relationship, or a healthy and happy one, is not easily known by people who simply think they need it.

TWO WAYS TO BE NICE

It assists us here to notice that there are two ways of experiencing niceness. There are definitely nice things that happen to us in life, and we love to draw them into our experiences, but when we *act* nicely and hope others will *act* nicely to us, we are covering up our awareness that Love is everywhere that we are; that is not so nice for us. We are wise to discover how we can uncover Love within us by exposing the "actions of niceness" that too often cover It.

Everyone can be truly helped by feeling Love, but Love is ordinarily not felt if It is approached with a sense of urgent need. This is because the urgency of need tends to result in one's "acting" nicely. Right then and there, if someone feels sorry along with "acting" nicely, what they do appears to the needy as all the love they can expect to experience. Fortunately, there is more love than this; there is Love and It can truly minister to need.

When we act nice to others, we are hoping others will act nice to us

Having meetings with the Lovefriend is a wonderful solution for any lack, but as long as a needy person thinks that Love is only that which gives him or her relief, it is not possible to bring

MEETING THE LOVEFRIEND

the awareness of the Lovefriend and those in need together. The
actual solution comes when a needy person begins to conceive the
idea that he or she really has no needs. This can be done because
Love is Self-giving and always has a solution, and it is impossible
to experience It without needs being dissolved. But an openness
with Love can only occur when one who feels he or she has many
needs becomes willing to turn his or her attention to the idea that
a solution exists. Imagination is necessary to accomplish this; a
person in need can imagine a positive experience; it takes Love
to think this way, but even the needy have it within them to do
that.

   If someone in need does not change the idea that he or she
is in need, Love is only met as love. Then people keep appearing
who are not truly nice, but who "act" like they are; personal
disguises abound.

   The Lovefriend is the greatest of all friends, but It only
gainfully assists us when we are truly desiring to express life
better. It is not that Love ever refuses to give Itself to us, but It
will not force Itself upon us, and so it cannot benefit us beyond
the strength of our desire to turn to It. When we lie to ourselves
about wanting to live better, we cannot discover the Lovefriend.
We have to be honest and sincere in our desire to meet with Love
and to experience It!

   Since there are always people who will be "nice" to us, even
when we do not desire their help, we can always experience
people who care; but that does not mean they all are truly loving.
Many of us have had that kind of care when others were "nice"
to us in more ways than we wanted to handle. So it is refreshing
to know that Love, unlike "nice" people, will not care for us any
more than we desire It to do. And nothing better than the life
we have had can happen with us unless we "turn" more toward
Love's presence. On the other hand, if we do not expect Good
loving care, we tend to make ourselves subject to people and
experiences that abuse us; and there are always plenty of people
who will carry this out.

   So long as other people feel sorry for us and "act" nicely to
us when we are strongly feeling our wants and needs, we cannot

find a friend of any kind unless *we see through* their "niceness." And the same is true when we look at the reverse of this, those times when we are "nice" to others and "try" to help them to feel better, while totally ignoring their real issues. When we help them materially here and there, and enable them to but limp along, they cannot resolve their difficulties unless they can dismiss our attention as unworthy of their consideration.

People who "act" nicely feel that other people might be offended unless they overlook certain facts about the careless ways those others live. We can rationalize such a behavior as though Love requires it, but Love does not know how to be "nice," if niceness is conceived as the belief that really Good care is not available.

Expressing Love and "acting" nicely are not at all alike. "Acting" nicely looks like Love, but it is deceptive. It too often judges the nature of something by the way it appears to be. People who are "very nice" are often hiding from themselves the ways in which they feel insecure. The actions of "niceness" cover up their concern that they cannot be liked for who they are, or "those actions" represent desires to earn sympathy from others.

Acting nicely looks like Love, but it is deceptive

"Nice" people may be rescuers or victims. If rescuers can act nicely to people who seem to be victims, they can appear to have good qualities that they have feared they do not have. If victims can pretend they are nice to others in order to have themselves rescued, they can feel justified in thinking that they are unlucky, and that they have the right to get help no matter how low their situation seems to be. "Niceness" exists because there are people who are comfortable thinking they are victims and others who think they can earn respect by being the protectors of these victims.

If we choose to court Love, and to express It, Love never accuses or withholds Itself, even if we have character defects that appear again and again. "Nice" people have not found this out; they hope that it will be through their "acting" nicely that they will experience Love.

When Love is ignored, harm comes to us. This is not Love's idea. We experience harm because Love's Good ideas about us are not being discovered and implemented by us. The result is that the forms of sickness, poverty, conflicts in our relationships, lack of confidence, low self-esteem and *all* of the many other ways that we feel hurt, burden us. When we feel these hurts, we usually blame other people, events and things that lie outside of the awareness that Love is being ignored. Other people can always try to help us, or we can try to help them, but help does not really come through our acting nicely.

Saying that we are sorry is "acting" nicely to others, and it would seem that it would be good to do, because the people who feel hurt appear to feel better because of it. However, this "nice" action assists them in justifying irresponsible actions, leaning on superficial kindnesses, and then ignoring Love all the more. It is a mistake--though a mistake is never truly a mistake. This is because a seeming mistake becomes an opportunity through which we and they can come to see that Love is needed, and that through It, a better way can be made possible; eventually we all discover these opportunities, but not necessarily within a particular lifetime. *We only come to know of our greater possibilities when we choose to believe that we have them.*

People who feel that they have been hurt will become truly happy only when it becomes unnecessary "to be right." Our "acting" nicely helps the persons who receive the nice acts to feel that they are justified in thinking and acting as they do, and therefore, ordinarily they continue to ignore Love. All persons can, in this way, live in a succession of efforts that prevents them from greatly feeling Love.

A succession of efforts to do better can be seen in the lives of many of us. We may do something which we hope other people will like; we then may wish that we will be told we are loved because of it; but then, regardless of what we are told, we will probably feel we are not loved enough. Following this, we will ordinarily press the situation so as to be seen more in the action we wish to have approved, until people tire of our wanting their attention, and we receive negative reactions from them; the end result is that we cannot help but feel that we are not loved at all.

The way out of feeling the need for approval comes as we discover Love within us. But, when someone always appears from somewhere to help us feel that we cannot improve upon our undesirable actions, we feel trapped in what we do. And we build a dependency upon those people while we are still feeling the need to be approved. As we accept the attention of the "nice" person who excuses us from responsibility, we feel underneath it all that we have failed, but that at least someone is nice to us; someone's being nice to us seems to alleviate our disappointment at not feeling self-fulfilled. However, the "*truly nice*" people are those who do not ever say they are sorry for us, nor do they feel sorry. They really feel Love towards those who hurt and they communicate the sense of Love well to anyone who is open to Love. But, if we are not open to Love, we turn away from those who really feel It, or we try to get them to share with us their regrets about our experience of failure; the truly nice people will not share our regrets because Love knows as them that there is nothing to ever regret.

Until each of us senses a personal responsibility, but not blame, for each time we appear to feel hurt, we cannot feel very much Love. To be unaware of Love is not a nice situation. It is even less so when friends "act" nicely by telling us that we should forget how we encumbered ourselves in a difficult situation, that it is the fault of other people, and that we should leave it at that. Such behavior is not really very nice because it dismisses the value of discovering responsibility and disguises the presence of Love with the thought that people who "act" nicely are all the love there is; it dims the idea that we only need Love.

None of this should be misconstrued to distract anyone from being gracious, understanding and appreciative of other people. Being nice in this true sense is admirable, and it is an activity that is prompted by Love.

CO-DEPENDENTS AND LOVE

Co-dependents keep insecure people immature by putting up with their addictions. Until we realize that people who are co-dependents are also experiencing insecurity, we may keep thinking they are nice. But, when we understand their real experience, we see that they cannot help themselves. They "act" nicely in order to cover up their own inability to know that marvelous solutions are always available to them and to others.

Those of us who play co-dependent roles need to discover Love. Let us fully understand that "acting" nice and loving people are not the same. To feel Love is to cease "acting" nicely. One may feel Love and be a very nice person, but niceness will not then be faked when someone needs to face up to why he or she appears to be hurting.

When we *admit* that we are "acting" nicely to avoid the responsibility of helping someone identify his or her addictions, we are already resolving the problem of being a co-dependent. But how can we feel good about following this up by not "acting" nicely to that person who appears to be hopelessly mired in the negative habit? (To refrain from "acting" nicely means to cease supporting someone who is letting a negative habit destroy him or her; it does not means to act with rudeness.) Love enables us to feel good while we are not condoning negative behavior. Because of Love, no co-dependent need support a person who is habitually choosing self-destructive actions.

Meeting the Lovefriend on a regular basis helps us to resolve our own problems and to assist others with theirs. Until we realize this, addicts and co-dependents have no solutions except partial ones. Full resolution of our problems can only occur through Love.

Does this mean that all people who have *truly* achieved a resolution of a serious problem have already met the Lovefriend? Yes, it does. Meeting the Lovefriend is the natural experience of being permanently healed of any negative condition. *However, if the healing is not natural or permanent, we have not met the Lovefriend through it. Being conscious of these meetings is a necessary step in our evolution, if life is to be totally satisfactory. Conscious awareness of "the meetings with Love" will be eventually experienced by all of us in this lifetime or another. It is nevertheless true that people already are having meetings with Love in connection with every situation that shows lasting improvement. And it is sensible to acknowledge that some people express Love frequently without being aware that they are meeting with It. Moreover, it is wonderful that they are doing this. Whatever way in which we bring the Love within us into our dispositions and activities is Good.*

SURRENDER

We do not know how to Love without Love actually moving us into Its uplifted expressiveness. As soon as we admit to ourselves that it is not possible for us to be amazingly kind, in and of ourselves, but that we desire such Self-expression, the nice person that we are emerges. It occurs as we surrender to Love.

Unless we surrender to the Lovefriend's presence in all that we do, we will never succeed in that which means the most to us. This surrender is accomplished through attending Love's meetings over and over, recognizing that Love is our most essential Friendship, and our only satisfactory guide.

Being truly nice to others is the most amazing kindness we can achieve. Otherwise, our "nice" actions are co-dependencies. Let Love act through us without restraint, and we inspire others to accept It too. Let us say to ourselves, "I surrender to Love all of the ways I have tried to help others or attempted to act as I think they desire of me." When we are truly surrendered to Love, we

may not always act as others think they want us to, but we act
lovingly. Everything then works out, however gradually, for the
Good of all. If people become critical of us, let us not ask how
we can please them more; rather let us declare to Love that we
surrender these concerns to Its guidance. Find the way to trust
Love. If this seems hard, let us speak words and join feelings with
the words, that Love now is acting as us; let Love simultaneously
be our actions.

*Let surrender be a passionate action. It is the nicest thing we can
ever do. It releases through our best thoughts and actions the real
inner sense we have of Love.*

UNRESOLVED ANGER

Before we become conscious of Love's meetings and attend
them regularly, unresolved anger builds a basis for "acting" nicely.
Because we may not desire to confront in ourselves or another
feelings of anger, often we bury the anger. We may believe that
the alternative is to visibly identify in ourselves or another a
problem that cannot be resolved. Included in this, we may fear
that we would not be loving to ourselves if we admit we have
done something, or could do something, that is unscrupulous.
And we may fear that we would appear unloving to confront in
someone else a tendency to act unkindly toward us and others.
Of course, it really means that we have not met Love or have not
realized Love's infinite capacity to provide a solution to anything.

Because Love is never angry, It can help us, but not for a
reason we are likely to conceive. Love is never angry inasmuch
as It always knows of Its innocence. Love views all people as
innocent of any wrongdoing, but not because It is naive. Rather,
Love knows we can all act in the way that is best for all, through
allowing Its guidance to express us. Love knows if we have not
yet turned to It for guidance, that in a similar future situation we
will. The Lovefriend simply awaits our turning to It for direction.
It waits for us as long as is necessary.

We easily misconceive Love's nature by thinking that It is
exceedingly patient with us. For Love has no patience at all. This

is because patience implies that something wrong must be endured for awhile; since Love never suffers, Its willingness to let us slowly accept Its direction is not a characteristic of perseverance. Love resolutely maintains Its confidence that we are discovering It as quickly as we need to. There is no concern in Love about any procrastination on our part.

When we become ready to accept Love's solutions for us, any pent-up anger dissolves itself. We can attempt to express that anger earlier, and we may think we will feel better to do so; we will be less nervous and less irritable. However, when we meet enough with Love, anger simply disintegrates as our sense of innocence or forgiveness takes its place.

It may be helpful to confront ourselves and others to avoid co-dependencies and resentments; both of these experiences disallow our being genuinely nice. However, our better course of action is to meet with Love regularly, letting It tell us what to do or allowing It to act as us. Ultimately, Love will be known as the solution for everything.

When the Lovefriend becomes our source of caring for all we do, the need to "act" nicely disappears; we then become amazingly kind. This kindness is natural because Love is our authentic nature.

MORE THAN AN EXAMPLE

When healing comes to us, we tend to naturally express niceness to others, but not to make them feel they must be "kept" in their disappointing conditions. The more natural expression of truly being nice is Love's Self-givingness.

We meet genuine nicety and Love in people who do not try to change us. They are nice but not forceful. Their most noticeable quality is their example of victorious living. They have met the Lovefriend often, which is why we meet Love in them. It is wonderful for us to discover people who are this way, but not so wonderful if we think we can only discover the Lovefriend because of them. Fortunately, our feeling of Love never comes about because of what happens with others; we meet Love in ourselves before we meet It in anyone else.

Love is not discovered by emulating others. To be sure, we are given helpful or unhelpful models for emulation depending on what our family, friends and associates are like. We have a better experience of life as more people live by Love, and their examples are a good influence on us. Yet Love is not discovered and implemented except as we cease trying to be like others, no matter what they are like. Meeting the Lovefriend is only achieved within our own thoughts; therefore, meeting Love in other people only occurs when we have first met Love within ourselves, and when we *then* see other examples of Its being expressed. Nevertheless, when someone else demonstrates that Love can be well expressed, we become more enthused about meeting the Love within ourselves.

Meeting Love in others only occurs when we have first met Love within ourselves

If we really feel Love, we desire to give ourselves away and to do all we can to help others to be lifted out of their difficulties.

What we can do is to spread among our friends and neighbors the sense of Love's presence that we have. As we build our own awareness of Love, we can inspire them to know that we desire that they have joy, good health, confidence, prosperity and peacefulness in their experiences. If our interest is sincere, Love will emerge in our relationships with them, and these benefits will begin to happen. However, as was indicated before, people cannot receive Love from another unless they first sense It in themselves. Nevertheless, when we are truly nice, sensitive, tender and interested in others' success, our personalities, our practices of goodwill and our uplifted ideas *become attractive* to those who are somewhat near to leaping from love to Love. Even as we are genuinely helpful through discontinuing former "nice actions," so we also assist others by being truly nice. It makes a difference to many people who are still looking for Love, because they observe Its resemblance in our dispositions. Then they look within themselves for It more than they have before. This does not mean we can help everyone we desire to, to really feel Love. There must also be a readiness on their part. It does mean that numerous people around us will experience and express Love, but not necessarily the ones that we might think would do so. Of course, if we continue to grow in Love, we will observe It growing within more and more of the people who we know.

INTERDEPENDENCY

If as co-dependents we choose to be truly nice, and we seek to really Love another who leans upon us, a revolution of our thoughts, feelings and actions occurs. It is "our surrender" to Love. As this happens, we release relationships from the way they seem to have strangled others and ourselves. Then we are free! When those who depended on us are also ready for this to happen, we may maintain the relationship, but on a higher and more authentic level of communication. However, this is not always the case; as we choose to be true in relationships, some former dependents leave us and reattach to new people who will "act" as nicely as we had been doing. We are wise to let that happen however it does, because some of our dependents may not feel ready to be free. And because we will be ready if we have met with Love (especially if we are conscious of It), our sense of Love's presence will guide us to relate to other people in ways that do not cause us to try to provide solutions for them.

When, as addicts, we choose to turn away from our addictions and let Love act through us, we meet the Lovefriend. It happens within us as we believe that our solution to habitual actions lies within our willingness to trust that Love is within us as our best friend, and as we want a truly nice experience rather than a dependence on someone who merely "acts" nicely. The most difficult action we must take to dissolve our co-dependency is to accept "poise," thereby freeing ourselves of the thought that we must cope with life. Finding another "nice" person never solves this. *Love is found by us when we act independently AND as we take interest in pursuing our innermost desires to do what most fulfills us as individuals, AND as we discover we need not cope with life because we can regularly experience it with ease.*

We need not cope with life because we can experience it with ease

When we live in a relationship with the Lovefriend, we no longer need to have dependents or to be a dependent. However, we do not become truly independent unless we attend meetings while we are growing towards interdependence. Interdependence is the state of relationship that we have with life, ourselves and everyone, in which we have no needs except for Love to be poured through us in all we do. We all need Love, that which Love alone can provide us, and that which Love alone can give through us. When Love is expressed by us in all we do, we are fulfilled and free. No dependencies are involved; we then live in a harmonious relationship with everything and everyone. When we let Love be us, It only knows to give us away, and then we in turn receive from others in a steady flowing manner.

When we let Love be our primary Friend we discover a relationship that will never end. Love does not make us a dependent or a co-dependent. It would seem, though, that then we have made ourselves a dependent on Love. But we have not! We will never make ourselves dependent on Love because we came into life at One with Love. Love is our essential nature. Once we accept Love's resourcefulness and happily meet with It regularly, any feeling we may have developed that we are dependent on the need to feel love ceases to be. Our interdependent actions and Self-reliance take the place of all dependency. This is because we cannot be dependent on anything which is not dependent for its (Its) own Good upon us.

Love is not dependent on us in order to be what It is, such as is the manner of a co-dependent. And we cannot feel dependent upon Love because our relationship with It is only established through our releasing ourselves from the idea that dependencies need exist. Love's expressing Itself through us is our acceptance of the nature we have always had, but which we could not know until we let go of dependencies. It is when we largely accept Love that we have our best meetings with It. We are interdependent beings thereafter.

Love is nice; but It is neither the experience of "acting" nicely nor the experience of feeling "niceness" from someone who provides for us, because Love's actions are always whole, perfect and complete, and happen entirely through us.

CHAPTER TWELVE

LOVE AND SYMPATHY

Can you use sympathy to actually help others rather than to merely console them? YES, YOU CAN! YES, YOU CAN! YES, YOU CAN!

The greatest resource we have is the Lovefriend. However, simply being told that we can gain the Good of life by trusting that the Lovefriend is with us does not mean we will easily express Its great resourcefulness. This is because we cannot live with great awareness of Its presence until we really feel Its presence. Even as the Lovefriend is described, there is probably a general unawareness of what It is.

Stated most positively, we are all forever unlimited in our ability to express Love, power, success and happiness. But, until we believe this, we appear to have an absence of some or all of these capacities, and an inconsistency in expressing them. On the other hand, when we believe we are as resourceful as has just been described, we manifest the evidences of this ability.

We express ourselves well as we focus our attention upon our potentiality. Even as a new automobile has the potentiality to take good care of our transportation needs, so we have the potential to take care of all of the needs and desires in which we have a natural interest. Even as a car can function ineffectively, we can limit our expression of the Good we ought to have by involving ourselves with that which causes us to be ineffective. We can resolve all of this when we discover how we impede ourselves. A car needs gasoline, oil, grease, water and additives to perform well; a car ordinarily must not be driven where its tires and underparts strike something that could be damaging, nor should it be neglected when care is vital. We can liken the care of our lives to the care of an automobile, of a living creature or of anything else. Yet there are major differences between our care and that of anything else. Although we, like things and creatures, need care, we are spiritually evolved beings who individually and personally choose our experiences from our wants and needs. Nothing else has that ability. Therefore the care we need to take of ourselves is different.

To give ourselves good care, we must first take the time and interest to provide our various capacities with the support that they need. We do this best as we open our awareness to what these capacities are.

Our unique capacities are to make choices and to creatively express Love to whatever degree we sense It. And everyone senses enough Love, even though It may be love for a long time, to choose many actions, and to express some awareness of Love creatively. Every nonhuman creature also has some sense of being loved or supported by life, and acts with various behaviors that show evidence of its being provided for. For all animals and plants, the experience of Love and choice is provided through something within them that is more interested in maintaining their species than their individual beingness. That Intelligence tends to maintain a similarity within their species and varieties, while at the same time supporting human beings to achieve increasing individuality. The Supreme Intelligence individualizes us according to our conscious choices of the things that we desire to think and do. While we are being made increasingly different from each other in our activities and behavior, our human ability to express Love is enabling us to be increasingly harmonious with each other and all life. However, our experiences of increasing individualization and harmony are achieved only to the extent that we accept them; the act of acceptance represents a conscious choice; all animals and plants accept themselves, but not consciously.

We could reduce our understanding of this intelligent activity to a study of behavior as related to genes and environments. Yet, for there to be an unending evolution of everything that is, and a possible harmonious relationship of everything with everything else, a Supreme Intelligence has to be inhabiting everything. Through Its presence, Love and choice must coexist within all that is human. So, what is unique about human life? Is it not that we are free to direct our own expression of Love, and that everything else is directed more by us than by Its own conscious choice? And could it not be that our conscious capacities to Love and choose are simply the enlightened activities of the Intelligence at work within us?

OUR GREATEST RESOURCE

Let us understand that although the Lovefriend is our great resource, our interest in expressing Its presence in our moment-to-moment experience is as essential to our resourcefulness and to our wise expression of Love and choice, as is the fact that It exists with us. We express the Lovefriend well as we conceive of It and believe in It as an indispensable reality, and as we regard anything else as non-essential. This may seem like an overstatement of Its value.   However, any lesser consideration of the Lovefriend is an unfortunate understatement of Its reality.

For example, when an artist paints, sculpts, writes or otherwise creates an image, that image has, already existed in his or her thoughts. For some artists, the image may exist in an already complete form in the conscious mind; it needs only to be translated from their minds into the particular medium they use, whether it be canvas, clay, music, words, or some other art form. For others, the complete image is less apparent. In these cases, the idea that it is there can be associated with Love's presence and then entrusted to Love's bringing the image forth and producing the art without a consciously conceived plan for it. It then progresses until it "feels" complete.   In either case, the achievement of producing art arises from placing attention solely upon the bringing forth of the images. The only work is in the experience of denying any place in the action to anything else that enters the imagination. Love acts as a resource here by keeping the artist's imagination focused on the original mental image until it is well represented. Love does this because It knows how to represent "us" well. When an artist meets enough with the Lovefriend, Love acts as him or her in the creative process; Love guides the artist's thoughts, feelings, and movements expertly and spontaneously. To the extent that the artist realizes Love's role in his or her creativity, the finished work will be that of genius. The artist's faith will have enabled Love to be his or her inspiration, in the truest sense of the word.

Inasmuch as the Lovefriend is to be understood as our source of living effectively, and the arts are only one example of how we can express Love, we could consider that we only need one friend, the Lovefriend. However, it is good that we have friends, and interests such as work,

The Lovefriend knows how to express us happily

food, hobbies, sports and other leisure activities. We must simply be careful not to allow them to control the way we live. *The point is that the Lovefriend knows how we can all relate to everything, but It will not act as us unless we are first of all committed to It in all we do.*

When we let our interests support that which is most lovable within us, the Lovefriend spontaneously acts out our lives as us. And our life experiences then include considerable interest in these other things. Let us understand that food, hobbies, sports, other leisure activities and our occupation are all good for us, and right for us to pursue. We simply need to be committed to expressing Love first! Unless we appreciate the Lovefriend most of all, the other things of life will spoil our experience in some way. This is a restatement of something said a long time ago: "But seek first his kingdom and his righteousness, and all these things shall be yours as well."[1] The kingdom and that which is right for us is discovered in the experience of having frequent meetings with the Lovefriend.

We can all fully express life as Love would do. Those people who succeed do so because they are feeling Love for who they are. Now this is a form of sympathy for oneself. Activating this form of sympathy sets us free!

OUR ONLY PROBLEM

Most people think they have many problems. Certain people in their lives seem to be problems to them. Then at times, their cars, washing machines, refrigerators, television sets and computers break down. They feel they could have problems with water, fire, air and earth; often they do. Their employment, relationships, education and health seem beset with problems.

We can all fully express life by feeling Love for who we are

Yet none of the disappointing conditions that are ordinarily described as arising from the items mentioned are fundamentally the results of them. Only as a secondary action does an automobile or refrigerator break down. Simply as a kinder substitute for the experiences of severe harm that would otherwise occur, does a common sickness or usual accident happen. I mean

---

[1] Matthew 6:33 (RSV).

by this that when we do not place our attention on the Love-friend, and as we do not let ourselves become who and what we are, the ability to express the Good of life is replaced by the results that are natural to our other attentiveness. And because it is most natural to express the presence of the Lovefriend as the persons who we are, the result of denying this to ourselves is often disappointing, to say the least.

Our only problem is that we think a lot about the idea that we have problems. When we think that people will hurt us, that our cars and appliances will frequently break down, that we could have plumbing problems and that our health is fragile, we set up the possibility of harm. But that which brings about the harm is not only the idea that it could happen; we also become hurt because we sympathize with ourselves when thinking that harm could happen. Sympathy is a major link between an idea and its action. Sympathy can hurt as easily as it can help.

Let us be aware that we must discover Love more than we have, in order to use power more constructively than we have. We can have a great sense of Love, and support ourselves well, but what we do with sympathy either helps or hinders us in supporting ourselves and others. *SO IT COMES TO THIS: WE WILL USHER IN THE REAL NEW AGE OF AWARENESS WHEN WE DISCOVER HOW TO SUCCESSFULLY SYMPATHIZE WITH OUR "AIMS" TO ACTIVATE OUR MEETINGS WITH THE LOVEFRIEND, AND WHEN WE DISCOVER HOW TO CEASE SYMPATHIZING WITH THE CONDITIONS THAT SEEM TO KEEP US FROM THESE MEETINGS. WHEN WE DIRECT THE POWER BY THESE BETTER SYMPATHIES, THERE WILL NOT BE MORE POWER OR EVEN MORE USE OF POWER THAN THERE ALREADY IS. HOWEVER, CONSTRUCTIVE ACTION WILL BE GREATLY REALIZED AND IT WILL BE ASTON-ISHINGLY BENEFICIAL TO US.*

JUSTICE

The universe is fundamentally made up of Love, Law (the Law of reaction) and Intelligence. Because there is as much Intelligence in Love as Law and in Law as Love, we can even more simply say, that the unity of Love and Law is the whole of our reality. But we will not describe the reality of the universe well unless we also observe that there are fundamental differences in Love and Law; they are wholly complementary, but nevertheless dissimilar.

Love is in everything and is everything. The nature of Love is to give Itself away. The Intelligence of life acts with Love to know that Love is giving Itself away. And for the gift to be truly given, there must be something that receives it. This is where we come in. Although we are Love and could not be otherwise, because there is nothing that Love is not, we must at first not know we are Love, *or there could not be a gift.* The greatest apparent mystery of life is the need to discover who we are. Deeper within our awareness we already know that we are Love in expression.

All people are here to discover that they are Love. Even when the consciousness of our planet has largely been lifted, and many people have come to know that they are Love, all people will still begin their existence here looking for Love and a connection between It and themselves. All the while that we search for Love and for our individual meanings, we are taken care of by a Universal Justice. The Law of reaction presides over us and forever moves through us. Aside from the written laws of people, the Universal Law (another name for the Law of reaction) of life enables us to function. There is a wide latitude in It for our choices to be expressed, and to be seen by us as they are. Yet there is a "bottom line" of harmful-

It seems like a mystery that we must discover who we are

ness that we can experience by our poorer choices. This is because we can only stay alive through having some sense of Love. When our sense of Love is little, or when we experience love and have no awareness that it is but a lesser sense of Love, the evidences of "our only problem" are in the many effects that severely disappoint us. We may then realize that our disappointments have arisen because we are either doing or not doing something essential to our well-being. If we sense this, we may use our awareness right then to discover the adequacy of the Lovefriend. But, if we do not, we may plant the seeds of our demise in this particular expression of life.

In between the great discovery of the Lovefriend with Its adequacy and the lack of any helpful discovery for better living, there is a large "land of nod," where many people live for a long time, unaware that their only one problem is that they think they have problems. They live in this unawareness while they blame themselves, other people and general or specific conditions for their misery. Because they have not assumed the responsibility for such conditions, no lasting help seems possible for them. Temporary help will lift people out of particular

The problem is you think you have a problem

problems, only to drop them into other ones. If we are in this state, we can examine how we think and we can gradually improve ourselves. But we cannot substantially succeed unless we cease thinking that our environment or other people are hurting us, or that there is something wrong with us. Our greatest assistance comes from raising our beliefs to know that the Lovefriend is helping us whenever we firmly identify ourselves with It. And, once again, we accomplish this by sympathizing with our aim to know the Lovefriend, but not at all by sympathizing with the experiences that seem to keep us from Love.

The Law of the universe (another name referring to the Law of reaction) is the power of life, and the power acts according to the ideas of Love to the extent that they are felt, believed and declared. When Love's better and higher ideas are ignored, the power of life carries on, on the basis of whatever degree of love is sensed, and always with justice. But, since most people feel they cannot trust that Love is sufficiently present, and they do not like the experiences that they have when the bottom-line of the Law shows itself, they construct civil laws on the basis of what seems fair to everyone. This humanly established justice is an attempt to provide a fair and equitable system of justice for all people. But, as we all know, it has many inadequacies.

This in no way means that it is a mistake to maintain civil laws, human government and equal liberties. It rather means that no matter how the judiciary process is carried out, some people escape just retributions and others are unjustly tried. Consequently, life appears unfair, and sympathies with its miscarriage of justice abound. Yet behind and within these appearances and experiences, the universe retains its justness. It is discovered and regularly experienced by those who unqualifiedly know that Love is ever present.

Sympathy and law enforcement are two of the most evident actions well-meaning human beings employ to help do the work of the universe in the everyday situations of life. They are necessary actions; however, they could be carried out in a better way than they have been.

Sympathy has been largely constructed around the attempt to

protect people from what is seen as victimization; sometimes they have been meanly treated by others, and other times they have seemed to experienced hardships which appear to have come from their environment or heredity. Sympathy has often included the belief that something unfair has been occurring. When others sympathize with the supposed victim's feelings over unfair treatment, a feeling of care is often experienced by the victim. Sympathy, then, may become instrumental in bringing about a temporary act of justice, and may console those who suffer. Sympathy with the solution exists too. Later we will examine how we can use it.

When civil justice involves the courts, both the accused and the accusers hope to win their case, and possibly a substantial retribution or some protection. *Often the basis for a favorable decision includes the ability of the accused or accusers to show that they have particular rights. Their rights are ordinarily earned either by something they have done, or by their not having committed moral wrongs. This is all reasonable; yet it disregards that the basis for good experiences is more to be found in sensing that all of us are Love, and that no one of us can feel hurt unless we are largely ignorant of our nature.*

Because the degree to which we sense Love, or the Lovefriend, constitutes the overriding natural justice, sometimes presumedly innocent persons who only know Love as love cannot seem to gain their rightful benefits through civil justice, and even if they do, new misfortune befalls them. Nothing can be done about this! It looks unfair, but it is not! It is not unfair because the natural Law of the universe (again, the same Law of reaction) in some way finally settles everything justly. However, before a final settlement is achieved, a series of actions imparted by the accusers in unconscious league with the accused often takes place. About half of the occurrences benefit the supposed victim and the other half appear to bring him or her harm. During this time, the way of justice can be earned: by building up the awareness of what is true and by believing enough that that one's rights should be served, the eventual right action prevails more quickly. Credits toward a quickened justice can be built up, then, through an individual's belief that he or she is basically good and therefore deserves fair treatment.

There can be an even "swifter justice." When a person has developed a consciousness of Love during the above process, something even more gratifying occurs; Love immediately resolves the situation, and the one involved is empowered beyond their "earnings." The recognition of Love enlarges the capacity to gain just treatment, and a "flow of Good living" is set in motion. Some people call this the "action of grace." One's sense of Love for Self -- or ability to greatly believe in Oneself -- is then the pivotal factor for natural and immediate settlements of justice. This is another description of the "Universal Justice" introduced in chapter four (under the subtitle "Love As Justice").

When one truly knows of this, the experience of earning justice is replaced by "immediate right action," and Love right then fulfills the Law. In other words, Love's Way immediately releases the one who accepts It; but Law's action, when Love is known as love, is to act upon credits that are earned and stored up. And whenever we think we have earned some rights, we may have or we may not have; justice acts according to the actual level rather than the perceived level, of these earnings. Whenever we truly express Love, we neither think we have earned rights nor do we wonder about it; we simply know that we are in Love's flow, and that Law provides Love's interests.

When it appears that we are earning justice, actually we are in some measure being open to Love's truly just actions. Although it seems in this that we have established credits, a greater recognition of Love's presence makes us aware that a deeper justice is supporting us, and will prevail with us in everything.

This does not mean that someone can simultaneously do evil things, Love the self, and live free from accusation. Rather, it means that the Law of the universe brings to a person's experience that which that person gives out. One's original thought about what should happen to others becomes the indictment for one's self! That is, if a victimizer appears to give out evil, a similar appearance of evil must be received by him or her. If a victim wishes a presumed victimizer to be hurt, the victim must be hurt all the more. When a victim or victimizer has cunningly manipulated that one's circumstances, or for whatever other reason, has avoided experiencing what is owed him or her (from the Law of reaction), there may be an experience of success for the manipulator in that situation, but the Law of nature always sees to it that the action will come back in some other situation, and probably from a different person.

Ultimately, the chain of events in which the Universal Law brings retribution to all is replaced by a happier action, wherein the bouts of punishment give way to better human relationships and experiences. But this does not happen until there is, in one's consciousness, a great sense of Love, be it in this expression of life or a later one. In all of this, sympathy plays an immense part.

OUR SYMPATHIES

Our sympathies are a particular kind of emotional reaction that we have toward people, living creatures and causes. Most people feel sympathetic when disappointments occur. Customarily these sympathies have been accepted as good for all. However, although it may feel comforting to the recipients of sympathy, sorrowful feelings do not do them much good.

Sympathy, as generally experienced, tends to help presumed victims feel all right about thinking that justice was not done to them. However, nothing ever happens without the underlying Law of the universe's acting to bring about a balance of justice to everything involved. It happens either through the visible actions of our policing and court systems or in some less obvious-but very real-way, so that the result is best for all. And because this is not generally sensed, many people think that they have to do something more about it, and if they cannot find a way to handle a vengeance, then they long to have other people console them.

We need to take a careful look at all this! Whenever we truly believe that justice is not done, we are right to act in some lawful way to settle a matter. But, if we go on and on without getting much of anything settled, we are wise to accept that justice has been done; that what it all means is that *something we had wanted to happen to others was simply being done to us* -- and that we should conclude the matter, because Universal Justice will finally settle it that way no matter what else we do. It often seems difficult for us to accept this, and so some of us have to experience one vengeful action after another throughout our lives. There is something more effective than vengeance to settle it! We do best to take time to meditate on Love until we have a better sense of each situation. Then our experiences of justice become happier and easier.

In the meanwhile, our sympathies continue to falsely, though temporarily, uphold some lawful practices that contain little Love. But this does not mean we are unwise to feel sympathetic. If we cease feeling sympathies, we will become cold, and our sense of Love will stagnate.

Too many sympathies give attention entirely to the conditions surrounding the disappointments that people have. They are merely a compensation or consolation to people who seem to have to feel disappointments. To some extent, these sympathies divert attention from the idea that justice has not helped a sufferer in the hoped-for way. Some of these sympathies are used by their presumed victims to directly harm themselves. They build up the idea that life is precious only when friends are consoling, that life is a struggle, and that all the love there is comes from friends who care about how much they feel hurt. The wonderful sense of Love that can truly help us is missed altogether in this: Love is reduced to love, and it keeps us from knowing that Love and Law are helping us. *All sympathy that is felt when we place our thoughts upon the experience of being hurt, or upon the conditions that surround us, denies us the privilege of discovering Love as we otherwise could.*

It is helpful for us to become aware that sympathy can be an empowerment of Love that will lift us into a happy, healing, and kind experience of life. This happens as we discover how the Law empowers us, how to direct our sympathies to relate well to it, and how to enlist It for our Good.

Our sympathetic nature can either enhance or detract from the well-being of our physical bodies, our relationships and our self-esteem. This happens through the way that we think about ourselves. But, because our thinking is often borrowed from others, we discover what inspires us or destroys us as we notice which people it is with whom we sympathize. If we sympathize with people who have trouble and are ordinarily not at ease with life, we are inviting difficulties and disease to be our own lot. If we sympathize with people who refuse to experience trouble and live in ease, we are attracting happy conditions and good health. However, this does not mean that we are wise to seek only the company of people who have no problems. This would be insensitive, and we cannot build a consciousness of Love if we are calloused toward those who suffer. Our best action, then, is to image our associates who continually feel trouble as being more interested in experiencing constructive solutions, ease and serenity, and then, to also be drawn to a larger number of positive-minded people.

Sympathy is an essential aspect of Love, but to equate the two is a mistake. Dictionaries would have us notice that the person who is sympathetic feels an affinity to others' problems by being sensitive to their emotions, and that a vibrational energy exists between people who are in sympathetic accord. Inasmuch as the general definition of sympathy tends to preclude our contemplation of solutions, we need to turn more and more to Love and combine our sympathetic feelings with Its confidence that Good is always with us.

Acting through sympathy, Love will bring us into close and wonderful relationships with people who have similar dispositions to our own. Also, where we feel a maximum understanding of other people, a sense of Love helps us support healthy resolutions to their problems. But if we tend to believe that many people cannot be trusted, our sympathies will lead us to agree with those who consider themselves to be victims. Again, if we take the time and interest to deepen our awareness of Love, to feel It as It more truly is, we will communicate It by sympathizing entirely with that aspect of peoples' feelings which is aiming for happiness and success. This is accomplished by withdrawing all thought that we need feel sorry for them, either because of their disappointments or because of the circumstances and conditions surrounding their failures or disappointments. To achieve a complete helpfulness, we will then direct our sympathies to the thought that they are discovering Love, trust and confidence and no longer need to place attention on experiences that have felt bad in their lives. Especially if such persons also desire to think and feel positively about their situation, they will have it within themselves to access the Lovefriend, who can help them directly in healing any presumed problem; we will do well to sympathetically conceive of them as working through their thoughts and feelings to believe this. We will understand that it may not feel easy for them to think of themselves as having a means of healing "just any situation"; nevertheless, we will think of them as being successful.

The marvelous truth about all of this is that it works. It may seem unfortunate that, when we sympathize with others' feelings of being victimized, they will tend to view our sympathy as providing at least partial justice for them. But that is the point. The power that Law provides to settle something appears quickly when sympathy becomes involved. By the same rule, Law provides people the ability to transfer their own idea that they must find justice by blaming someone else, TO the viewpoint that Love is coming through them and acting as them, and that no more blame is necessary. That is, if we sympathize with someone's experience of being hurt, the person may appreciate our concern, but this does not help. If we sympathize with the idea that such a person can turn the event into the ability to trust others, this person will be helped if he or she is open to our presence. Carrying this even further, Love acts through the person receiving this better form of sympathy and rather instantly rebuilds that one's attitude with confidence, positivity and a new well-being.

If readers feel this form of helpfulness could be exciting, be aware that this kind of result has become ordinary for many of us who use it regularly. It means that no people need feel themselves victimized any longer, and none need to continue in any form of disease, be it physical, mental or spiritual. But it also means that we all have spiritual and mental work to do to change our thoughts from thinking about problems as though they must last, to thinking about the presence of the Lovefriend who is always with us, and to open ourselves in every way to feel Love.

LOVE'S LIKENESS TO SYMPATHY

Love does not enter into our tussle with conditions. This is because Love knows that no condition can harm us. Our acceptance that Love is with us provides us with the wisdom, resourcefulness and serenity to be healed of our experiences of feeling hurt by anything at all. Love never directly makes a condition change. When we recognize Love's presence and let It help us, Love simply adjusts our thoughts so that we relate to our conditions in ways that the Law uses to terminate our problems.

Love is never sympathetic with our conditions. The way Love is

We can victoriously rise out of the problems we have with conditions

like sympathy is in Its confident feeling that we can victoriously face the challenge of rising out of the problems we think we have with our conditions.

The Lovefriend is something deep within us that knows how to be all we truly desire to be. And It knows how to express our sincere desires, while maintaining perfect harmony with all people and everything, in ways that make for happiness, peacefulness, success, wholesomeness and abundant living. The Lovefriend helps us with being sympathetic insofar as we let It lift our sense of Spirit upward. Through the Lovefriend, we can discover how to live in a natural manner that enables Good to be experienced with everyone whose lives we touch. A sensitivity, receptivity, responsiveness and resonance occur with everyone with whom we achieve this feeling of close relationship. And the close relationship happens through a vibratory activity in which an attraction pulls together all who feel it.

The emergence of the Lovefriend into our outward life causes an irresistible attraction to develop in us that pulls people and experiences to us that promise joy, peace and abundance. The Lovefriend causes us to sympathetically vibrate with the highest feelings, thoughts and interests of others.

What we desire to accomplish, then, is to place our thoughts and feelings on pulling up the Lovefriend through ourselves. We desire to be sympathetic to discovering how this may be done. We desire not to sympathize with our weaknesses or sense of obstacles or blocks in achieving this. We desire to turn away from thinking of anything that might prevent this successful unfoldment of Love through us. We desire to express the Lovefriend and nothing else, to let It be us as It knows is best for us. Our earliest steps toward this accomplishment are to choose to have meetings with the Lovefriend, and to open ourselves to the high ideas It will give us and the positive feelings It will prompt within us.

LOVE'S DIFFERENCES FROM SYMPATHY

To the extent that we greatly feel Love, we will not vibrate with someone else's despondency, hurt, resentment, anxiety, hostility, inadequacy or thoughts of being a victim or victimizer. It is Good for us that when we let ourselves vibrate deeply enough with other people, there is always a perfect inward sense of their not ever having been disappointed, confused or fearful. But to find that uplifted affinity, we often have to take the time and interest to become quiet enough to know there is nothing of life with which we need to struggle. When that gets clear, we can say the name of anyone else to ourselves and find a troublefree and loving affinity with that one.

We do best to establish a sensitivity to any other person with whom we desire to vibrate, from a deep enough place within us so that it does not become a lower emotional experience for us. Sympathetic vibrations, until the present time in human history, have included many strong feelings that have been associated with the lower emotions, such as those of feeling cheated, abused and ignored. When we react sympathetically with someone to something we both dislike, we tend to build mutual feelings of dissatisfaction. Love knows a better way; Love inspires people who seek to build harmony with ideas for agreements. Love matches our thoughts and bring us into cooperating activities. But this will not happen if we make the customary type of sympathies the basis of our attraction. In the sense of the higher emotions, there is a connection among us all, a place of resonance, where we can all vibrate harmoniously.

Love expresses Itself through the sense of sympathy we have deep within ourselves. Again, Love is never hurt; Love is never disturbed or excited; Love never feels sorry, never pities anyone.

Like empathy, Love never enters into the feelings of suffering sympathy's disappointments. Unlike empathy, Love never considers sympathy's disappointments as hurtful. Love listens **through the Law** to the pathos of a disturbed person, and whenever such a person begins to believe that Love is there, It replaces the seeming suffering with Its solution to the extent that the person becomes receptive. To the degree that we sense Love greatly, we listen and sympathize with any person, but no matter how poignant and moving such a one's experience may be, we feel no pity; we are not in the least alarmed; rather, we place our attention on seeing the Lovefriend emerging in that person's life.

OUR CRITICAL SYMPATHIES

We have too long been thinking that we need to sympathize with people who feel disappointment by feeling their disappointment with them. We have too long been equating sympathy, as it has usually been defined, with Love. Feeling sorry for the abused is a form of such sympathy. Feeling sorry ordinarily means that we think he or she is stuck in a bad situation. If we feel we would like to help, but do not see how we can, we easily feel sorry for the person; we may even try to help because we think the friend is an unfortunate victim of life.

Sympathy has often been used to consider the experiences of hardship as obstacles that are necessary due to circumstances. Even if the circumstances are only there because the people who feel hurt do not know better, sympathy has often regarded that ignorance as necessary. Then it has falsely accused their environment or heredity. This form of sympathy cannot be a great expression of Love because Love does not have to cope with environment, heredity or any other circumstance.

This kind of thinking has been primarily negative. This is because sympathy has too often been an agreement with the belief that neither we nor other people have the power to be lifted out of conditions of misery, except as luck or money might be used to do so. When we have thought this way, our thinking has temporarily prevented us from inviting Love to find positive outlets through us that are commensurate with Love's qualities. Love knows that, when It is truly expressed, nothing can appear hurt, but the form our sympathies have often taken has tended to prevent us from inviting Love's healings. We cannot believe in Love as the great answer and also believe that such traditional ideas of sympathy are necessary.

When we desire to, we can inspire ourselves with positive thinking. It comes out of a deep loving place within us. It is already in everyone's consciousness and is brought forth by our recognition of it. It is the conviction that Love makes everything whole.

When we have not acknowledged the loving place of our thoughts, we have felt inadequate. Then we have turned to look for outside support. Our reactions have followed our disbelief. We have reacted to what is around us and forgotten what is within us. That has set us up to be sympathetic to conditions. We have often thought something was wrong in our communities because nothing seemed resourceful there. Actually, we have not allowed our latent resourcefulness to come through us; therefore, blaming some aspects of our surrounding community seemed to be the only thing we knew to do. Trying to change the community seemed like an authentic act of Love because we believed it would show that we care.

Let us analyze the reasoning of our sympathies. We may right now become critical of something in our community. We may think we are loving persons by setting out to improve it. We may believe that something we see as very negative should be attacked. The center of our interest is, in such an instance, a need to resist or change a negative condition. Such thought and action assist the growth of that which is negative and at the same time, reduce awareness of the positive core of Love within us.

Love is the source through which all the power comes into constructive manifestation. The only permanent solution to any problem comes from Love as the Lovefriend. Love is affectionate. It adores and takes care of all Its objects. But how can the affection and adoration of Love help the things we desire to benefit, when our relationship to them is entirely to attack people and practices that are associated with them? Love cannot help us when we proceed that way! Rather, when we become critical, we form channels for the lower use of power, not Love, to go to work on the conditions that surround Love's objects, so as to expand these undesirable conditions and to make them worse. This happens because the Law of the universe makes conditions for us that are like the thoughts we have of love.

Let us notice again that Love knows what is best for us, and that Love is the authority and Intelligence that uses power constructively. But Love is not the power! There is no forcefulness in Love! When we become critical of someone or something because we are sympathizing with someone or something else, we are circumventing Love's presence; Love is no less, but we are using Love less; power is no less, but we are directing power with a vengeance to hurt someone or something. That which we oppose will then oppose us. "What we resist persists!" Love is not drawn upon! But power is activated, and made to focus upon a condition which enlarges itself, simply because we have given it much attention.

FOCUSING LOVE

Can we direct Love upon a negative situation and change the situation into something positive? We definitely can! We can accomplish this by thinking of the potential Good in the situation. *As we remove our focus from the negative condition, and place it on the condition's potential Good, and as we think of Love and power working together to express and expand our experience of that Good, it happens! However, let us understand that when we simply focus Love upon something, we are not focusing power as such.*

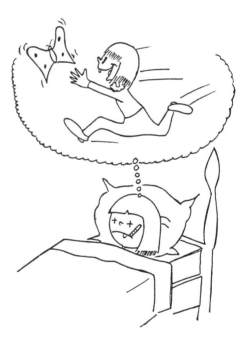

As we redirect our focus from negative conditions to positive potential, Love expands our experience of Good

We are feeling Love's presence; at the same time, we may focus the power to help something if we so choose.

POWER IS FOCUSED BY THINKING OF SOMETHING WE DESIRE AS THOUGH IT IS ALREADY ACCOMPLISHED. LOVE IS FOCUSED BY FEELING ITS PRESENCE AND FORMING AN ATTITUDE THAT IS HARMONIOUS WITH IT. LOVE AND POWER CAN BE FOCUSED TOGETHER, AND WHEN WE DO THAT, I CALL IT THE ACTION OF "LOVEPOWER." WE WILL SOON EXAMINE THE NATURE OF LOVEPOWER, AND WE WILL SEE THAT EVEN DURING USE, LOVE IS NOT A POWER OR THE POWER.

Before we look for the Good, and encourage It to emerge from a situation, we do best to seek guidance from Love. This is accomplished by meditation, by turning to the Intelligence of Love, and by increasing our sense of the reality of Love. Then, as we bring all our thoughts and feelings into the order that allows Love and power to act through them together, we can focus our best thoughts and feelings on what we most deeply desire. That order of thoughts and feelings is a channel through which Love greatly gives

The blueprint of desire
+
The feeling of Love
+
Power of Law
=
LOVEPOWER

Itself.

Here is an example of focusing Love: suppose we desire to know whether we should marry a particular person. We bring our sense of Love and our thoughts to a focus about the idea that the wisdom or foolishness of our contemplated marriage will show itself. Because we may have become very emotionally involved with our "special other," we may not receive guidance as easily as if we had not been feeling so much emotion. To focus Love on such a marriage, we do best to take a period of time -- at least thirty days -- to contemplate several times a day the idea, "The wisdom or foolishness of the marriage I am considering is showing itself to me." In this way, Love is given the means to rise through all our emotions and to expand our sense of wisdom greatly. If it is not wise for this marriage to take place, the sense of foolishness will soon show itself. If the marriage can be Good if we change our thinking, those changes required in our thought will be made obvious to us. Of course, we have to be sensitive to discover that guidance. We are made sensitive to the degree that we make the Lovefriend our closest companion.

Because our other emotions may strongly intrude upon our ability to focus the Intelligence of Love, we may not wish to meditate on the idea that Love will show Itself as wisdom and guide us in a decision about marriage. Nevertheless, it is still best that we meditate about it daily! Gradually we will discover that all seeming problems are not, in and of themselves, difficult to resolve. The only real difficulties that we have are the result of living too much in our lower emotions and contemplating Love's presence too rarely.

Here is an example of focusing Lovepower: let us conceive of helping someone or some cause in our community, and discover how to help that situation by beginning in the place where we so often are, that is, in our lower emotions. We first acknowledge our lesser use of sympathies, and then turn away from them, centering our thoughts upon the idea that the Lovefriend is One with us conceiving ourselves as being willing for It to show us how to better care for the situation. Then, as we focus our thoughts upon Love's solution and expect the power to act upon our thoughts as we desire, it will, unless we disbelieve it. Focusing power successfully is achieved as we think expectantly about our interest, and as we assure ourselves that, because of Love's presence, the desired result is surely accomplished.

As we aim high, the people and needs of our community will be pulled into the resolutions of that which previously had troubled us, or the person we wanted to help will find his or her way. We are wise, then, to credit the people or person with being loving, because Love will thereby be more evident. And because Love heals, we did nothing willfully to help; rather, we recognized that the presence of Love is there for all of us.

Here is an example of such a process: we can ably express Love by examining some sympathy we have; perhaps, we want to help some person; we may feel we can provide a solution to that person's problems by reducing the degree of involvement that one has with some other person in his or her life who has appeared to be harmful. Perhaps we may even conceive of separating the two of them entirely. Although Love can completely heal the situation, It will not heal it through what we do, until we change from being sympathetic with the condition of the relationship to a better form of sympathetic thinking. It would be something that regards both of those persons as feeling a harmonic convergence or a happy parting, whichever is known by Love as truly best for their particular situation, as It uses us to assist them. This is accomplished as we admit to ourselves the extent of our criticism, and then, as we see *anew* the people or the situation that had seemed to be at blame.

Because Love cannot, of Itself, ever hate or hurt anything or anyone, It will not choose to assist us in destroying anything, not even an enemy. Therefore, whenever we attempt to focus Love upon people or a situation, but think vengefully because we sympathize with someone's being hurt, our sense of Love is reduced to love, to a lower emotional reaction. Whatever happens from there is not an activity of Love, even if we insist that it is. But, when we use sympathy in the way most people have, we will not easily notice that we are this unloving.

Our sense of how greatly or minimally we are feeling and

thinking with Love's presence will ordinarily not be obvious to us until we become aware of our attitude about Love, or until the actions of Law become uncomfortable to us. If we make ourselves aware of Law's action but think vengefully, we will eventually notice that our life experience is becoming uncomfortable, because we will be recipients of experiences that are like the ones that we are mentally placing upon others. If we are really motivated to discover Love, and a better attitude, we will sooner or later develop a new interest in thinking higher thoughts and giving to all others that which is a kind action. A new awareness of responsibility will emerge; we will think and act towards others in accord with what we most deeply desire to experience in our own lives.

We are responsible for the way we think, and our responsibility increases as we discover and prize the way Love thinks. Our responsibility then requires us to see everything in a new light, with Love, and to act accordingly.

When we begin to frequently focus with a large sense of Love's presence, we discover how to express Love greatly. Focusing with a substantial sense of Love's presence causes us to become conscious of how to think better, to aim for positive targets and to enable power to function more beneficially in our lives.

The focus of Love is the form that our attitude takes. If we greatly sense Love, our attitudes will be marvelous: we will passionately desire our own and other people's happiness, well-being and serenity. If we sense Love as love, our attitudes will mostly be blameful toward others' actions, or blameful toward our own, and will not be helpful in resolving the disappointments in our lives and the lives of friends whom we may wish to help. *To enhance our ability to focus on Love's presence,* we must assume responsibility and eliminate blame. This may not seem easy to do. Nevertheless, it need not be hard! It becomes an experience of ease as *we make it our greatest interest to court the Lovefriend.* As we discover how we can believe in the presence of the Lovefriend, and as we take time to form a Friendship with It, our sense of Love grows. When we sense Love enough, assuming responsibility, thinking positively, and focusing Love become much easier to accomplish.

The focusing of power is different. It means that we attend our thoughts....that we believe we can have what it is that we think about. Unlimited power is always present. However, if we want to succeed, we need to direct it more effectively. We also need to think with a greater purpose. *BRINGING OUR FOCUS OF LOVE AND POWER TOGETHER THROUGH SYMPATHIZING WITH A POSITIVE AIM WILL THEN BECOME ESPECIALLY CONSTRUCTIVE.*

FORGIVENESS

As we *see anew*, we first discover that often when we have been sympathetic, we have fixed too much of our attention upon undesirable conditions. We then declare that we do not want to keep doing that! We notice that we have been thinking in a critical way, and we ask ourselves why we have developed such a manner. We reason that our attitude would be different if we were not so often reminded of something we consider unacceptable in ourselves. Something we did, or might do, disturbs us. Our attitude and reasoning about ourselves resemble the conditions we see and dislike in the experience of a person with whom we are sympathizing.

IF WE CANNOT MAKE OURSELVES AWARE OF HOW WE ARE ACTUALLY SPEAKING OUT AGAINST OURSELVES, WE CANNOT FIND IT EASY TO TAKE OUR ATTENTION FROM THE NEGATIVE ASPECT OF A CURRENT SITUATION. IT IS SIMPLY OUR SELF-JUDGMENT THAT KEEPS US FROM EASILY CHANGING OUR NEGATIVE MANNER.

This does not mean that we should cease being sympathetic! Sympathy is a great quality. It does means that we do best to let go of sympathy as we have learned to experience it from people in general. We can become sympathetic with ourselves and others without feeling vengeance!

Once we are familiar with our self-judgment, we become more able to sense Love and to let It help us to use power constructively; we do so by forgiving ourselves. It is useful to use a blend of thoughts

*We tend to speak out against ourselves
through our self-judgment*

and feelings to do this; if we take enough interest, and become sufficiently imaginative, we can substantially dissolve the blame and guilt in our thoughts about ourselves. We can tell when we have made considerable progress, by taking time to be alone, and then telling ourselves exactly what we have criticized about ourselves. We then repeat further statements of self-forgiveness. We will gain the most from this if immediately afterwards, we engage ourselves in laughter, dancing or other natural pleasures which motivate us to feel glad that we are alive. Artificial stimulants or depressants such as alcohol or drugs should not be included in this activity. They are unnatural, and they rob us of the ability to examine thoroughly our judgments and our thoughts of blame; they diminish our capacity to forget the past and to establish self-acceptance, which we need in order to celebrate Love as our healer. When we have done this so completely that there is no return of anxiety or guilt, we are ready to focus Love, to direct It upon the positive ideas that enable us to help ourselves and others in a constructive way.

Our forgiveness will be more effective as we additionally declare many times a day for two weeks, "I am letting Love act as me to forgive myself," and then cease using the declaration thereafter. This method of forgiveness will largely free us from anxiety, guilt and excessive use of the lower emotions. It will enable us to focus our thoughts, to govern our feelings and to trust Love and Law to act wonderfully as us, unless we continue using it after its original impact has lessened. If we do, its suggestiveness *may* give us a reverse action, **unless** we have built a substantial conviction of Its being helpful.

As we feel released from negative thinking, we then help ourselves to let high thoughts of Love take the place of those we have let go. Whereas we have often thought that Love could not exist or that we had to do good deeds, we can now establish a Friendship with Love and entertain Its high ideas, thinking of them as our greatest sense of reality and letting Love assist us in forgiving ourselves for previously ignoring It.

Love will always assist us in doing what is best for us as we focus our sympathies on the greatest potential Good in any situation. We can specify what that is by describing the most positive and constructive state of being that we can think of, something that is always the opposite of the undesired negative condition. Love assists us, as we place our attention upon It, in realizing that nothing unlike Love is with us; this causes a channel for Love to totally express us as only It knows to do. The Law will automatically do the rest.

When we sympathize with our own interest to be at One with Love, everything undesirable falls away from our experience. Expressing sympathy without having much awareness of Love's presence is often a painful experience; but when we sympathize with the idea of Love's being everywhere present, we are freed of all pain, because It is everywhere we are. Its unlimited helpfulness is experienced by us as we notice Love, and then as we meet with It. The experience of innocence replaces all need to forgive ourselves again, because the meetings help us to discover that we are Love, and nothing less.

Through attending the meetings over and over we come to know that Love's sympathizing through us keeps us focused on solutions. We cannot do this effectively without Love. As with "Self-givingness" and our taking the interest "to be truly nice," once again, let us be aware that we do not know how to Love until we surrender our lesser sympathies and let Love be our entire thoughts, feelings and actions.

Sympathizing with troubled conditions is an act of love; sympathizing with the interest to experience life's loftiest possibilities is Love's action that frees us from troubled conditions.

CHAPTER THIRTEEN

LOVEPOWER

Can you imagine Lovepower helping you and your friends? Can you experience Lovepower in an incredibly helpful manner? YES, YOU CAN! YES, YOU CAN! YES, YOU CAN!

Let us understand that although many people describe Love as the greatest power on earth, Love, as explained in chapter twelve, is not a power, or the power. To comprehend this, consider how many people in the last few decades have been spiritually assisted through acquiring the belief that "there is a power greater than I am" and "I am not the power." They have risen out of dysfunctional behavior through declaring this idea because the conception implied by this is that they are users of power rather than being power itself.

It is true that people who know they are not the power are spiritually empowered. This knowledge helps establish authority in them; and when power is equated with authority, it could be said that they have power. However, power itself is an energetic force that is the work that life does in us, through us and around us. Power moves through us according to our higher desires when we admit that, of ourselves, we cannot make our interests occur as we want; but we can make ourselves channels for power to function well through us. When Love is greatly recognized and felt within our desires, the Law (or the power) acts through us as constructively as we need it to.

In this chapter, I want us to understand that although Love is not the power, when we allow Love to greatly express us we are empowered. In order to know that we are Love, we do well to realize that we are not power; as quickly as this understanding arises in our thinking, we act as though we are fully empowered. Power is always in our lives, but the power is scattered or misdirected when we think we can be powerful without letting Love express us well; when we believe that we are Love, power is not increased, but it is focused and directed, and solutions thereby abound for all of our needs and desires.

Love, then, expresses us resourcefully as we conceive that we are Love but not power. Amazingly, we then live as though we *are* Love and power, but we achieve this by declaring the Love state as so and the power state as not so. As we shall soon see, when we become clear enough about this, we experience Love and power as though they are altogether One. Thereafter we may think they are inseparable, and we will be right. This is because we will have no further need to acknowledge that we are not the power as we will then have no intention of misusing it. The concept of Lovepower will then explain our relationship with Love and power. Therefore, I cannot disagree with anyone's statement when they declare that Love is the greatest power there is....unless they think they are the power. If we equate ourselves with power itself, our arrogance will make us less likely to seek guidance and inspiration from *THE SOURCE (LOVE). THEREFORE, UNTIL WE HAVE THE ATTITUDE THAT WE ARE NOT THE POWER, WE WILL NOT BE OPEN TO KNOW THAT WE ARE LOVE.*

Some people, without consciously thinking that they are not the power, believe that Love and power are inseparable. Most people have not achieved this. How does it happen for the few? It is because they do not need to move their consciousness away from the idea that they need power. If we know that all the power we need is flowing through us, we no longer feel the need for it; for then, unlimited power is already giving itself to us. When we Love enough, we have no problem with power. Unless we *know* that power is not a problem for us, we are wise to emphasize that we are not the power, or separate the idea that we are the power from our interest in expressing Love more.

Another way to grasp this is to simply turn toward our experience of life expecting that we have the possibility of expressing Love in a way of splendor. It happens to the extent that we have a great sense of the presence of the Lovefriend. When Love is expressed in Its splendor, there is a great empowerment of the people who express It. This happens because the Law of the universe, that which makes everything function as it does, actively enables Love to manifest all we believe It can do. But even when Love is poorly expressed, so that love is all that is sensed, there is no less power! The Law, or the power, then acts to enable whatever else is believed in, to be demonstrated. Whether the results of our beliefs are those of Love or love, at any given time they are empowered to reflect our consciousness of Love (or love).

Life's reality consists of this dynamic activity of whatever understanding we have of Love, being expressed through Law. *Great empowerment lies in the expression of Love's ideas; just as much power acts through love's thoughts.* Not all power is as greatly conceived; but all power is equally forceful.

If the Law or the power were to act only when Love is deeply sensed, we would have been living up until now in experiences of life that would have been rather unfruitful and inactive (because most of us have not sensed Love greatly before this time). It is clear to all of us that such is not the case; the power, activity, vigor and fruitfulness of life have always been present. But there has been a tendency, where people are involved, for the activity of our empowerment to contain more of a destructive element within its movement than has been understood or appreciated. When Love is not sensed, then, power is still everywhere active, but constructive activity is not as prevalent as it could be. *LET US NOW DISCOVER THE LOVEFRIEND, AND THE CONSTRUCTIVE EXPRESSION OF LIFE WILL ASTONISH US. FOR LIFE'S POWER WILL CONSEQUENTLY EXPRESS ALL THE GOOD WE CAN CONCEIVE.*

The authority that causes our experiences to be happy, successful and harmonious, is Love. Power that creates both our positive and negative experiences is Law, not Love. That which I call Lovepower is neither Love without power nor power without Love; It is the combined expression of Love and power, and is perfect action. Until we discover Lovepower, we experience

*Discover the Lovefriend, and we will
express all the Good we can conceive*

"lovepower," which involves the lower emotions and consequently is not perfect action. On the other hand, Lovepower is not only perfect action, but is the underlying cause of the Good experiences that happen whenever Love is giving Itself away through people who are empowered by It. These experiences occur as Love's higher ideas are thought and felt; a clear and untroubled channel is thereby formed through which Love is well expressed. Lovepower is also the perfect action that is the cause of Good experiences when Love is received without any intrusion of other considerations; in this instance, no channel is formed because Love is the entire action of someone.

THE NATURE OF POWER

Let us go back a few centuries when little was known about power. Then, people depended almost entirely on animals, physical strength and material means to do everything. Gradually, various mechanical devices were developed and mechanical power became important. It was not yet understood that great power could be harnessed through chemicals, steam, magnets, electricity, atoms, etc.. In a short while such understanding was acquired, and its benefits are now commonly utilized by most countries of the world.

The power of Law (the Law of reaction) could never have allowed the present rapid advances of these apparent physical powers except by reason of Its own nature, which is twofold: 1. The *Law is a reactor to our thoughts.* 2. The *Law is the complement of Love.*

The *Law reacts to our thoughts (1): The Law has always reacted to human thought in a mathematically precise manner.* But, since people have generally been unaware that they could use this reaction to benefit themselves, the action of the Law has occurred without their noticing it very much. But then, some early explorers of the idea that there are universal laws began to believe that they could discover a mechanistic universe that operated independently of their thought. They were on the right track, because we now know that the Law is always impersonal, fulfilling our wishes only if we believe It will. It cannot act apart from our underlying expectancies. The Law does not care what It does; It acts mathematically and mechanically, but Its actions are always reactions to our thought. Its manner of action is to serve the ideas we most embody or appreciate. Our connection to the Law comes through our use of the subconscious Mind, because the Law reacts every instant to the sum total of that which we think into the subconscious Mind.

Can the Law, or could It ever, act without reacting to thought? No, It cannot, It has not and It never will. There have always been thoughts telling the Law what to do. They have always come from the same Mind that we use today.

It is inconceivable that the universe could exist without Mind, because It is Mind. If the Law of Mind could exist without thoughts placing demands upon It, It would have to be inactive or dormant, because Its particular nature is to specifically act on thoughts. It does this without ever making choices about these actions.

It is true that the actions of the Law are carried out in many mechanical ways that we can observe. We can explain those actions as being the results of physical laws, such as the laws of motion explained by Newton and the laws of relativity described by Einstein. But that does not explain the basic reason *why* they happen. The reason why Law reacts to our thoughts, by lawfully doing everything that It does, is because Law is unified with Love; Love is a givingness and therefore desires to express Itself (or because Its nature is "to give," It has the need to be expressed), and Law is always serving the interests of Love (and love).

The *Law is complementing Love (2): Together, they constitute our entire experience of thought, emotion and life.* The Law creates forms and experiences that are like all the ideas we conceive, according to our acceptance of these ideas. All the ideas are conceived by Love; however, because we think our own ideas after Love has first thought them, and as the result of our generally sensing Love as only love, we usually receive them with considerable doubt and misunderstanding, and the Law provides us experiences that are rather poor copies of the originals. Law thus reacts creatively to our ideas just as fully as It would if Love contemplated them without our negative reservations. *THAT IS, LAW MAKES OUR CONCEPTIONS OF THESE IDEAS INTO OUR ACTUAL EXPERIENCES, SOLELY FROM THE DEGREE TO WHICH WE BELIEVE IN THEM. SOMETIMES THE EFFECTS ARE BEAUTIFUL; UNTIL WE KNOW MORE ABOUT LOVE THAN love, OFTEN THESE RESULTS ARE NOT SO PRETTY. WE CAN EXPRESS THEM BETTER SIMPLY BY COURTING LOVE.*

We can conceive that there could have been a more rapid revealing of Love within us, so that people would not have lingered as long sensing Love merely as love. We can presume that had Love made Its nature and values more immediately obvious to our imagination, we would have sensed Love's qualities more easily, quickly and completely than we have. Accordingly, by now it could have meant that our use of physical power would include more constructive action. We would then have already acted to slow or stop the destructive activities of war and planetary damage. We would be letting Love better guide us in our use of power. But Love has not unfolded Itself more quickly through us or as us, because the Law has been bound by Its nature to serve the ideas of Love exactly as people have contemplated them (rather than as rapidly as Love could have revealed the greater magnificence of Its ideas through people). Love could not have made Itself more obvious through us than It has or Love would have been forcing (not a manner of Love) Its way upon us; we would then not have been *choosing* to turn to Love's presence with free thought. However, had people before now responded more quickly to Love's presence, and believed in It, they would have expressed themselves more constructively and peacefully. By the same reasoning, we can *NOW* conceive a much more rapid unfoldment of Love through ourselves, and choose to believe that it is happening with us; such a higher conception and acceptance can resolve problems for which we otherwise could see no solution, and help to restore the planet.

We did not sufficiently notice Love's presence before now because we were ignorant of our need for Its guidance. But Love would not have been Love if we were required to accept Its guidance and to live by Its Supreme Intelligence; freedom of choice is inherent in Love's nature. *Love, through us and as us has a devotion to uphold that we CHOOSE to either feel aware of It or not. We can help ourselves today to make better choices for our needs and desires, by developing our awareness of what Love can better express as us. It will happen as we individually find reasons to appreciate Love enough to more completely express It.* We will have to do this without its being greatly obvious to us that It is our greater wisdom to do so; if it were more obvious, it would not be a free choice. For Love to give Itself fully through us, It has first had to *hide* Itself within our dispositions.

As we become more fully aware of how Love and Law work together to maximally benefit us, we turn more to Love's presence for guidance; that is, we lift our sense of love to Love and we think with higher Intelligence. As we do this, we discover that

Love and Law are unalterably intertwined within us, that they are all about us and are in everything that exists. As we turn more to Love, Law automatically reacts to our better thoughts, and life is experienced more wonderfully by us. Turning more to Love's presence includes that we take a deeper interest in both Love and Law. As we do, we discover major differences between them, although they work together for our Good.

Because Law is mechanical, It simply serves any use we make of It. But Love contemplates how life is happy, whole, successful, peaceful and abundant, and Law's service to and through us therefore includes our discovering and appreciating Love's objectives. To give all that It is through us, which is Love's central interest and Its essential reason for being, Love has made Its home within the center of each individual self. Why? *It is the nature of Love to totally give Itself through us. It is the nature of Law to serve us experiences that are like the level of Love or love that we have grasped in our thought and accepted in our feelings.*

What are we doing with the gifts of Love and Law? So far, we have somewhat greedily chosen to take what we feel we can have that will satisfy our instincts for pleasure and safety, and disregarded the rest. Once again, we are wise not to feel guilty or wrong because of these actions. We could not have done better unless we had met more with Love. Feeling bad about our behavior will keep us feeling Love as love. Whenever that happens, we are wise to tell ourselves that we have done all that we knew to do, because the higher wisdom could only have been better known to us had we turned more to Love's presence. So we are presently experiencing just what we have expected. And we can lift our future experiences by going to Love's meetings now.

As we let Love guide us and enrich our actions, at first it seems that we have found a greater power than before. Eventually we discover that there is never more power or less power, but that all the power of life is Law, and Law is universal by nature. Yet when we think, feel and act with a large sense of Love, power acts more and more constructively through us. Gradually we find that Love and Law can work through us just as masterfully as they have in the making of planets, stars, oceans and forests. They can act as though Love is power and power is Love; when we really feel Love, It actually shows Itself to be at One with power and power actually shows itself to be at One with Love. And when that awareness is experienced, we become constructive and loving in all we do. But until we have a large sense of Love, we tend to use whatever understanding we have of the Law only to increase our power to get things, to horde, to compete and to control others.

Where we go from here is up to us. Our possibilities include an even greater development of materialism or the unlimited expression of our Spirits. We do best as we focus our thought on peace and a positive life-style; it is especially good for us to focus on Love, that is, to seek the guidance of Love. But regardless of where we place our attention, we shall never lack for Love or power. Love and power are here to stay; they are as close as our thought.

ATTITUDE OF NONRESISTANCE

The reason Love is not power (although It is at One with it) is that Love is specifically the attitude we have about power when we choose to care about peace, harmony and well-being.

Lovepower is an attitude that is dedicated to harmonious living

Lovepower is the combination of (1) an attitude that is dedicated to harmonious living and (2) the power which enables it to happen. We cannot be forced to experience the attitude of

Love, but neither can we have world peace, abundance, success and happiness for all people unless we desire this attitude.

Lovepower is the right exercising of power so that the attitude of Love may prevail. Until Lovepower is widely used, just as much power will be used by us, but less constructively. Love's ability to use Law's power is natural and necessary because Love has no force of Its own. Still, Love's needs are not dependent upon force inasmuch as It has an even greater empowerment, that of nonresistance. Lovepower is the effective tool of people who believe that Love is surely empowered by not being forceful. Nonresistance is the most powerful action that can be taken, but it is not ever a power that coerces. *Love and power seem contradictory until we understand that loving is the greatest expression of power by virtue of Its not being power in and of Itself.*

Meeting the Lovefriend becomes the basis of understanding Love and power; through our meetings with Love we learn how to let life be just as it is. Lovepower acts through our willingness to not resist any-

Lovepower acts through our willingness to not resist anything, but to believe that Good is in all

thing, but to believe that Good is in all. An attitude of nonresistance opens us to the experiences of Lovepower.

ONE PRESENCE WITH TWO BASIC CHARACTERISTICS

LOVEPOWER IS A UNITY, THEN, OF LOVE AND POWER; LOVE AND LAW CAN BENEFIT US GREATLY AS WE CON-CEIVE OF THEM TOGETHER. YET OUR USE OF LOVEPOWER IS CURTAILED IF WE EITHER THINK OF LOVE AS WEAK, OR IF WE THINK OF LAW AS A SUPERVISOR. HEREIN LIES THE GREATEST DIFFICULTY THAT PEOPLE HAVE EXPERIENCED WITH THEOLOGIES OR TRADITIONAL RELIGIOUS TEACH-INGS. The idea of God, which in truth includes Love and Law, has long been taught without a full sense of truth, so that many people think of a being of Love that is not everywhere comple-mented by Law. They think Love must suffer, because It is beset by troublemakers who temporarily weaken how much people can sense It, or they think that Love is sometimes not as strong as trouble. Other people believe in universal reality of Law that acts judgmentally toward us; to them, God is not going to greatly Love us unless we comply with "His" demands, and only then will "He" give us all that Love can.

As quickly as one reads or hears the word God, ordinarily one or the other image (Love or Law) emerges in our reflections. It is as though a Universal Intelligence must either be weak "for us" or overpowering "to us." But, suppose we turn away from this traditional concept of God.

Suppose we discover Love as an Infinite Intelligence and as unlimited care. Now let us conceive of Love as being everywhere, including the place where we are and every other place we could be. Think of Love as something that can think and feel through us and as us. Accept that Love acts through us, and all about us, by our thinking and feeling high ideas and by our expecting and desiring that they can be experienced everywhere. Accept that Love in life is all of that, and that as we live with this understand-ing, we discover that Love is being us. Conclude this definition of Love by thinking of It as nonjudgmental and sympathetic.

Now let us think of Law as being necessary to Love, so that Love has a means to manifest the ideas of Good that It conceives and can be expressed and maintained everywhere. Conceive of

Law as serving all the ideas thought through people, whether of Love or love. Even as Love does not judge anything, so Law does not judge the people's thoughts. Law reflects the ideas of Love, including those of love, by creating experiences and things that are like the ideas thought. Law does not think of Itself as a Self or even a self. Law is a mechanical and impersonal action that enables Love to be expressed. Law takes nothing into account, considering nothing at all except that which Love, including love, speaks.

If we believe that Love is real 'and is the nature of the givingness of the universe, if we believe Law is just as real and is the creative force of the universe, then we have defined two very different conceptions about the arena of our existence. It is Good for us that we do this.

If we declare that Love and Law are One, somehow unalterably intertwined, and if we believe that, since we have defined reality, we are therefore referring to God, we are wise. One aspect of the God reality is Love; the other is power. Love is not power. Law is not Love. It is essential for our well-being that we remember this when we join them in one word. Then, when we speak of Lovepower, when we believe in It and when we let It express us, we experience something nonjudgmental that can and will do that which is Good for us. Lovepower only knows how to express us constructively; Law or power by Itself only knows how to express Its

Lovepower only knows how to express us constructively

forcefulness and does not care if It is destructive or constructive. We use the Law every time we think in accordance with how we feel our thoughts. But we only use Lovepower when we recognize that Love is with us, in us, through us and is acting as us.

The greatest thing we can do is to recognize Lovepower and express It. When God means Lovepower, our lives function happily, peacefully and harmoniously. When God largely means Law with judgment, we function with just as much power, and we can be very effective, but we must be burdened with stress and disappointment. When God largely means Love that must suffer because there seem to be forces that contend against It, we still function with just as much power, but we are much less effective. We worry about how our protection can be arranged; and although we may still believe that Good will ultimately win out, we unfortunately conceive that we must suffer, sacrifice and struggle in the NOW.

When we speak of Lovepower, we gain little benefit unless we remind ourselves many times every day that both Love and Law comprise It. This does not mean that there are two Gods or gods. It simply means that the great reality we live in cannot be comprehended in Its Oneness until the way we think about life is lifted much higher. But in the meantime, we can believe and express Love very well by recognizing that both Love and Law are within us and around us. We can also maintain faith that they are One, and then simply admit that the extent of our conscious-ness is not yet substantial enough to explain how they are that way, but that someday it will be.

As we think and feel Love and life this way, there are moments when we know Love and Law are One. When they happen we cannot amply explain Lovepower to a critical person who wants to hear It all rationally and logically, but we can explain that Love and Law are complementary; this will make sense to anyone who is ready and desirous to meet Love.

We can also become aware that Law is never judgmental; as we do, Its creative mirror shows us that It creates our experiences entirely out of the judgments and acceptances we make about ourselves. We can discover, too, that Love is not the result of suffering, but the cause of harmony and ease. All this, we can know and express RIGHT NOW.

The presence of Love and Law is the characteristic way that our "life reality" presents Itself within us. Whether we desire to name It Lovepower or God, we do best to think of our reality as being Love and Law. But since the lawful characteristic is mechanical, our meetings with the Lovefriend are our best opportunity to *feel* at One with It. *Recognizing that what we call Lovepower is that One reality can suitably simplify all of It for us.*

LOVE'S WILL

There are three activities of Love's will for us. All can be expressed in our own behavior, and we are wise to accomplish this. The first of them is to long for positive experiences to happen. The second is to choose experiences that well represent our individualities and to contemplate the nature of these experiences. The third is to imagine these experiences as being consummated. Lovepower is what gives birth to, sustains, and keeps active these experiences. The creativity involved is Law's method of acting by reacting to Love's initial activity. Love is the underlying causative motivator, and Law is the creative activator. Altogether, the results are Lovepower's means of expression.

The Lovefriend teaches us about these actions when we turn to Its presence with a willingness. Our individual wills have to become willing for Love and Law to well express us. When we are sufficiently willing, we experience Lovepower as making anything that we desire. When we meet with the Lovefriend, It comes into our awareness through our willingness. It is then that we long for really Good things to happen; we choose them in accord with the integrity of our inherent loving nature; we imagine and allow Love through Law to construct them. It never happens as magnificently when we have made ourselves willful. This is because willfulness is the attempt to act creatively without sensing Law's creative expertise or Love's guidance and presence. The Friend is most observed and the Law most helpful to us when we are in states of willingness.

When we are willing, we experience
Lovepower as making anything that we desire

USING POWER CONSTRUCTIVELY

We live in a universe wherein power is made available to every person to do anything we can conceive, whether we Love each other or not. Of course, we cannot conceive our best experiences unless we are aware of Love. Therefore, we tend to be somewhat destructive until we meet the Lovefriend; then we spontaneously choose to be constructive. Until then, Love has given us the privilege to be alive and to use Law's power as we desire. It seems like a risky venture on Love's part. Certainly, many people have appeared to greatly hurt themselves and others because they did not know Love. And yet Love is so very present that we are not likely to ignore It until we have irreversibly hurt our planet.

Although it may seem as though we have come terribly close to that, as we sense Love more and more, by our own choices, we use power very constructively; we discover Lovepower. This enables us to be especially productive in our development of further energies. The greater evolution of all of us awaits this awareness.

Let us discover the Lovepower, which enables us to use power with Love's authority; the Good we will then do with It will benefit everyone. We live our lives most effectively as we live with a substantial awareness of Lovepower, and we live our lives least effectively as we wield power without much sense of Love. We mislead ourselves if we think that acts of power indicate that we are loving people. When we are greatly empowered, be it for good or evil designs, it proves to us that we know how to direct our thoughts toward certain ends. When we are less empowered, but feel Love to an extent that is greater than our lower emotions, we have much greater authority; as we continue in this way, Lovepower gradually provides us with as much empowerment as we desire.

Let us discover that we can use our thoughts, whether or not we sense Love or love, to get the specific results that we desire. But, let us be glad that our best experiences of life happen as we increase our sense of Love, and as we express ourselves toward ends that are for the Good of all.

Using Lovepower is then the means for living the greatest life conceivable; it can only be experienced as we sense Love's presence enough to act with Its authority. To the extent that we know we are Love, that we understand Law and that we know we are not Its power, we are able to meet Love with the awareness that provides us with Its authority. Alternatively, we may live equally in magnificence by simply accepting that we are Love and that Love is power, while simultaneously having no need to act as the power except as Love guides us.

Lovepower is the ability to easily, successfully
and constructively express Love's inspired ideas.

CHAPTER FOURTEEN

BLUEPRINT FOR LOVE

Say to yourself, *"THE LOVEFRIEND IS EVERYWHERE I AM. THE LOVEFRIEND IS EVERYTHING I AM. UNTIL I KNOW THIS, I SPEND MY TIME AND ENERGY SEEKING, AT FIRST FOR love, AND LATER FOR LOVE."*

Because we could not be free if we were to *automatically* discover the Lovefriend with all of Its unlimited helpfulness, we begin our lives questioning ourselves and others as to what life is all about and why it seems love is not as present as we think it should be. Authentic answers elude us as long as we search for love. But, once we lift our idea to the expectation that Love is to be found within, our sense that love is with us becomes obvious. In the same way, when we expand our conception of the reality of Love to the idea that the Lovefriend is Love, Love brilliantly shows Itself.

For a time, through imaging the idea of the Lovefriend, we sufficiently satisfy ourselves with the awareness of feeling Love here and there. No matter how this happens, because Love is perfect for us in all ways, periodic experiences of It provide the happiness and confidence that make life worthwhile.

Some of us discover the presence of the Lovefriend along with our earliest awareness of Love, but Its presence is not as evident to us on an everyday basis as happens later on. The sense that Love is ever present may be with us from the moment of our first meeting with the Lovefriend or It too may come and go. Others of us have no awareness of the Lovefriend until Love has been obvious to us for many years. It is not an important difference, however this occurs. All that means anything as regards Love, is that all people are evolving a great sense of It, and that we will all become aware of the Lovefriend somewhere in our evolving awareness of Love. Of course, many people will not do that in this lifetime. And for those who disbelieve that immortality is an aspect of existence, a sense of feeling secure about Love, and the possibility of expanding a friendship with It may seem dim. Consequently, some people may spend this present lifetime only searching for an experience of Love now and then, or only searching for love or in some instances, questioning that love can even greatly be.

Believing that we have been alive before and that we will be alive after this lifetime is completed, is a challenge to many people. The amazing thing about it is that many who sense Love to a considerable degree are atheistic or agnostic. An everlasting life ordinarily seems impossible or dubious to them. Still, if Love for them is sensed enough, even they will come to the realization that of Itself Love is something that is forever; and the idea that Love carries us on from one life to another eventually will build into some of their philosophies. However, discovering Love is generally more directly linked to believing that life is not a lucky interruption of nonexistence. Our meeting the Lovefriend removes all doubts of whether the Love within life is a continuum.

The most significant point we need to know about our various awarenesses pertaining to love, Love, the Lovefriend and Lovepower is that we are all evolving an increasing sense of Love, and that therefore, if we regularly contemplate the idea of the Lovefriend, we cannot fail to reveal Love to our doubts, and sooner or later the awareness of the Lovefriend also. It is a natural unfoldment of our consciousness. But, nature may be slow to show us the Lovefriend unless we image It frequently and build our expectancies. This is because we would not be free if we experienced something that we had not chosen. We must choose to believe the Lovefriend exists before It will make Itself evident.

Many things that we experience are explained by us according to how they appear. When they are physically apparent, we see them according to how we have learned to think about things.

If they have no physical appearance in and of themselves, such as love or Love in Love's abstract definitions, we judge them according to how we think that they could feel to us. If no one else tells us how they feel, we can only imagine how they might feel before we describe them.

EARLY IMAGES

It may seem mysterious that the Lovefriend's presence can be felt by anyone; yet, it is natural and normal, because sensing the Lovefriend is simply being aware of Love as It most truly is. It will not happen as long as we try to figure out who we are or what we should be doing, or by our doubting that something in us already knows our mission for being alive. *The means through which we open ourselves to the awareness of the Lovefriend lies in our believing that something in ourselves knows how to think, feel and take action in the ways that are best for us. Because that something is the Lovefriend, in opening ourselves to this idea of It, we establish the means to be evolved into an awareness of Its being with us.*

When we conclude that our own calculations about life have not explained it well, and when we expect a deeper and better answer to emerge from within us, we discover Love speaking through us and as us. We then feel that the understanding that comes from the depth of our beings is from something that seems like a Friendship of Love. When this much is felt, the oneness with the Friend is greatly building itself.

At first, we think that the Lovefriend must exist because It is a sensible explanation of the way life's Intelligence could best communicate Itself. Or we feel that the Lovefriend must be with us in everything we do because life gradually feels friendlier; we feel protected by an unseen presence which we presume is in someway the greatest reality of all. We do not think or feel this way very long before some kind of image shows itself; the image but briefly appears; still, it deeply impresses us. Or within our imagination of the Lovefriend, "something of Love" is conceived as being more authentic than contrary thoughts about it. The Lovefriend is sensed in one way or the other, depending on the particular nature of our personality.

These early meetings of the Lovefriend are real to us; however, we cannot sufficiently describe their reality to other people who have not yet evolved their interests to be One with Love. The meetings are not ordinary and therefore appear not to be explainable to them. Other people can even make us question the wisdom of our saying that such meetings have occurred. *Yet we will always know that they happened.* Perhaps it is best that we keep them somewhat private, for a secret knowledge of how happiness and well-being come about is easily prized; and the early gained sense of Love's presence is more treasurable than our being bantered about by the public. However, in time, some people will truly desire to discover Love's meetings, and will approach the subject with this in Mind. As we let Love assist us, we will know how to share the way.

A good way to begin to prepare ourselves to experience the presence of the Lovefriend's image is in our talking with ourselves while looking in a mirror. If we practice this everyday, the Lovefriend's image will gradually become apparent. In this preparation, we are wise to clarify the nature of the image. Some people will actually observe both their reflection and still an extra image, as though it is moving in and out of the physical body, but others of us will find the image entirely that of an idea, yet one that will become more definitely believed simply by doing the exercise. *It does not make any difference if we see an additional image or if we think of the Lovefriend as an image which we simply believe could be; either way, the Lovefriend has meetings with us.*

Look in the mirror and tell your reflection that it is your inner Friend. Then "act" like the idea that a mirror-image can speak back. This is not an act such as when you *try* to do something--for that is what you do when you disbelieve. This is the action of listening to something within yourself which is always telling you that you have Its constant companionship. The idea of the "Friend image" hearing you speak, and of Its speaking with you, is imaginative to say the least. Since images are made from imagination, what you see and hear with your physical eyes and ears is less significant to you than what you imagine would be

Good for you to observe. None of this is meant to replace common sense and usual speech, hearing or other awarenesses. It is meant to complete your experiencing life by including all the words, images, symbols and objects your entire sense of life makes possible for you to recognize. The Lovefriend can use your usual ways of relating to life AND It can heighten your sense of everything, while increasing your awareness of images based upon the greater reality of Love.

Although a mirror may become your most tangible method to achieve the awareness that an inner Friend is always there for you, you can achieve the meeting in other ways. You can feel the presence through your discovering somewhere deep within yourself an adequacy you

Tell your reflection that it is your inner friend; then "act" like the mirror can speak back

never knew you had. Especially if you were born into a family where it seemed that you would not be able to compete with a popular brother or sister or that you would never be able to copy the example of a successful father or mother, you may feel inadequacy. Love is a high level of adequacy which waits for you to talk with It, so that you can overturn your false idea of inadequacy. Such "high level" adequacy *is* the Lovefriend.

LOVE BROUGHT ME ADEQUACY

My first distinct experience of the Lovefriend came in my youth. As I described earlier in this book, I turned from the conditions of a teenage romance and found the Lovefriend simply waiting for me to experience Its Love *as* me. Before the experience, I had but dimly noticed that something within me of high character was standing or sitting near me wherever I went. It desired to escort me into a growth of spiritual splendor. It was a prototype of what I was to be. I was generally oblivious of it until sixteen years of age.

The experience came to me at a time when I was feeling sorry for myself. I felt little approval from my family and peers. Moreover, I was severely judgmental of myself; no one around me seemed just right either. I was quiet about it. My awareness of the world was troubling me, and I kept it to myself.

I never really was an unhappy child, nor did I ever think to abuse myself. I believed life was very good. But I also felt I was letting my family and my peers down. I tried to be a good person but I feared I could not be good enough. This was because I did not feel I had an adequate identity. I did not realize then that people who felt like I did were everywhere I went.

That first experience of my meeting the Lovefriend was my resolution of apparent trouble that I originally felt in an incident that occurred on the day of my birth. I was to have been a girl named Rose Marie. My parents planned for a girl and Rose Marie was preselected as my name. After my birth, they discussed this with friends and selected a new name. The experience of choosing a new name became the basis of what they thought was a humorous story that they told to me and to others.

On hearing the story over and over, I came to feel that I was initially a failure. I felt I had to find someway to correct this. I reasoned that if I had been a girl I would have been all right. But I was not a girl. Therefore I concluded that my birth disappointed the people whom I prized the most. But what could I do? I was also feeling that my family was giving me but little attention. I had an older brother and sister; my brother received the most attention; my sister and I were taught that he was great and that it was special for our family that one of us was great.

The strongest thoughts I had about myself were that I was inadequate and worthless. Then, while yet a very young boy, somewhere between the ages of seven and ten, I thought of a way to solve my presumed problem. I would make myself worthy and adequate by marrying a girl by the name of Rose Marie. I felt that would make me complete and satisfy my idea of the requirements I believed my family had for me. That plan sank deeply into my thoughts.

I had no way of feeling certain that I would be adequate because of my plan. I simply hoped I would be. I put as much of my confidence as I felt I could muster into the naive idea.

By the time I was some past ten years of age, I was already feeling quite frustrated, for I had not met any girl by that name. As the years passed, I felt increasingly anxious. As a young boy I knew I would not even want to marry anyone for a long time, but I wanted to at least know that the girl who could fulfill me existed, and where it was that she would be.

At the age of sixteen, I met "my" Rose Marie. I dated her several times, and I was immediately convinced that she was the one for me. I had dated various girls, and I had been turned down by several also. But, when my Rose Marie ceased dating me, her refusal became my personal trauma.

Late on a Friday evening, when it was clear to me that she was definitely not going out with me anymore, I returned to my home from a party. I quietly slipped into my upstairs bedroom and there spent several hours, most of the time in tears, because of my disappointment.

I felt a poignant sense of self pity and I talked repetitively to myself about my discouragement. I told myself I saw no valid reason for my Rose Marie to turn away from me. I was certainly a gentleman and generous; I had even provided an automobile for our dates (which was considered special in those times and in the actual small town where it all happened). However, the question of why it was that she did not want to see me again was less important to me than the one of how I was going to establish my sense of sufficiency. I was only partly aware of having that thought. But, I was very aware that I was putting stock in the idea that something was shattering my sense of ego. I felt a lack of confidence; that part was a terribly conscious experience. On the other hand, the only way that the evidence of my inadequacy became obvious to me was in an even more emotional manner; I felt it, and then I did not; I felt it again, and then I did not. But, the empty feeling kept coming back. On and on, I cried. Never have I felt myself so full of anguish.

As I moved back and forth between conscious and unconscious states of mind, I was telling myself that the only opportunity I had ever found where I could feel I would be all right had been taken from me, and that I was feeling serious regrets for having tried to achieve it. My thoughts were entangled with very intense feelings of my frustration. It was so very real that I was constantly shaking. I can remember, that after some period of time, I began to feel so much inadequacy that I gave up the consideration that there could be any solution for me that contained common sense.

I cried continuously for about two hours; I then breathed a thought as though it concluded the matter. After all, what could I do? It seemed hopeless!

What happened next could not have occurred except that I changed my feelings from caring about the relationship with the girl to not caring that it could not now be. Love used my thoughts as a channel for its greater expression through me. It was because I let go all sense that the situation in any way remained important to me.

Quite suddenly, I found myself coming into a completely different experience! My tears rather instantly dried up. My mouth opened with a very big smile. I laughed and laughed. Shivers went up and down my spine. I felt so good that I spoke with a quickness. I felt enthused about my self-identity, because I was rapidly becoming aware that my life had a wonderful mission.

Love poured through me. Peace of Mind filled me. My entire body felt ecstatic with a joyousness unrivalled in all the experiences I had known before.

What happened to me was that for the first time in my life, I turned my thoughts to the idea that something, call it God, or Love, or whatever--was talking with me and giving me a new direction. I had been raised to believe in God. I had often said memorized prayers. But for the first time, I just simply found myself talking with this invisible presence as though It was interested in me and in resolving my problem.

I probably thought of my invisible partner as being with me from the moment that I came into the room. After I had poured out everything I could think to say, after I had cried until my eyes were very reddened, I found It speaking with me. It used my thoughts and my lips. It simply assured me that all was well. It was entirely all right that Rose Marie had turned away from me. Surprisingly, I did not question her withdrawal any longer. I now knew my life was functioning perfectly. There was nothing

w r o n g . Nothing had ever b e e n w r o n g . This archetype of me was assisting me to s e e m y whole life in a new way. The old ideas were discarded with ease. It was easy to do because I was being given an idea that I

We can exchange a lower idea of Love for a higher idea of Love

was adequate, that I had worth, that life was as great as it could be, through me. *I was exchanging an old idea that had never worked well for me, for a higher idea, actually a much older idea of me; I instantly knew it was to enable my life to be happy and whole.*

It was then that I became clear about my Friend. I knew I

was talking with Love. It also felt like what I had conceived that God would be. But Love was the best way to describe it. I called it God and Father and by other names. Still I identified it most of all as Love. I knew then, that everybody has this Friend; perhaps the Friend would feel somewhat different for different people; yet I knew Love is everyone's Friend. Love was coming from within me, and at the same time was surrounding me. The room was thick with Love. I could really feel Love! This feeling gave me more confidence than anything else ever would or could!

I soon announced to myself that I desired to help other people feel this Love. I wanted to assist them to experience and enjoy the same deeply-felt serenity and well-being. Then I confidently told myself I was to be a wonderful minister; I was to teach people about Love and everything It means. These people would feel Love on a high level where they could find out what It really means.

The experience lasted for many hours. Then I closed my eyes; my thoughts became less conscious; a very restful sleep followed. On the dawn of the next day, I discovered an incredible capacity in myself. I was greatly interested in improving my education, to Love people and to appreciate the opportunities of my life. I was assisted from within myself to set out to do these things and I accomplished them with ease.

Every evening afterwards, I walked for an hour. I had never done this before. I found places to walk where I was alone--so far as people were concerned. Yet I felt myself in the company of Love. I talked with It wherever I walked. I listened as It told me who I was and what I was to do with my life.

I realized that Love was not separate from me; Love was not even some small part of me. Love was my real nature, and had always been watching out for me--from within me.

The more I talked with this inner sense of Friendship then the more I felt Love. Wonderful results followed this. There were numerous magnificent healings, both of myself and other people in my life. Did I believe I could lift up my lower ideas about life and myself? There is nothing I believed more! Moreover it became an everyday experience.

TURNING OUR LIVES AROUND

I am convinced that all of us are sheltering magnificent solutions *within* our sense of disappointments. The opportunities of joy, adequacy and direction are waiting for us to join them. They are within *Love,* which is the place of our deeper feelings and thought. We have waited long enough to make the discovery that we can meet with the Lovefriend, and that Love desires to express us far better than we know to do without our being aware of It.

We need wait no longer! *Love* encourages us to become who we have always been. As we look up, as we expect joy and peace, as we find our mission for being, we are attended by our Friend.

Let us be aware that all of life always becomes more of what we see it to be. Let us know that *Love* through Law is making our thoughts and our interests come true. Our attention is watched by *Law*; the experiences of our lives are being crafted out of Law's reactions to the choices we make with the Lovefriend or love.

Love is a high emotion. Because of It, we need no longer judgmentally react to the way other people and our environment seem to be. *Love* is reaching through us to give us away.

As we give of ourselves to everyone, our strengths become known to us. As we give of ourselves, we quickly learn what we give best. *Love* is with us in giving more and more of what we give best because *Love* is our Friend. This makes us into persons of power. And always, we receive a likeness to that which we give, and that which we gain is more than we supply.

We must keep looking at our potentiality if we desire to fully lift up our experience of Love. However, if we keep thinking that what our five senses tell us is all that there is to know, we cannot be lifted up from love. We must change that way of viewing reality or stay stuck in our disappointments. It comes down to this: "No one can serve two masters....You cannot serve God and mammon."[1] Choose this day to serve Love.

What will this be like for you?

Love as you, feels your ideas and your intents about them; It then serves you experiences as copies of what It has felt of you. Love does this because Love wants you to have what you think you desire.

How about this kind of response? Let yourself really feel Love in your life. Then serve Love the kind of life you find It to be.

The feeling at first, that I was experiencing the emotion of love with Rose Marie, gave way to the feeling that I had lost my love. This is the usual pattern of all transmutations. There is a sense of thinking that we are losing something we have. Feeling that kind of disappointment either ends with a sadness that remains unhealed or a transmutation takes place. Our experiences have been full of instances where we chose to believe no

Everything changes for the better when we believe something within us has a resolution

answer was available. Here is where we can do our most definite personal work. *We can come to know that in what we fear to lose there is contained the resolution. It is in there somewhere.*

Everything changes for the better when we believe something within us has a resolution!

---

[1] Matthew 6:24 (RSV).

THE BLUEPRINT

What is this Love within us? It is the original idea of who we are. There is a simple activity we all can learn. We can visualize the idea of a person (the Lovefriend) who looks like us; we can tell ourselves It is there within us; It goes with us all our days on earth. It is like the blueprint of every building that is well-constructed. Contractors do their best work when they study well the blueprints and build a good likeness of them. We must do the same if we are to feel adequate and realize fulfillment. That is, our adequacy is realized as we develop our lives out of an expectancy that we have a Lovefriend.

When we begin to think we could not be on planet earth without a map, we understand ourselves better than ever before. As we begin to think there is an ideal person from whom we are being made, we think correctly. As we sit somewhere, we should always feel our Friend sitting by us. As we walk, we should believe our Friend is at our side, or behind us, or walking in our body in the way we are. We should think this way because it is true about us.

As we believe that there is an inner person with us wherever we go, we also do well to remind ourselves that this inner person is perfect. As we think it, as we let ourselves feel it, at times we find our lives functioning perfectly. This is because Love has found in these thoughts the way to be us as we are. Then Love builds in us a majesty.

Those times that Love is realized majestically by us come and go for awhile. At first it is as mysterious to us that they go as that they come. Then we study how we may establish our feeling of Love and how we may keep the feeling. Gradually we find the way to bring this sense of Love out of us more often. Eventually the feeling stays for long periods.

Love's action as us and our acceptance of It, become habitual when we cease chasing after It. Visualizing Love as the person we really are is not chasing after Love. It is becoming still enough in our thoughts and very focused so as to let Love rise up from within us. We do this best as we cease searching, as we simply believe Love is there. It is natural to Love others and to feel Love within ourselves. All that is ever unnatural is for us to try to make it be. Love is felt by us as ever present when we are convinced Love could be no other way.

Love wells up and bursts forth from within us because It is the way life is best felt by us. The way we feel about ourselves determines how authentic this awareness of Love is. Love comes from within us; we provide our own experience of Love; as we do, we come to know Love is outside of us too. But we cannot know Love anywhere around us, in Its real majesty, until we let It rise up within us and show us that It is everywhere. As we do, we provide Love great channels of action that release a mighty sense that people can feel of It all over the earth.

We have not yet seen what Love will do,
until we open our thoughts and let Love through.

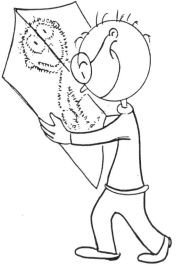

The blueprint of who we are is forever contained within us

Letting ourselves live receptively to the enriching ideas of Love may seem to be something better than we have thought could happen with us. We may be slow to accept that we are worthy of It. We often tell ourselves that it is possible for some people to really feel Love, but that it is not for us. Some of us have even said that it was possible for one, but no other. We sometimes think it cannot happen except to special people, and with this we fail to see ourselves as special.

We have to let go all ideas that Love is not truly within us, or otherwise we will gradually see increasing numbers of people express Love while we linger in our thoughts of inferiority. The belief in the blueprint is our great resource to dissolve all doubts. Confidence in the idea that the blueprint is our Lovefriend brings us into the real feelings of Love.

The blueprint of who we are is forever contained within us. Regardless of what we think, feel and do, we are being made into a perfect copy of the blueprint. Because the Lovefriend is the blueprint and is without a mistake, as we open ourselves to Love we speedily become as much of what and who we are, as is the quickness of our accepting It. As the blueprint is duplicated outwardly the features of its pattern manifest the essence of Self and dignify the individual. Every person is different in the particular combination of characteristics that are demonstrated. These distinguishing attributes have the same primal base, but they otherwise have individualized constituent ingredients for each particular Self-fulfillment. They have not been sufficiently noticed before because they are the maturation that we have kept from our awarenesses.

THE MEETINGS

The reason for having meetings with the Lovefriend is to build up our sense of Love, and to be fired up with a great interest to express Love's presence in all that we do. The meetings have already been detailed in chapters two and five. I am readdressing the procedure of the "solitary ones" here.

In the solitary meetings, the opening words are generally stated by the outward self. A good way to begin is by exclaiming, "I am Love." It is good to repeat that phrase a few times.

Love is always ready for the meetings and is always there. Love's attention is never divided or distracted. Love is always ready to talk with us, and always hears us.

In some of these meetings, Love presents Its ideas of what we can do to achieve our interests. However, we do not hear Love's talk about this unless we are aligned sufficiently with It. Although the Lovefriend is always listening, It already knows what our interests are.

On the other hand, in some other meetings, Love simply inspires us with a grand sense of Its supportiveness. And this sometimes means that we do not know what to do when a meeting is over anymore than we did before. However amazingly, Love then acts as us as though we know.

We speak with Love at every meeting. Our reason for speaking is to clarify for ourselves that which we desire. The clarification is best achieved as we speak to why we have a specified interest. Love's presence assists us as we do; we are then filled with an awareness of Its supportiveness. As we let ourselves feel Love's presence, an ability builds for us to sense the conviction that we have that which we desire.

In the meeting, we do best as we increase our interest by asking ourselves as to whether our stated desire is our greatest aspiration, and as to whether it represents our thinking right then more than anything else. If it does, Love's communication with us is empowering and preparatory to our success with our achieving the desire.

After the soul's sincere desire is established, surrounded and filled with Love's energizing empowerment, a meeting continues by our affirming that Love is surely expressing us through our deepening interest to be active in this way. The affirmations are concluded by our declaring that Love fulfills us as we prepare ourselves to act in accord with our interest.

We then think and feel the idea that we cannot make our interest happen. We open our thoughts and feelings so that Love and Law, or so that Lovepower, manifests the interest in our lives. We declare that our willingness represents our interest to cooperate with Lovepower.

Love supports us between our meetings, as we teach all our feelings that either arise during the meetings or between them that we desire all expressiveness to be in concert with Love's Intelligence. Whenever necessary, we do well to speak strongly, but never disparagingly, to dissenting feelings; nevertheless, we urge them to be agreeable! This is essential, because Love never forces us to feel Its essence; it is up to us to build enough enthusiasm so that we will feel compliant with the idea of being at One with Love.

We are wise to neither oppose the idea of having to urge our feelings to cooperate with Love nor to use self-accusation to enable the cooperation to take place. Many people keep themselves from Love's ease for very long periods because of using one or the other of these errant actions. To understand this, we must first believe that we are right to direct unordered feelings to adjust their sense of action so as to cooperate with our more deeply desired aims. Next, in encouraging the cooperation of our feelings, we are wise to be sensitive and understanding of the fact that we could feel deprived of lesser interests we have been feeling, ones that we think we want or need to continue experiencing. This releases us from self-accusation, which places blame upon us everytime we feel too greatly challenged in the setting and following of higher goals than before. If for the time being, the only way we can find to urge our feelings and our stray thoughts to go along with our thoughtful aims, must include our experiencing blame, shame, guilt or punishment, we are better off to temporarily settle for accepting ourselves as just fine in whatever less demanding ways we are experiencing our behavior.

ALTHOUGH WE MAY HAVE TO ACCEPT OURSELVES JUST AS WE HAVE BEEN FUNCTIONING OVER AND OVER, AS WE WORK WITH IMAGINING THE PRESENCE OF THE LOVE-FRIEND, GRADUALLY THE ACCUSATORY CONDITION WILL FALL AWAY FROM OUR THOUGHTS AND FEELINGS. IT IS ESSENTIAL THAT WE TREAT OURSELVES LIGHTLY, AND NOT LET LOVE'S HEIGHTS BE FELT WITH A SERIOUSNESS. THEN, AND ONLY THEN, WILL OUR FEELINGS EVENTUALLY COMPLY WITH LOVE'S HELPFULNESS.

In a meeting with Love we will always establish the feeling of innocence. It is the result of self-criticism's demise. When we become aware of innocence, we will tend to know that Love is talking with us. All that I have just explained about the procedures of the meeting spontaneously occur with us when we have become familiar with them AND sensed innocency.

We conclude the meeting by saying that we are willing to be guided to whatever understanding of our expressiveness is best for us, even if it is different than we have declared. And we thank the Lovefriend for Its guidance, whether we feel it right then or for whenever we will. We go out into our life situation, whatever it is, and we act as though Love is with us. AND IT IS!

It may seem from this description that our meetings with Love are complex in nature. However, all of this happens easily, naturally and without the slightest sense of complexity. This is because the Lovefriend guides us through the meetings. Everything I have written is known within the depths of Mind and is revealed as the meetings occur. Therefore, we gain by familiarizing ourselves with this explanation, but we need not try to figure out any exacting details that could require effort. It simply is helpful to simulate this model to some small extent.

Sometimes when we attempt to meet with the Lovefriend, it seems that Love is not there. If this happens often, we are wise to examine whether we have met frequently enough; gradually a sense of the presence announces itself to us through our developing an increasing interest in the meetings. Always, our willingness to let the Lovefriend assist us is necessary. And our feeling innocent "is the key."

Some meetings may occur spontaneously. We may be frequently drawn to this presence. However that may be, we are wise to establish meetings, and be regular about it for the rest of our lives.

AFTER THE MEETINGS ARE OVER

As we attend our meetings with the Lovefriend, the character-istics of the blueprints are shown us. They are revealed to us a little more at each meeting. After each meeting is over, they are actualized in our experiences. If we do not respond to the availability of each actualization possibility, the meetings happen further apart. If we respond with much commitment and enthusiasm, the actualizations happen quickly and the meetings naturally occur closer together.

Through actualizing the essence of ourselves into the lives we live, our lives generally unfold about us as follows. We discover that all the love there is is Love, and that no one at any one time experiences love and Love. When for us, love ceases to be, we find that Love is all there is. When Love is not felt, It is still there with us, but It feels like love. When we experience love we desire to get something from others. When we express Love we are giving ourselves away. All the deep-abiding joy we will ever know is that which happens with us in those moments that we really express Love. Since Love as love is the least of Love that we can experience, there is never a time we do not feel some eventual satisfaction from an experience; I mean there are always satisfactions in love; nevertheless, the greatest satisfaction for everyone is to really feel Love. All lesser satisfactions are feelings that we are getting something or several things. But, no one can ever get all the things they want at once. When Love is really felt the satisfaction of getting something is converted to the ecstasy of giving the Self away.

When we experience love we desire to get something from others;
when we express Love we are giving ourselves away

Whenever we give ourselves away or ponder the idea to do so, we sense our spiritual identity. This awareness of why we are alive is at the center of every thought we have. Although we are all born with the blueprint of who we are, we do not tend to truly discover our identity until we become committed to being lifted from love to Love. The next several pages explain the sequential order of how this spiritual Self-actualization takes place with us (there is the element of summary in it of the preceding chapters).

We notice that Love is unconditional early in our earthen lives, but many of us dismiss this observation because we are afraid to experience anything in which conditions are not named. This is the result of listening too much to the opinions of others who fear life. Still, we confront ourselves with the idea of unconditional Love along with conditional love, over and over again. We gradually settle for experiencing everything as coming from conditional love. We do not observe unconditional Love again until we choose to rise out of the particular comfort zone that love has set for us.

When we choose to rise upward with Love, we change our thinking about justice and what is fair in life. Life is felt as absolutely Good to us; everywhere it is just, although it often seems unfair. As we continue to actualize our essence and as our unfoldment continues, that which appears unfair no longer matters. We lose sight or interest in the occurrences that seem to favor others. We change our view from our cries about injustices when we let Love come through us, because we have realized our innocence and turned to a higher interest. We have become interested in what we can give and not in what we can gain. There are no conditions placed upon this interest because the Love we now feel is not only unconditional, but unconditioned.

All of this includes that for a long time we care about our negative experiences. Then we care less and less, until our stress is greatly reduced by not caring about our circumstances. Again, we discover how to care, but not as we experienced care before. From deep within ourselves Love acts as us, caring for ourselves and others in a high way of life.

Our higher sense of Love and Its caring is a tenderness that goes out (It is felt as though we are giving It away, but Love never actually leaves us) toward everyone and everything; this is a higher emotion; now we are in "the Meetings" frequently. Suffering is dissipated; blame is forgotten; reactions are no longer necessary. We feel friendship: the Lovefriend is at One with us. Our cares are gone and our capacity to most truly care has developed itself within us and acts as us. We notice our desires but do not feel our happiness is any longer dependent upon them. Now our desires are simply the names we give to the recognition of our potential and the bringing forth of our essence.

Sacrifice is no longer necessary; still we give ourselves away. Our joy is full because our givingness is our relaxation. We simply take the action that we feel from the innermost prompting of Love. We do not support others in their burdens; yet we support them in their turning towards their opportunities. We do not "act" nice, but we are nice to everyone.

We come to know what is best to do so as to Love people who are feeling hurt, and without feeling hurt ourselves. Lovepower is our tool to help; It flows through our sympathetic feelings and joins us with people who feel distraught, through our agreeing with them that they can have that which they are aiming for in their most noble longings. We know they can achieve it because Love is our connection with them; their negative conditions are unknown by Love and so we only see their disappointments as that which they are letting go.

Our spiritual identity includes then, for all of us, our letting go of the circumstances and conditions that otherwise are the only trouble that can be. As we do it with others it is done with us too.

After being in as many meetings as it takes to raise consciousness to a sufficiently high sense of spirituality, an awareness dawns upon our imagination that our sympathy towards positive and constructive thought will result in such change as is desirable. This is the avenue through which Love achieves anything of interest to us. Because this action, which is the most powerful action possible, is necessary for bringing everyone to a great experience of well-being, until love is raised into Love the world must suffer. For the same reason, when this greater sense of sympathy is discovered, suffering will cease to be.

It was written that people described Jesus as compassionate. Many people have also believed that he was the greatest lover of humankind. But, if compassion is to be understood by the dictionary definitions of it, either Jesus loved others more constructively than is generally implied by his having been compassionate, or a better explanation was needed but was not comprehended by his reporters in their explaining his practice of Love. The usual explanation of compassion includes "taking pity on someone." If we pity other people, it is because we sympathize with their conditions. Unfortunately, until we have had enough meetings with Love, we do love other people through our pitying them; this is not helpful, because the attention that we give to their problems encourages those problems to grow. If we truly Love others we will not be compassionate, but we will sympathize with their interests to experience their deeper and higher desires.

*By pitying the problems of others we encourage
those problems to grow*

    I do not find that a third view of Jesus which conceives of him as the ideal of what a very good man would be, but one who never actually lived, as worthy of my interest. It may be that "the son of righteousness," (described in the Dead Sea Scrolls) who lived in the same region a century earlier than Jesus, actually spoke and acted in some of the ways that later were attributed to Jesus. However, if that were true, it means to me that two people in ancient history, rather than one person, are thereby credited with having developed a great sense of expressing Love and life. Other evidences of modern scholarship indicate that there could have been even more than two such persons. Also, great leaders taught loving ways in many places other than Palestine. Most of the great world religions included high teachings about Love. Again, some people who have not had any religious leanings have developed a constancy of high Love as their consciousness. When people are permanently healed or genuinely helped, it *usually* happens through high Love and precludes the presence of pity and ordinary conceptions of compassion and sympathy; and high Love is much more than empathy.[2] High Love is powerful; high Love is Lovepower and It is very real and very present.

To become sympathetic is an essential step in our growth if the awareness of Love is to abound among us and other people. But, to experience sympathy so as to place blame on conditions is to ignore that Love is unconditioned and unconditional. Always we must remind ourselves of this or Love will remain love to us when we think that is the best It can be.

Having pity is feeling love; sympathizing with conditions is feeling love; feeling love is a low emotion; the Lovefriend never pities, never sympathizes with conditions and is the highest expression of emotion that exists. Although we do best to remind ourselves of this again and again, we need to attend the meetings of the Lovefriend to discover how much more there is to Love than love.

---

[2] As I mentioned in the chapter on "Love And Sacrifice," a *few* people have greatly loved others while being sacrificial and feeling pity toward them, and so again I acknowledge that some exceptions exist. For this reason I have employed the word "usually" here. However, the mixture of great Love with pity, ordinary conceptions of compassion, sympathy or empathy, rarely happens, and so occasional examples, no matter how moving they may be, are not the kind of leadership which will implant Love permanently into our practices. And empathy may include sympathy without the empathetic person's having to feel the despair of the other person, but unless the sense of the Lovefriend's presence is included, empathy by itself cannot truly help or heal in a permanent manner. That is, the empathizer can only truly benefit another or the self by attending Love's meetings.

There are many "anonymous meetings" that people attend in these times; in them they hope to get support from other people, to get a lift and to resolve addictions. Those meetings help them enough so that they have been proven to be the most beneficial experience known today to many people of the western world. With all due respect for those many support groups that become "necessary crutches" for awhile, the meetings with the Lovefriend are the next step; they will prove to lift us higher, but not until we are ready for them.

Meetings are necessary for every person who is to be happy, successful and well. Support groups are excellent means to take first steps; much can be done through them that is very helpful to many people. Yet, most support in them up until now has been of the experience of love. When we are ready, willing and interested to really feel Love, there is a greater inward supportiveness that is awaiting us with the Lovefriend. Meetings with the Lovefriend are not only possible for everyone, but eventually all people will attend these meetings at least several times a week. Within these meetings, Love finds the openness to flow through all the thoughts and feelings that enable anyone to thereafter be happy, whole and complete. However, one meeting or a very few meetings are not enough. Because every meeting lifts us higher, we need not have many of them, before we become committed to meeting with the Lovefriend regularly.

After each meeting is over, a great sense of how to give ourselves away and feel Good about it develops. When we understand how to do this and we act accordingly, we are not deprived of anything. As I have repeatedly stated, Self-givingness is not sacrificial. When the meetings have become regular for us, all that we give is replaced within us with more that we can give. The meetings remake us into Love; then we give because Love always gives, and Love is never unable to give. The one who Loves the most, in every fresh moment, has the most to give.

The meetings we have with the Lovefriend enable
us to fall out of love and into Love.

CHAPTER FIFTEEN

REPRESENTED BY THE LOVEFRIEND

S ay to yourself, *"I AM BEING GENTLY PULLED BY THE LOVEFRIEND, AT FIRST INTO ITS LIKENESS, AND AT LAST INTO THE IDENTITY OF IT. I CAN MEET THE LOVEFRIEND ANYDAY, FOR IT SHOWS ITSELF TO ME, THROUGH ME, WHENEVER I AM WELL EXPRESSED. AS I STOP MYSELF RIGHT WHERE I AM AND LET MY SENSE OF WHO I AM BECOMING SPEAK TO ME, I FEEL LOVE ALONE. THIS HAPPENS TO ME TO THE DEGREE OF MY TRUST."*
Our trust is sufficient as we determine that we are becoming who we are and that we have not been made from what has happened. We are made of what will be, and what will be has always been. LOVE IS IN ALL OF IT! As long as we feel we must be able to explain It, we cannot really feel It. When we let ourselves really feel Love, we need no explanation, for we easily and simply accept that it is altogether all we can truly be, all we have truly become and all we have truly been.

That the whole population of our planet could live in peace has not only forever been a possibility; it has always been in the blueprint. As we become who we are individually, we discover that Love has always been in perfect communication among us from within us.

Already there is One of us. You and I have never truly been apart though it has seemed that way. We cannot really come together though it appears we should. Your Lovefriend and my Lovefriend and every person's Lovefriend altogether are gently pulling together our thoughts of oneness until we recognize that we have never been separated. As we feel these tugs, we come to know our unity.

We have a Lovefriend; we are becoming It; we are Love.

The Lovefriend unites us as One

ONE LOVEFRIEND

Our sense of having Lovefriends suggests that we each have One and that therefore there are many. That sense of the Lovefriend is a misunderstanding of our unity. Our greater sense of who we are enables us to feel unified. *THERE IS NOT TRULY YOUR LOVEFRIEND AND MY LOVEFRIEND; THERE ARE INDIVIDUAL AWARENESSES OF THE ONE TRUTH OF OUR BEING. BUT UNTIL WE KNOW WE ARE IN NO WAY DIVIDED, WE FIRST FEEL THE ONE AS MANY.*

EVERYTHING IS EVOLVING

Animals and plants do not have Lovefriends. Neither is there a Lovefriend for a stone or a drop of water. This is because everything other than human life is already expressing the life within it in the way of its nature. All of it is already feeling its unity with us to the extent of our acceptance of what it truly is. However, the complete sense of its nature and unity with us is not fully expressed until we give it our transmuted understanding. Nothing in nature holds anything from us that we do not hold from ourselves.

Everything is evolving into more of what it is; as we involve our higher ideas, Love greatly evolves us, and along with us, all the creatures, plants, minerals and experiences of our lives. Everything has come from Love and is unfolded from the idea that Love has given it; by this I mean that everything begins with a perfect pattern, or a divine blueprint. But, the greater evolution of nature has also awaited the awakening of human appreciation for our Lovefriend. That appreciation is achieved as our Lovefriend is acknowledged and invited by many of us, to both specialize us and unify us.

BEING LED BY CHILDREN

We do not feel the presence of our Lovefriend when we use our thinking to misrepresent our nature. We have often done this by thinking in a lowly way about ourselves, but our Lovefriend is that aspect of us that has never been spoiled by false thoughts. The Lovefriend is like a secure child who might mature without losing its vivid imagination and sense of trust. Such a child would know nothing of materialism wherein it would try to meet its wants from things alone; nor would it ever feel a need to. It would only know how to succeed in being what it is. When we regard the Lovefriend as we would regard that kind of child, we truly appreciate ourselves. When we seek the company of the Lovefriend in that kind of Spirit, we bring our whole selves together.

*We do best by opening ourselves
to the imagination of a child*

Many of our little children have shown us the way, but we have then steered them to our false realism. We have persuaded them that their inner playmates are not there. We have talked them out of believing in their images. We do best as we follow what they first said to us. We do this by opening ourselves to their kind of imagination. It is largely through a childlike imagination, *one that is positive,* that we discover how to read our own blueprints. Thinking, feeling and acting in this way, we greatly unfold ourselves.

IMAGINATION

The Lovefriend is always with us, but we cannot know this unless we become imaginative. Even then, we may find it difficult to employ our imaginings in place of what we have established before, because we tend to habitually follow what we measure by our five senses. However, that does not matter, unless we believe that our experiencing Love, joy, serenity and feeling Good about ourselves is a valueless activity. Such would mean that because we are cynical, we think we must prove that there is a basis for believing these experiences could benefit us. But, even if we have felt that we have to prove something, can we not now discover our increasing happiness, achievement of other goals and the ways this inspiration benefits us as enough proof that Love is taking care of us? If we can, then let us let go of anything that keeps our imagination from being lively and credible. Let us be open to expressing Love because It leads us to harmony, happiness, wholeness, success, peacefulness and joy.

Think of the Lovefriend in the most personal way. Think of It as your Friend. Let yourself feel your Friend's presence.

Conceive your Lovefriend as often standing behind you. Believe It is sometimes seated beside you. Other times think of your Friend slipping in and out of you. At still other times when you are in perfect accord with Love, suppose your Friend simply is you; expect that you are One with It. KNOW THAT YOU ARE! YOU ARE!

YOU ARE ONE WITH LOVE! Therefore, be easy on yourself. Your Friend smiles all the time. You are becoming all your Friend is. You have never been lonely. You never will be. Your Friend never leaves you.

YOU ARE ONE WITH LOVE! Therefore, you may sometimes feel you are getting a glimpse of your Friend. Right then, your chin is up and your head is high. The fleeting form is a pattern of perfection. Always a radiant smile, a cheerful disposition and a positive action are there. Then, suddenly, that One disappears.

YOU ARE ONE WITH LOVE! Therefore, carry the ideal sense of your Friend forward! Be convinced that you will glimpse that One again! It will take a lot of imagination and enthusiasm....but then the Lovefriend will show through you. Think positively and expectantly. Let yourself be interested in how wonderful you can be. Your Lovefriend will show you who you are and who you were made to be, as you believe...as you believe!

Say, "I AM ONE WITH LOVE." Tell yourself this over and over.

If you reach out to touch your Friend, you will not find an object there, as though another person, chair or tree is near you. Still, your Friend is touching you in your thoughts of yourself.

Your Lovefriend is never absent. The original blueprint of who you are is nearer than your hands and feet.

To know you are at One with Love, you must first imagine that you are. You need not cause yourself to do this all of the time because some of the time you are more naturally in an imagining mood; in your other times you are quite naturally feeling the result of what you have been imagining. Therefore, think your Friend is there. Then let yourself feel it must be true. IT IS TRUE; YET WITHOUT IMAGINATION, THE FRIEND WILL NOT REVEAL ITSELF!

Act as though you really are with your Friend all of the time, for you are. Groom yourself for your Friend. Do not ask yourself, will other people like the way I look, but rather do I feel better about myself and my appearance? Ask, does my appearance unmistakably reveal the Lovefriend's presence? Is my Friend expressing me better because of each thing I am thinking, feeling, saying and doing? Think about whether you are wholly open to expressing Love, to receiving Its expression and giving Its expression, for right then your Friend is being you in all ways.

This use of imagination is not for the purpose of deceiving ourselves. Never forget; the Lovefriend is real. The Lovefriend exists in fullness in every human life. As us, Love is us. The purpose for using imagination is to awaken us to greater Self-reality which we cannot know if we live in a mere analysis of thoughts, feelings and actions. When we imagine the Lovefriend, we give It the opportunity to privilege us with Its Friendship. Through this activity of thought and feelings, we open up to the inner sense of Self that we have otherwise largely closed off to our critical thought.

SUPPORT GROUPS

The support system of "anonymous" groups and a multitude of other support groups "seems" to promise us that the future of Love for us lies entirely in our supporting each other during those crises of "unfair" experiences....of feeling hurt. However, the harsh experiencing of crises is the result of people's not feeling Love; no crises feel harmful to those who know the Lovefriend. Although present day support groups readily attract many people who seem to experience numerous crises, there could be a better emphasis in group supportiveness, one that would not focus upon negative conditions. The ability to focus entirely on living by positive and constructive ideas everyday could be the greater avenue for support groups to pursue. It might seem that if tragic conditions were not the cause of people's coming together, support groups would not exist. However, support groups will continue to be popular; and gradually they will have positive reasons for meeting rather than negative ones.

I am misunderstood if this is interpreted as though I am saying that present support groups are not using positive steps in their procedures. To the contrary, there are many positive measures that are being used by them. And I believe they have been unique, because they have been more fully instrumental in reconstructing torn lives than has been any other single aid except for our individual contemplations. However, when people gather together to focus upon their problems, a very negative atmosphere easily tends to form with them for a long, long while. On the other hand, when people gather to focus ***ENTIRELY UPON THEIR SOLUTIONS*** and choose to rarely review their disappointments, but rather seek means to believe in their potential Good, they hasten their being able to feel Love's presence, Love's Way and Love's answer. We are wise to replace the long time we have so often taken within group experiences to admit our conditions and to build sorriness for ourselves and others before reconstructing our experiences. The better activity is to begin by cultivating an awareness of the Lovefriend, to allow Its feeling of confidence, serenity and Love to build more rapidly with us.

As we become aware of the existence of the Lovefriend, many of us will spend not a few hours alone with It. There cannot be a substitute for our giving regular solitary time to this deepening of our awareness that Love is a presence that supports us; however, group work to build a conviction that Love is always with us is an essential activity too. Rather than an eventual reduction of the great many people who are presently in support groups, the understanding of how to meet the Lovefriend will enlarge their numbers as It becomes a major focus with them.

And support groups will turn their sympathies more toward seeing their friends succeed. Already, this interest in *elevating* sympathy is happening with some groups. We are wise to include this in all groups because when we otherwise sympathize with blame, shame and failure, not only our innocence but Love, remains undiscovered by us.

Support groups will do best as they become centered in the experience of having their participants share in One Friendship. Exchanging conversation about the growing awareness of how self-esteem is greatly raised whenever we court the Lovefriend, brings all people who participate into a wonderful new focus.

Support groups can find right now that the sharing of the common Friendship they have with Love will not build denominational differences. People who are Jews, Catholics, Protestants, Buddhists, Islamics, Hindus, animists, those who are of other religions, those who dislike organized religion, agnostics and atheists will all find a meeting ground when Love is their basis for meeting. Whether we believe in a traditional idea of God, another understanding, none at all, or simply wonder what God could be, does not make much difference when we desire to discover the Lovefriend and meet with It. (It is true, as I stated before, that the people who believe in their ability to meet with the Lovefriend are also those who tend to believe in immortality. The idea of God will more generally be conceived by them. However, if energy is believed to have Intelligence, that alone will suffice for some.)

Support groups who desire right now to center their attention upon Love, by means of using an elevated model of sympathy and a positive, constructive approach of Self-giving, will find their sharing of the philosophy presented in this book a major tool. Particularly if they desire to feel their oneness with the Lovefriend, support groups can be an effective means of discovering Its presence. Experiential evidence of this is building for me inasmuch as I have been assisting support groups to center their interests in meeting the Lovefriend.

We all have many interests, unless we have but a little love for ourselves. Our interests in enjoying life and experiencing harmony with each other is growing because we are feeling love more and more, and because an increasing number of us have already had awarenesses of meeting again and again with the Love that is within us.

The insatiable need to only have things is gradually dropping out of the concerns for many of us. It is because the consciousness of love has been raised in people generally, so that many of the people who used to think that the more they had, the more they would have to get, are now expecting that their greater richness is more that of an uplifted experience of character. Especially good character includes our experiencing a richness of Love, joy, peace and faith.

The greatest treasure of all time is the Lovefriend. Everyone can meet with It as often as is liked. As support groups build themselves up around the idea that Love can be found inwardly, a growing contentment with spirituality will inevitably show itself. Again, everything we do is of some interest to us; the Lovefriend knows how to do it all, constructively--simply anything that we want. There is no limit to what It can do as us.

The greatest treasure of all time is the Lovefriend

But we may sincerely wonder how the Lovefriend, who it has seemed meets us best while we are in solitary spaces, can meet with groups? To be sure, we are entering into a new spiritual territory when we gather a small group of people together to explore their individual potentials rather than their plights. To complicate the situation, many of us who have met the Lovefriend have confused others about Love's presence by acting as though we had some "special spiritual happening" that they perhaps would never understand. Often we have not thought that we wanted to imply this, but the description of our experience immediately made it sound too mysterious, strange or esoteric to others. Yet, the Lovefriend knows how we can talk with others about Love and remove the walls we have built around this magnificent experience. We are wise as we focus on how we can support others to discover Love, and in a way that they can enthusiastically accept. It is not satisfactory to live by love, when Love is waiting at everybody's door.

These new support groups, or Love's meetings with two or more people, begin best as we explore how we can Love others one at a time. They cannot begin at all until we meet Love individually. If the reader will work with the ideas of this book until the Lovefriend is truly experienced, a group can then be formed, because he or she will know that Love is a true and everpresent Friend. However, anyone who comes to know of Love's presence must proceed without boasting about his or her spirituality. This cannot be emphasized too much.

LOVE'S GROUP MEETINGS

In the support group meetings, we need to share with each new person the explanations given here. It is best to build these groups slowly so that each new participant gains understanding of how to conduct his or her own solitary meetings. This is because the group meetings cannot enable all participants to really know of Love's presence unless each one has more than one solitary meeting between the group meetings. Success then in group meetings necessitates many individual meetings.

Love's group meetings will build around the experience of meeting the Lovefriend. For first time participants, they will include a brief description, of no more than five minute's length, of the need to be in the group. All should be encouraged to connect that need with the interest of having Love flow through them for their good and for the good of others. Such encouragement cannot occur unless the purpose of the support group is first and foremost to express Love, and only secondarily to resolve problems. Most people join support groups to overcome addictions, abuses, hurts, loneliness or other negative experiences. The desire to find solutions to problems outweighs all other reasons combined. However, the recognition of the Lovefriend cannot be achieved if group members focus upon anything other than It.

It takes creative thought to say, think and feel the desire to express Love. But it can be achieved, even when other reasons, stemming from some seemingly deep hurts, are the basis for participating in a group. The person who begins a group will have to have this clearly in Mind and not ever lose sight of it in order for success to follow. Most new group members will have to be supported through the process of changing their focus from a problem to expressing Love. As has been explained, Love expresses grand solutions as we focus on the possibilities of It; as the reader's conviction builds around this understanding, the

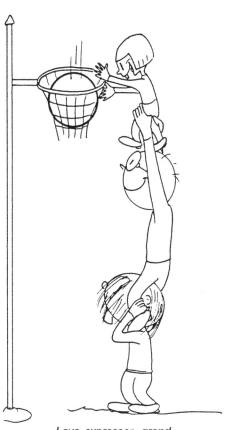

Love expresses grand solutions as we allow It

idea of having support groups built around the Lovefriend will be increasingly credible.

People who are familiar with traditional support groups will readily notice that their usual kind of supportiveness and procedures can only partially apply to group meetings with the Lovefriend. For instance, *the usual need to help a person turn away from denial of a problem is much less involved. THIS DOES NOT MEAN THAT THE GROUP ENABLES A PERSON TO DENY AN ADDICTION, ETC.. NOR DOES IT MEAN THAT A GROUP ALLOWS ANYONE TO PRESUME HE OR SHE IS AMPLY FEELING AND EXPRESSING LOVE IF PROBLEMS CONTINUE IN THEIR LIVES. RATHER, IT MEANS THAT SOLUTIONS TO PROBLEMS FOLLOW A DIFFERENT COURSE. It includes that when a person takes the time and interest to meet with the Lovefriend, Love reveals to that person a perfect sequence of actions that brings correction gently, firmly and on time, but without the group's being able to predict the how and when of it. There is a permanent group leader; however, no one ever sees the One; control is nonexistent; only the Lovefriend provides unquestionable authority.*

Love's group meetings will be the new basis of spirituality for groups in the twenty-first century. The different procedures will also include that any old Lovefriend support groups will easily integrate new members in any meeting. This is true because there will not need to be as much privacy about the seeming hurts that have been shared, inasmuch as they will not be discussed as much. How to allow Love to be felt and expressed will be the main conversation. Building an ease for a new entrant will happen with quickness. The most essential experience of the groups will be the joyful activity of supporting each participant's interest to believe in Love's presence as they altogether grow into their potential.

In every meeting, everyone will declare that they are loving themselves; they will gradually learn to talk out loud with the Lovefriend. Some discussion and affirmations about Love's perfect nature and immediate presence, will be included.

In Love's group meetings, we do best as we keep in mind that the Lovefriend is primarily interested to represent our individualities. That which all of us most sincerely desire is to simply be who we are. The Lovefriend is most obvious to us when we approach It with this design in our thinking.

LET US JOIN IN GROUPS AND FIND OUT FROM EACH OTHER HOW WE CAN DISCOVER THE LOVEFRIEND MORE. LET US EXPLORE TOGETHER HOW WE CAN BE SYMPATHET- IC WITH OUR GREATER POSSIBILITIES THROUGH MORE SELF-GIVING AND BEING TRULY NICE. BUT, LET US NEVER FORGET TO HAVE MEETINGS WITH THE LOVEFRIEND ALONE. WHATEVER IT IS THAT WE DESIRE TO DO, THE LOVEFRIEND KNOWS HOW TO DO IT CONSTRUCTIVELY. THE LOVEFRIEND IS READY TO ACT WONDERFULLY AS US; THE LOVEFRIEND KNOWS HOW TO EXPERTLY REPRESENT US ALL.

No one need ever be out of work again, be impoverished or diseased, feel lonely or not know how to do something, because OUR Lovefriend is right where we are, knows perfect solutions for all our situations and desires to give them away through us, by expressing as us the lives we most desire to have.

WHY I AM ALIVE

Why am I alive? It is for the reason that I can express Love. It is because I am Love. I am living on earth to give myself away.

I cannot discover who I am or give myself away until I free myself from other ideas about me that have held me captive. But, should I succeed in releasing myself from living in accord with societal and parental demands, and not yet know that I am Love, I must become imprisoned again with other societal forces. Therefore, simply being free may feel very good momentarily, but it does not necessarily deliver me into a realization of who I am or into the manifestation of my true Self-expression.

If my first interest is to be free, I will eventually loose myself from the more apparent demands of the usual human bondage. And I will think I have gained the best that life can give me. However, it is inevitable that I will have simply prepared myself for a new form of bondage, one that merely has a different appearance. The chains will be made from new interests, but ones that cause me to conform my attention to some form of material-ism, to something rather limited in spirituality.

Numerous people have freed themselves from the restrictions of today's habituations and addictive patterns, only to be confronted with the confusion of trying to identify what a reasonable and satisfactory alternative life-style could possibly be. If we were not already Love, the frustration of trying to make sense of life would forever confine our Spirits to a search for something we would want that could not be found. Fortunately, *WE ARE LOVE, ALL OF US!*

If my primary interest is to express Love, I will discover the truth of who I am.   As I go about expressing Love, I will increasingly open up my sense of Self-essence. This will release me from everything except my Self-givingness. Although Love will act as me in all I do, I will also be truly free, because Love is free.

LOVE IS FREE, SUPREMELY INTELLIGENT, INFINITELY RESOURCEFUL AND UNLIMITED IN FRIENDSHIP. THIS IS WHAT I AM, WHO I AM AND ALL THAT I AM!   IT IS MY DESIRE AND MY SELF-WORTH TO KNOW THIS AND THIS ALONE!   IT IS MY PASSION TO LET LOVE ACT AS ME!

CONNECTION OF THE ROYAL IDEAS

All of the Royal Ideas are unified. The unity connections are in our awareness of Love's coming through our attentiveness with them. In "Second Reflections," meditation through contemplation establishes the silence in which all thoughts that do not host Love's presence are discarded. That silence is the backdrop to our being able to be aware of Love's presence. The end of "Second Reflections" was a great beginning for us, because once the silence is regularly known, our recognition of Love's presence as the ultimate experience of greater livingness can come through it. The end of "Meeting the Lovefriend" is now the great beginning for our actually bringing Love's awareness up through the Silence.

GLOSSARY

GLOSSARY

I define the following words and phrases differently than most people have been doing. Therefore, it would be helpful for the reader to become familiar with the glossary.

"ACTING" NICE - A counterfeit action which outwardly resembles nicety, but is actually a covering up of disbeliefs that the recipients are worthy of affection.

AFFECTION - The expression of emotion resulting from the extent to which Love's presence is sensed or felt.

AWARENESS - The openness towards knowledge and discovery. When used to feel and express Love, it increases the capacity for having spiritual consciousness.

BECOMING - The awareness that we are Love, that we are the Lovefriend. Statements about becoming Love actually mean that we are "becoming aware" that we are Love. Until we become deeply aware of being Love, our greater lovingness is latent.

CARE - Love's continuous expression. Is provided with kindness and gentleness to the extent that Love is conceived as Self-givingness.

CARE AGENT - Every person on earth. Care is channeled through everyone in accordance with the level of each person's awareness of Love's nature.

COMMON SENSE - Practical consideration, which along with logical thinking and sensitive action, places a person at Love's door where poise can be experienced and an openness toward experiencing Love's presence can be maximized.

CONCENTRATION - Placement of one's attention upon the "idea" that a meeting with the Lovefriend is occurring; essential for the awareness to take place. Not to be understood as the means of causing the experience to happen.

CONDITIONAL love - Love given with the proviso that the object's prior and present actions must first be made acceptable to the giver.

CONSCIOUSNESS - Usually conceived here as the degree to which a person is permitting Love's uplifted Intelligence, sympathy, solutions, Self-givingness and kindness to be his or her philosophy and practice of life. This explanation carries validity because Love knows the whole Truth of being and is life's integrity. Is sometimes alternately presumed as one's awareness and explanation of life's experiences.

CONTEMPLATION - The practice of and degree to which thought is focused upon a particular idea, with the conviction that the idea will unfold its meaning and will benefit the contemplator's experiences. Utilized most specifically here to place one's awareness upon Love's presence and Its being greatly expressed through and as the contemplator.

CONTROLLER - One who takes charge of one's experiences. Best control lies in permitting the Lovefriend to act as or through the self, but this awaits our choice to let go of the belief that we have to control ourselves.

DEPENDENCY - The experience of one's relying upon some other person, persons or conditions, for care.

DESIRE - Can be a yearning for something that will temporarily satisfy a frustration. In its deeper and more positive nature, a desire is a longing for Self-fulfillment through authentic Self-expression, and is the motive power that permits the Love-friend to act as us.

DESIROUS NATURE - Refers here to the natural state of our desiring to express Love in all the ways that fulfill us.

DIVINE BLUEPRINT - The authentic, individual and everlasting idea of our potentiality to express Love.

EMOTION - The affective motivation for expressing oneself. All emotions stem from Love. When this is known, Love unifies us with everyone and everything so that we can live constructively, resourcefully and beneficially. To whatever extent this is sensed, to that degree we live harmoniously with people and with everything that is.

ESSENCE - Our true nature. It is hidden from us until we know that we are Love and become willing to allow It to emerge as our livingness.

FEELING - Means here the sense of Love or life that we have. Everyone feels love and life; everyone can feel Love and aliveness. More than the five senses are involved. However, they are very much included, because Love in us activates us to feel Good in all the ways that are natural with us.

FLOW - Movement without restriction. Love moves freely through us and as us. However, until we know this and go with the flow, we feel Love as love; we then think we have to construct love. Love already is and knows only to flow.

FORGETTING - The liberating adjustment of dissolving mistaken assessments of blame, shame and thoughts held against ourselves and others.

FORGETIVE - An inventive, imaginative, creative way of thinking anew so as to live constructively. Occurs as we forget old emotional fixations and elevate our thoughts to greater possibilities for action.

FORGIVENESS - Frees us of resentments and makes it possible for us to truly Love ourselves and others.

FOREMOST EMOTION - Love. The motivating presence which, when we surrender to It, causes us to feel the consciousness that all is Good, to desire to express this feeling and to succeed in our expression of It.

FRIENDSHIP - The constant companionship within the heart's center of every person. Its name is the Lovefriend. As we believe in It and expect It to assist us, we meet It in Its perfect ideas about what we may think so as to successfully solve any of our challenges. Capitalized because Love's Friendship is distinctive.

GOOD - The greatest possible experience of life; inherent within us and given through everyone. Our Good comes to us through the Lovefriend's companionship to the degree that we recognize Its presence. Capitalized except for instances that may refer to a comparative state.

GUILT - The result of feeling inadequate and fearing we have done wrong. It is resolved through feeling innocence or forgiveness.

HIGH ACTION - The coming into one's experiences of a most desirable expressiveness through meetings with the Lovefriend and drawing upon Its supreme knowledge.

HIGHER JUSTICE - Sometimes taught as "grace." Ordinary justice is the action of receiving the exact or "fair" equivalent of either ordinary or low actions, plus the penalties that arise when guilt feelings build a low idea of what one deserves. When high actions are expressed, the resulting higher justice provides us experiences which are free of penalties and which also contain the joy of trust, harmony, peace and Love.

HUMAN METAMORPHOSIS - Results from our discovering and accepting Love as our foremost spiritual emotion. It enables us to experience Love's higher expressiveness through our being Self-giving and living by high ideas that bring about greater living. Occurs as we allow the Lovefriend to be the whole of us.

IDEA - An opportunity for better living. Every idea is first thought by Love's Intelligence. As we receive any idea into our awareness, its pure state is diminished according to any low sense we have of Love's presence. We can trace the cause of our thinking impure thoughts to our allowing "love" to dominate our relationship with those others who are similarly naive toward higher thinking; our meetings with Love will lift us out of such influence.

INNOCENCE - Placing no blame or shame upon the self or another; carries no resentment. When one is aware of "carrying" these negative practices, innocence can still be gradually achieved through forgetting, forgiving and being forgetive.

INTELLIGENCE - Knowing what to think and do to maintain complete harmony, unlimited resourcefulness and wholeness. Love's presence is Supreme Intelligence. Always capitalized because of Its essence.

JUSTICE - See Higher Justice, Ordinary Justice and Universal Justice.

LAW - Nature's method of creating our experiences by manifesting through us and as us the reactions of its Universal Intelligence to all our thoughts, especially of the underlying intentions of them that we conceive. Is continuously creating the circumstances of our lives. The complement of Love. Capitalized because It refers to the grand actions of the creator and creativeness.

LOVE - Self-givingness, Intelligence, emotion, Friendship, resourcefulness, guidance, sympathy, tenderness, kindness and life's greatest strength, though it is totally nonresistant. The complement of Law; unlike Law, Love only acts through us to the extent that we sense It and expect It to; the result is that we experience Love as Love or as love. Capitalized because of Its divine nature.

LOVEFRIEND - The friendly and unconditional presence of Love sensed when It is allowed to flow from one's deepest inner feelings into all of his or her thoughts and onward into all conversations and actions. Capitalized because of Its divine nature.

LOVEPOWER - Love and Law acting in concert. When nothing is forced, but the confidence that a positive and constructive resolution of anything can be, and when Love is allowed to express such an outcome, Lovepower is that action. Lovepower is the greatest of forces, or especially forceful, through Its not being a force. Lovepower is the activity of unlimited resourcefulness which results from one's masterfully using Law by allowing Love's guidance and presence to be the Law's basis for action. Capitalized because of Its being the combined expressiveness of power and Love's guidance acting as One.

LOVE'S ANSWER - Love's perfect solution in action in anyone's life.

LOVE'S FRIENDS - Those of us who have accepted Love's Friendship as the entire solution for our needs and desires, and who express Love's Friendship with those others who feel they have unresolved needs or desires and seek Love's empowerment.

LOVE'S GROUP MEETINGS - Resemble existing support groups, but have major differences. Purpose is to assist each individual to meet with Love privately, regularly and to successfully receive Love's guidance. Group atmosphere is established around the recognizing of inocence, "talking with Love," and allowing Love's solutions to members' needs and desires to take place.

LOVE'S MEETINGS - Extraordinarily serene and encouraging experiences, because the Lovefriend's presence is sensed. Feeling adequacy and either innocence or forgiveness; allowing Love to provide solutions to needs and desires; becoming greatly aware of one's loving nature.

LOVE'S PERSONALNESS - Love's acting with especial resourcefulness through and as persons; however, Love Itself is not a personality.

LOVE'S PRESENCE - The Lovefriend. Love is always present and Its Friendship is big-hearted, high-minded and unlimited in resourcefulness. Love's being felt or sensed as close, friendly with everyone and everything, in every place, in every moment.

LOVE'S WAY - The expression of Love through us which sympathizes with solutions, gives without reservation of Self, and is amazingly kind.

love - The common, familiar and popular expression of Love. It is giving for the purpose of achieving gain. While a person presumes that love is as much Love as there is, a maturing of the self is needed. Everyone who lives by love is evolving the self into an expresser of Love, no matter how slowly Love may show Itself through each one.

LOW ACTION - The manner of life which reflects the kind of attentiveness that is largely affixed to physical emotion.

MEETINGS - Here explained as the experiences one has with Love wherein the Lovefriend's presence provides a person with Love's consciousness, resourcefulness, Intelligence and Self-givingness.

MOTIVATION - It is inspired living, and is greatly felt through meetings with the Lovefriend.

NATURE - The inherent character or essence of Oneself, which is predisposed toward expressing Love's consciousness. However, it is necessary that we meet with Love and evolve our natural tendencies through the meetings before nature allows Love to greatly express us with regularity.

NEW ACTIONS - Replacements for the repetitious tendency of reactions to habitually occur with us, through our turning toward Love and focusing upon the idea of Its being the actor of us.

NEW THOUGHT - Thinking which makes new actions possible. All new thoughts result from our allowing Love to guide our thinking. They may arise from a deep place in us which we discover through our being "in the silence." They may be "in something" that we hear from others, or "of something" we read or observe or simply appreciate. However, merely hearing new thoughts from others or being quiet does not mean that we are coming from Love. All of this requires us to spend "enough time" in the silence, and that we become increasingly honest with ourselves, as to when we are truly allowing Love to guide us.

NICENESS - A kindness that deeply satisfies us, but is not genuine unless Love inspires it.

ONENESS - The relationship every person has with Love and all other people, but is only outwardly experienced to the degree that Love's presence is greatly sensed. One is capitalized when It represents unity rather than relationships between presumed separate beings.

ORDINARY JUSTICE - Either the experience of inequality that results from prejudiced reactions or "fair" treatment that happens when we compromise ourselves for gain. Penalties are added, and when all is considered, this usual experience of justice often seems unfair because it is not provided in consideration of the efforts made to experience something better.

PASSION - The action that is expressed when a desire is felt with strong commitment. The passion to express Love is the greatest feeling we can have. All other passions need upliftment, which can only occur with oneself through maturation.

PHYSICAL EMOTIONS - Lower affections which we feel when fear and a presumed lack of Self-identity control us.

POINT OF POISE - The sense of imperturbability which is wonderfully felt and operative to the extent that we flow successfully with life's situations, through our sensing the Lovefriend's presence or when we are at heart's door (on the verge of meeting the Lovefriend).

QUIET - The peaceful, confident, loving and quieting experience that happens with us through our letting Love act as us.

REACTION - The mechanical and beneficial form of response by the Law to our thoughts. When we personally and mechanically react to people and situations, Love is unfortunately felt as love. Love will change our unfortunate reactions to new actions when we desire this.

RELATIONSHIP - An involvement requiring commitments if happiness is to abound. There is but One relationship with Love; we are all unified (One) in Love's Friendship. In love, we have many relationships that are based upon our reactions.

SACRIFICE - The low state of expressing Love, although a very few individuals have managed to be sacrificial and Self-giving at the same time. When one's understanding of the personal compulsion to sacrifice is matured, Self-givingness becomes that one's normal behavior.

SELF-EXPRESSION - The bringing forth of one's inner unique beingness through a sharing of Self (Self-givingness).

SELF-FULFILLMENT - Allowing Love to express Oneself in all ways.

SELF-GIVINGNESS - The high state of Self acting from the awareness that Love is paramount and desires individuals to express It; does not need to act sacrificially.

SELF-PUNISHING HABITUAL DEPRESSANTS - Low desires that are substitutes for natural, normal, necessary or legitimate desires. Hurtful, Self-rejecting thoughts. Occur as mistakes that we make when we struggle with life.

SENSING LOVE - Deeply feeling an awareness of Love's presence. Involves the five senses, intuition, and allowing Love to increasingly express through us.

SENSITIVITY - The kind of response to one's experience and that of others, which along with logical thinking and common sense, can enable a person to discover Love's presence.

SPIRIT - The Lovefriend within us when capitalized, and the seeking aspect of Self otherwise.

SPIRITUAL BEINGS - All people are spiritual beings whose natural state is to recognize Love's presence and perfectly express Love's high ideas of Good. Everyone will ultimately succeed in achieving this through acquiring Love's consciousness. The human community appears to be something of a lesser nature than it is until its individuals achieve Self-recognition.

SPIRITUAL EMOTIONS - The higher affections which we feel and through which we function masterfully to the degree that Love is recognized or sensed as our Self-identity.

SUBSTITUTES FOR LOVE - Addressed in this book as sacrifice, sympathy with problems and "acting" nice.

SUPREME CAUSE - Love's ability to maximize Good.

SUPPORT GROUPS - See Love's Group Meetings.

SYMPATHY - The affectionate, emotional responsiveness to oneself or others in which sorriness and concern about problems can be terribly involved. Love's sympathies, however, feel no element of being sorry or concerned in the sense of an anxiety, but rather feel deeply interested in solutions and in focusing entirely upon them.

TENDERNESS - The sensitive and intimate manner by which Love expresses through us the extent of our recognition of Its presence.

TEN NORMAL HABITUAL ACTION NEEDS - The necessary, regular experiences along with having meetings with the Lovefriend which are involved in our living a normal and natural life. Expressed as legitimate desires.

TRUST - The experience of allowing Love to build in us confidence and appreciation of ourselves, others and Love's presence and solutions.

UNCONDITIONAL LOVE - The basis of Love's actions. This means that sympathy with solutions is Love's entire affection, because conditions are never given the attention by Love that allows them to restrain, hurt or control.

UNIVERSAL JUSTICE - The naturally provided Good experiences which occur with those who cooperate with nature. They are as beneficial as are the willingness, interest and action of the recipient to harmonize with the universe.

If one's intentions are limited in scope, one's rewards will be similarly limited. If one's intentions are rooted in Love, then one's rewards are limitless.

Universal justice acts as "ordinary justice" when a person has not discovered the greater possibilities inherent in cooperating with life's flow. Universal justice acts as "Higher Justice" when anyone "goes with the flow."

INDEX

Introduction through Glossary

LOVE'S MANAGEMENT

Love finds Its way
      into the heart
as we let go
      and let Its part
be guidance
      and nonresistance.

Love changes us
      cares for each need
as we allow
      growth of Its seed--
the Friendship
      of Its unity.

Our ideas
      form attractions
inspiration
      then new actions--
bringing forth
      amazing kindness.

All becomes true
      as the Lovefriend
emerges through
      our thoughts to tend
the manner
      of the things we do.

ONE WORLD, ONE LIFE, ONE LOVE

One world has always existed;
    until now we could not accept it or believe.
Becoming aware of the Lovefriend
    lifts us to know, but not to be naive.
No utopia, nor is it escape,
    rather it is the truth that we conceive.

Imagination serves us well
    as the old facts and each precedent we let go.
Thinking anew about innocence
    opens us to Love and living in which we know
Nothing hard can continue with us longer
    than Love remains as love to us and low.

Encouraging high perspectives,
    dissolving mistakes, misfortunes and pollution,
Uniting with Love's mystic presence,
    finding there the oneness that ends intrusion,
Thinking better of ourselves, Love feels close;
    we express Self-givingness, solution.

ABOUT THE AUTHOR

Royal Satterlee began to feel adequacy when he had a mystical experience at 16. His feeling of inadequacy all but disappeared from his life for awhile. However, he allowed some inability to experience a complete social ease to interfere with his other achievements. As he matured, this one condition hindered his self-expression. Eventually he identified himself with the idea that the "Friend" spoken about throughout this book could marvelously assist him with all his needs and desires. The outcome has been to increasingly allow the "Lovefriend" to think, feel and act as him. This, then, is Royal's teaching to every seeker. To meet the "Lovefriend" is to become a finder, to discover who we are and how to live in deep personal satisfaction, in harmony with people and in cooperation with the planet.

Royal is a minister of the United Church of Religious Science. Previously he was a Methodist minister. Between the two ministries, he successfully conducted his own business in Southern California. He loved his experience with business. However, his commitment to assist people in discovering their spiritual nature has always been his deepest interest.

Royal was married to Noreen in 1950 and cherishes his marital experience. He and Noreen have two children, Rhonda and Clarence. His family life is important to him. Numerous people who have become his other close friends are all special to him too. Again, the experience of the Lovefriend along with his feeling "at One" with It, is the cement of his life, that which fulfills him.

Books

(Immediately available from the author unless otherwise specified)

LOVE'S GROUP MEETINGS - (64 page booklet, available in 1992)
Teaches how support groups can enable participants to sense Love's mystic presence daily. Includes definitions of Love's nature, of Love's activity in the lives of individuals and groups. Contains guidelines for establishing group meetings with Love. Explains the experiences of feeling innocent, of being at One with Love, of surrendering self-control to the Lovefriend, of talking with It. Four group exercises included. Shows these meetings as wholly positive, productive, peaceful and practical. Illustrated by Dick Hannon.

MEETING THE LOVEFRIEND - (384 PAGE BOOK)
Describes Love as ultimate reality; as creative of everything, in concert with Law; as entire cause of the direction our experiences take. Shows that Love's actions are best formed in our lives to the extent that we recognize Its presence. Recognition occurs through discovering Love as our Friend. Then, we allow Love's Friendship to act as us, through Its inspired ideas for living constructively, effectively, peacefully, productively and happily. Illustrated by Dick Hannon.

SECOND REFLECTIONS - (224 page book)
Explains that appearances seem to diminish the intrinsic value of everything. Shows that Second Reflections from a "deep place within," clarify this conception: all is inherently Good and perfectly formed. Method is meditation by contemplation. Enables us to know ourselves as absolute equals of everyone.

TALKING WITH LOVE - (96 page book, available in 1992)
Talking with Love begins as we accept It as our Friend. At first, we talk "to" Love. When we feel at One with Love, we talk "with" It. Includes directions for discovering Love's high ideas of how we can magnificently express our sincere desires. Love guides us.... tells us how. As oneness takes form, Love acts as us. Illustrated by Dick Hannon.

Audio Cassettes

HOW TO BE AMAZINGLY KIND - (one audio cassette, 60 minutes) Tendency in relationships is toward dependencies. Some depend on others for receiving care; some depend upon being able to give care. These arrangements "appear" to be nice, but, they are actually motivated by people's trying to gain happiness from others. Love's inner friendship releases dependents; provides them with amazing kindness. Methods are explained.

(1) LOVE'S GROUP MEETINGS and **(2) TALKING WITH LOVE** - (two audio cassettes, 60 minutes each, in a Deluxe Album) First tape: Explains how Love's Group Meetings (support groups) can be formed and experienced. Participants encourage each other to believe in Love's presence. Lovefriend is leader and supports everyone who fully participates.

Second tape: Shows how conversations with Love can heal, be productive. Assistance given to sense Love's presence, to allow Love's friendship to act through and as the self.

THE GENESIS OF EQUALITY - (two audio cassettes, 90 minutes each, in a Deluxe Album) Tells that all people are unlimited and equal in potential to express sincere desires. No struggle, suffering, sacrifice or stress is necessary. Inner message about Adam and Eve and Garden of Eden is that they represent consciousness. Teaches how we can "return" to equality and paradise through discovering the consciousness that recognizes Love and cooperates with Law.

MEDITATION BY CONTEMPLATION - (three audio cassettes, 90 minutes each, in a Deluxe Album) Theory of contemplative meditation (tape one), its procedure (tape two), and its results in action (tape three). Examples provided. An active form of meditation allowing guidance and higher actions to "come through" meditator's thoughts, feelings and activities. Love is expressed through anyone interested in evolving consciousness in this way. Recognition of Truth of Being is paramount.

*Buy the books from your local bookstore
if available, or order from:*

ROYAL IDEAS PUBLICATIONS
P.O. Box 1663
Manchester, MO 63011-1663
Tel. 1-800-628-LOVE (5683)

Books:

Love's Group Meetings *(available in 1992)*	$2.95
Meeting the Lovefriend	14.95
Second Reflections	9.95
Talking With Love *(available in 1992)*	6.95

Audio Cassettes:

How To Be Amazingly Kind   9.95
One tape, 60 minutes

Love's Group Meetings
Talking With Love
Each, one cassette, 60 minutes
Sold only together in a Deluxe Album   19.95

The Genesis of Equality
Deluxe Album: Two audio cassettes, 90 minutes each   21.95

Meditation By Contemplation
Deluxe Album: Three audio cassettes, 90 minutes each   29.95

Please address inquiries regarding lectures, seminars, telephone consultations or other services to Royal Satterlee at the above address. Telephone orders can be placed by calling 1-800-628-LOVE (5683). Please fill in the order form so that you will have all the information necessary at the time of your call. Prices are subject to change without notice.

Name:
Address:
City:
State: Zip:
Telephone: Home:
Work:

Order by Phone
1-800-628-LOVE
1-800-628-5683
Orders only please - Inquiries taken by mail
Please allow 6 weeks for delivery
Prices subject to change without notice
No cash or C.O.D. accepted

X	Serial#[1]	Item	Qty	Price	Amt
	B-103	Meeting the Lovefriend		$14.95	
	B-102	Second Reflections		9.95	
	B-101	Love's Group Meetings[2]		2.95	
	B-104	Talking With Love[2]		6.95	
	AC301	How To Be Amazingly Kind		9.95	
	DA203	Love's Group Meetings & Talking With Love		19.95	
	DA202	The Genesis of Equality		21.95	
	DA201	Meditation/Contemplation		29.95	

Charge Card Orders	Subtotal	
☐ Visa ☐ Master Card Exp. Date: _____ Card # Signature:	MO residents add 6.225% sales tax	
NOTE: New Address **Royal Ideas Publications** **P.O. Box 1663** **Manchester, MO 63011-1663** **Tel. 1-800-628-LOVE (5683)**	Add $1.50 per book/tape for s/h	
	TOTAL	

[1] B = Book;   AC = Audio Cassette Tape
DA = Deluxe Album Cassette Tapes;   [2] Available in 1992